Black Rice

Black Rice

The African Origins of Rice Cultivation in the Americas

Judith A. Carney

HARVARD UNIVERSITY PRESS

Cambridge, Massachusetts
London, England

Library of Congress Cataloging-in-Publication Data

Carney, Judith Ann.
    Black rice : the African origins of rice cultivation in the Americas / Judith A.
Carney.
        p.   cm.
    Includes bibliographical references (p.).
    ISBN 0-674-00452-3 (cloth)
    ISBN 0-674-00834-0 (paper)
    1. Rice—Southern States—History   2. Rice—Africa, West—History.
3. Slaves—Southern States.   I. Title.
SB191.R5 C35   2001
633.1'8'0975—dc21   00-053941

To the memory of D and of my parents

Contents

Figures

Preface

Unbeknownst to me at the time, this book originated more than fifteen years ago in two disparate geographical settings. The first glimmering appeared in the West African country The Gambia, where I conducted my doctoral research on the impact of technological change in rice production on female labor and access to resources. Hoping to understand better the history of rice cultivation in The Gambia and its evolution as a crop grown only by women, I spent several months in the country's national archives. In a moldering musty room one rainy summer day in 1984, I stumbled across a reference from 1823 that enthusiastically proclaimed that Gambian rice cultivation could rival that of Carolina. The geographical basis of the comparison puzzled me, and only many years later did I learn the significance of this statement.

The second incident to bear on this book occurred while I was a Rockefeller Foundation postdoctoral fellow with the International Maize and Wheat Improvement Center (CIMMYT) in Mexico. On a research trip along the Gulf Coast in 1988, I came across a road sign south of Veracruz that caused me nearly to veer off the road. The name of the approaching hamlet was Mandinga, the same as that of the rice-growing ethnic group with whom I had worked in The Gambia. A stop in the village revealed a Mexican population of mixed African descent and the presence of some abandoned rice fields. Only in 1993, as an assistant professor at UCLA, did these strands come together when I discovered that rice formed the basis of the plantation system in coastal South Carolina. The argument of historians Peter Wood and Daniel Littlefield that Africans brought with them skills crucial in the making of the Carolina rice economy proved a revelation to me and charted the direction of my work over the years that followed.

This book is the result of my continuing effort to examine the history of rice cultivation in the Atlantic basin from an interdisciplinary and cross-cultural perspective. The research presented tells a previously untold story of the African presence and legacy in the Americas. Rice, not only an important crop but the basis of an entire cultural system, traveled across the Middle Passage of bondage through African growers and pounders of rice. These men and women, enslaved in the Americas, saw their traditional agriculture emerge as the first food commodity traded across the ocean on a large scale by capitalists who would later take complete credit for the innovation. The amazing story of these African rice growers and their descendants throughout the Atlantic basin is the subject of this book.

As with any project of this scope, there are many whose encouragement and critical judgment were vital to the completion of the manuscript, even though responsibility for the interpretation is solely my own. Let me begin first with Peter Wood, whose compelling scholarship inspired me to cross disciplinary boundaries and attempt my own contribution to his pioneering work. I am deeply grateful for his incisive reading of the book manuscript. I also thank Joyce Seltzer, Elizabeth Gilbert, and David Lobenstine at Harvard University Press for their critical comments and support for this project.

There are many others to thank on both sides of the Atlantic basin. For their help with research on South Carolina my gratitude extends to Sharon Bennett, Joyce Chaplin, Peter Coclanis, Leland Ferguson, Mary Galvin, Fritz Hamer, Karen Hess, Daniel C. Littlefield, Alexander Moore, Richard Porcher, Amelia Wallace Vernon, Don West, and the staff at the Avery Research Center for African American History and Culture in Charleston.

My research in West Africa was made possible with the assistance of Kumona Baba, Musa Ceesay, K. F. Demba, Chris Elias, the late Chief Mboge, Julia Morris, Salime Moukhtara, Patrick Pieyre, Sandra Russo, Modi Sanneh, and Axel Thoma. I would also like to pay tribute to my own tutors in the rice fields of Senegambia, who include villagers too numerous to name, many of them female. This book could never have been written without the knowledge they imparted to me. I also wish to thank David P. Gamble and Paul Richards, whose extensive knowledge of rice cultivation in The Gambia and Sierra Leone and whose patient responses to my endless queries contributed a great deal. I am grateful as well to Neil Brady, Derk HilleRisLambers, Deborah Pearsall, and Duncan Vaughn for assistance with technical questions on rice cultivation. In Brazil, I thank Rosa Acevedo Marin, Mario Hiraoka, and D. Michael O'Grady for their assistance with fieldwork and archival references. I additionally wish to thank the research library staff at the Muséum National d'Histoire Naturelle in Paris for locating documents pertinent to botanical research on rice in francophone West Africa.

Many scholars provided critical encouragement and feedback. They include Kat Anderson, Jeremy Ball, Tom Bassett, Ira Berlin, Tom Gillespie, Susanna Hecht, Kairn Kleiman, Don Mitchell, Sarah Morris, Ben Orlove, Haripriya Rangan, Jim Scott, Michael Storper, Ferro Trabalzi, Matt Turner, Michael Watts, and Karl Zimmerer. I also wish to express my appreciation to Chase Langford for preparing the graphics for this book.

Critical funding was provided by a Wenner-Gren Foundation for Anthropological Research Fellowship and a President's Research Fellowship in the Humanities from the University of California. Several travel grants through African Studies, the Latin American Studies Center, and the International Studies and Overseas Programs of the University of California, Los Angeles, helped make possible some of my fieldwork.

I have also drawn on several of my previously published articles: "From Hands to Tutors: African Expertise in the South Carolina Rice Economy," *Agricultural History*, 67, no. 3 (©1993 by *Agricultural History*): 1–30; "Landscapes of Technology Transfer: Rice Cultivation and African Continuities," *Technology and Culture*, 37, no. 1 (1996): 5–35; "Rice Milling, Gender, and Slave Labour in Colonial South Carolina," *Past and Present: A Journal of Historical Studies*, no. 153 (November 1996; world copyright: The Past and Present Society, 175 Banbury Road, Oxford, England): 108–134; "The African Origins of Carolina Rice Culture," *Ecumene*, 7, no. 2 (2000): 127–149. I thank the journals for permission to use these materials here in revised form.

As the first in my family to earn a college degree, I would like to pay homage to the teachers who gave me a love of learning and inspired me over the years to continue my education. This book represents my effort to give something back to that broader community. Another source of inspiration has been the encouragement of family and friends outside the academy. Among those whose love and friendship sustained me over the years are my brothers, Lou, Tim, and Gary Carney; my sister, the late Margaret Sanchez; Doris and the late Martin Goetz; and Lou Truesdell. Two people especially deserve acknowledgment for making this book possible. One is Don Goetz, a companion in life's journey for over twenty-five years, whose love, compassion for others, and courage inspired me. Sadly, his untimely death did not grant him the opportunity to read these words of appreciation. The other person I wish to acknowledge is Richard Rosomoff, for his unflagging encouragement over the long period of writing. He weathered the uncertainties involved in bringing a large project to conclusion, and most important, he believed in the book and in me.

Finally, as the dedication states, this book is also for my parents, Margaret G. and Louis J. Carney, whose passage in life was brief. Their abbreviated lives catapulted me from an early age into a special odyssey as an adult, with full awareness of the brevity of time and the meaning of love. My research for this book has made me acutely aware of my privileged position in being able to honor them. This was not the case for the millions forced into Atlantic slavery, as the following pages testify.

Black Rice

Introduction

> The millions of Africans who were dragged to the New World were
> not blank slates upon which European civilizations would write at
> will. They were peoples with complex social, political, and religious
> systems of their own. By forced transportation and incessant violence
> slavery was able to interdict the transfer of those systems as systems;
> none could be carried intact across the sea. But it could not crush the
> intellects, habits of mind, and spirits of its victims. They survived in
> spite of everything, their children survived and in them survived
> Africa.
>
> —Sidney W. Mintz, introduction to the 1990 edition of
> *The Myth of the Negro Past* by Melville Herskovits

$\mathcal{T}$HIS BOOK is about rice and the origins of its cultivation in
the Americas. It is, in fact, a narrative of the Atlantic slave trade whose
telling assists in the recovery of a significant African contribution to the
agricultural history of the Americas. As the following pages reveal, this
contribution was to prove considerably more than the standard view of
slaves as a source of unskilled labor. Through their cultivation of rice,
slaves reinforced an African identity by adapting a favored dietary staple of West Africa to tropical and subtropical America. But even more
critically, the knowledge of how to grow rice provided the enslaved
with the ability to negotiate the terms of their bondage while providing
a subsistence staple to maroons throughout Latin America.[1]

Of the more than twenty species of the rice genus *Oryza*, only two
were domesticated, *glaberrima* and *sativa*. Most likely both types were
introduced to the New World in the century following the voyages
of Columbus. The conventional interpretation of rice history in the
Americas assigns Europeans the role of ingeniously adapting a crop of
Asian origin to New World conditions. This perspective, however, ig-
nores the role of Africans in establishing a preferred food staple under

slavery. The development of rice culture marked not simply the movement of a crop across the Atlantic but also the transfer of an entire cultural system, from production to consumption.

Drawing upon diverse historical and botanical materials, I argue for
the primacy of African rice and skills in the crop's development in the
Americas. My focus is on treating the transfer of rice as the diffusion of
an indigenous knowledge system. The method involves a close inspection of the agricultural strategy of rice growing and its techniques—
an agrarian genealogy—and their evolution over time. A knowledge
system long practiced in West Africa was brought with slaves across
the Atlantic. This book draws attention to how its diffusion has been
misunderstood and misinterpreted in ways that diminished the significance of the African origins of the crop and of the people who grew
the rice, processed the grain, and prepared the food. Recovery of this
African knowledge system promotes our understanding of rice history
in the Atlantic basin and the African contribution to the Americas. An
agrarian genealogy of rice demands an intellectual journey through the
Atlantic basin that reverses the direction of enslaved persons across the
Middle Passage.

THE PAST SEVERAL decades have witnessed an increasing willingness
by scholars to concede that Africans may have played a significant role
in shaping the cultures of the Americas since 1500. Among the long-
standing themes in African-American history is the debate over cultural survival and acculturation. This dates to the early twentieth century, when anthropologist Melville Herskovits first tried to show that
to believe that the African and the African-American had no past was
to perpetuate a pernicious myth. In his 1941 book, *The Myth of the Negro Past*, Herskovits challenged the notion of sociologist E. Franklin
Frazier and his students that slavery had stripped its victims of their African heritage.[2] Over the next decades Herskovits and his followers
identified various cultural retentions they viewed as African, particularly in relation to religion, language, and the arts. Much of this research, however, drew criticism for treating Africa as a single cultural
area, a concept of culture very much in fashion at that time, but inaccu-
rate in portraying the diversity and complexity of cultures found in just
West Africa alone.[3] The search for vestiges of an African culture in the

United States consequently proved so generalized that it provided little understanding of the distinctive black cultures that formed in the Americas. Nonetheless, Herskovits's field research in West Africa, the Caribbean, and Suriname made him the first scholar to examine populations of African descent from a perspective focused on the Atlantic basin.

Rejecting the value of identifying African traits for explaining the distinctive black cultures of the Americas, anthropologists Sidney Mintz and Richard Price emphasized instead the process of cultural change. In *The Birth of African-American Culture: An Anthropological Perspective* (1976) they argued that cultural fragmentation and the formation of plantation societies of slaves from disparate ethnic origins resulted in syncretic cultures. Slaves survived the brutal and dehumanizing experience of bondage by developing hybrid cultures. Enslavement thus forced them to create their own culture within a setting where plantation owners exercised an absolute monopoly of power. The social experience of being African and a slave, Mintz and Price argued, proved far more significant in structuring the black cultures of the Americas than any traits or retentions associated with specific African ethnic groups. The emphasis of Mintz and Price on the syncretic cultures slaves shaped from their African origins profoundly influenced studies of black cultures throughout the African diaspora.[4]

Until the 1970s interest in the role that Africa, and West Africa in particular, may have played in the shaping of certain aspects of society and culture in the Americas remained largely a concern of anthropologists. This changed profoundly in 1974 when historian Peter Wood published *Black Majority*. In a radical departure from previous studies of the coastal South Carolina plantation economy, Wood moved blacks from the background to the center of the analysis by showing the context in which slaves of different ethnic groups forged a new way of life around the cultivation of rice. He argued that the emergence of rice as the chief plantation crop owed a great deal to the fact that many West Africans, unlike the European colonists, grew rice before crossing the Middle Passage of slavery. Wood's brilliant insight was to emphasize the skills that Africans brought to the Carolina frontier through a critical reading of early accounts of rice cultivation, written by slave owners, that attributed such knowledge to European ingenuity. His work shifted the research emphasis from cultural *change* to cultural *exchange* while challenging the long-held notion that slaves contributed only unskilled labor to the plantation economies of the Americas.[5]

Historian Daniel C. Littlefield's book, *Rice and Slaves*, published in 1981, added several innovative directions to Wood's research. In the spirit of Herskovits, Littlefield placed his analysis of Carolina rice origins within the context of the Atlantic basin, identifying the area of West Africa where rice was planted and thus the geographic origin of ethnic groups familiar with its cultivation during the Atlantic slave trade. He documented the preference among rice planters for slaves from specific ethnic groups, thereby revealing their awareness of those skilled in rice cultivation. Drawing upon evidence from shipping accounts and newspaper ads for runaways, Littlefield contended that planters were aware of ethnic differences among Africans. Documentation shows that plantation owners, even if not always able to obtain Africans skilled in rice growing, sought to use this knowledge of rice cultivation for their own purposes.[6]

The emphasis of Wood and Littlefield on the diffusion of skills from West Africa to South Carolina in rice cultivation explored new terrain. Instead of examining the impact of one culture upon another, they emphasized how Africans from diverse ethnicities, thrown together in slavery, created a new way of life in coastal Carolina, where a crop known only to some of them became the plantation staple. The association of agricultural skills with certain African ethnicities within a specific geographic region opened up provocative questions concerning the black Atlantic and called for a research perspective emphasizing not only culture but also culture in relationship to technology and the environment.

A perspective on culture and environment in Atlantic history was already being developed by historian Alfred W. Crosby in his book *The Columbian Exchange*, published in 1972, as well as in other volumes that appeared over the following decade.[7] Emphasis on the cultural and biological exchanges that radically transformed New and Old World ecosystems in the aftermath of the voyages of Columbus served as Crosby's point of departure. His work chronicled the transatlantic exchange of peoples, plants, animals, and germs, drawing particular attention to the impact of seeds of New World origin on the Old World, and the role of Europeans in their global diffusion. Crosby's original notion of this

"Columbian Exchange" has become central to our understanding of the transoceanic plant exchanges that accompanied European voyages across the globe. An enduring legacy of his research was to place culture and environment in a new relationship through the dramatic transformations that occurred in Atlantic world ecosystems.

The exchange of plants of African origin and the plausible role of slaves in their adaptation to New World environments, however, has only recently begun to receive consideration among researchers. Much of this neglect has derived from the racial and gender biases of so much inherited scholarship, which cast Africa as a backwater of the global economic system, intrinsically devoid of civilization. As bondage placed males and females in the social category of slaves, scholarship dispossessed them of their preexisting ethnic and gendered forms of knowledge, robbing them of their real contributions to the Americas. African food systems, the foundation of civilization, were similarly ignored. The historical botany of West Africa's chief food staple, rice, for instance, was not widely known in the anglophone world until the 1970s.[8] The question of whether enslaved persons brought with them any inherited knowledge and skills from the African continent would await the research of Peter Wood and others.

Although the research of Wood and Littlefield has chipped away at the notion that slaves brought few skills across the Middle Passage, those contributions are still too frequently conceptualized as minor. Little ground in fact has given way over the issue that slaves may have transferred crucial technologies to the Americas, such as milling devices or systems of water control for irrigation. Consideration of this proposition strikes deep into the widely held belief in Western culture that attributes the political-economic hegemony of Europe and the United States to a preeminent mastery of technology, which in turn distinguishes Europe and its culture from all other societies. In this view the direction of technology and its advances diffuses across geographic space to non-European peoples.[9]

But serious problems develop with this view when one considers agriculture. The modern urbanized world that characterizes the twenty-first century makes it difficult to recall the worlds in existence over two hundred years ago, when life was lived in largely rural environments. In the not so distant past the relationship of culture to environment was one where agriculture provided the connective tissue. Agriculture represented distinctive repositories of knowledge transmitted through practices and technologies to make nature yield. Such knowledge systems were not the same in all places and followed different paths of development. But they all involved ways of knowing, ways of manipulating nature with hands, tools, and mechanical devices to ensure the availability of food for survival. In mediating the relationship between culture and environment, these indigenous knowledge systems linked food to cultural identity. One such indigenous knowledge system that would prove of enduring significance for the Americas emerged on West African floodplains with rice.

Here the words of geographer Carville Earle merit repeating for their bearing on the role of rice in African-American history and the agricultural history of the Americas. Recovery of this suppressed narrative of the Atlantic slave trade demands an intellectual odyssey, "a reacquaintance with the rural worlds of American history, a patient tracing of the manifold agrarian connections between nature and culture in worlds we have lost, a suspension of modernity's disbelief in the extraordinary power of prosaic agrarian systems, and, in the process, an exposition of a new interpretation of the American past."[10]

This book draws attention to the knowledge system underlying the cultivation of rice in the Americas and West Africa. It investigates not only food and cultural identity but issues of indigenous knowledge and epistemology, human agency and social structure, seed transfers and the diffusion of cropping systems, agricultural innovation, and the power relations that shape agrarian practices. An examination of these issues in the context of rice history in the Americas demands rethinking the meaning of the Columbian Exchange to include not only the seeds that transferred throughout the Atlantic basin but the cropping systems as well. People and plants together migrated as a result of European global expansion. And among these were millions of Africans whose enslavement forced them to become involuntary migrants to the Americas. Rice figured crucially among the seeds that accompanied their migration, and slaves planted the crop wherever social and environmental conditions seemed propitious. In adapting a favored dietary staple to local conditions, slaves drew upon a sophisticated knowledge system that informed cultivation and processing methods. Such practices in West Africa have long been ethnic and gendered. This indigenous African expertise mediated the diffusion of rice cultivation to the Americas and offered a means to negotiate the terms of labor in slavery.

Recent advances in biotechnology bring to the fore the relationship of systems of knowledge to ideas developed by different peoples in specific regions of the world, an issue often forgotten in considerations of the Columbian Exchange. Over the past decade the increasing number of patents filed for genetically modified plants have resulted in numerous disputes over intellectual property rights, whose legal adjudication demands the evaluation of prior and regional claims to knowledge.[11] These claims frequently bring into conflict representatives of ethnic groups who domesticated a plant that bears desirable traits with firms in industrialized countries whose subsequent tinkering establishes the legal basis for ownership and profits.

Considerations of prior knowledge and its geographical basis, unfortunately, are not yet a central concern for understanding the significance of the global plant dispersals of the Columbian Exchange. In fact, emphasis on seed transfers has inadvertently removed the knowledge systems developed by specific peoples from the agricultural history of areas revolutionized by the plants they domesticated. The emphasis on seeds over the cropping systems as they diffused throughout the Atlantic world consequently fails to reveal the ethnic and gendered dimensions of indigenous knowledge, which figure importantly in this account of the early history of rice cultivation in the Americas. In disregarding the techniques and processing methods that developed in specific geographical regions with plant domestication, agricultural history is reduced to the mere exchange of seeds by the group brokering their transfer, thereby privileging that group by attributing to it the ingenuity in "discovering" the principles of cultivation. In the case of rice, this position has resulted in a serious distortion that has obscured African technological contributions to rice culture in the Americas, especially where the crop was grown under submersion. Tracing the diffusion of agrarian practices, water control, winnowing, milling, and the cooking techniques associated with African rice cultivation across the Middle Passage to the Americas enables us to place ingenuity in its proper setting, that is, with the West African slaves already skilled in the crop's cultivation.

The establishment of rice cultivation characterized most regions settled by slaves or runaways in the Americas and attests to the crop's significance for cultural identity. In much of West Africa to this day, a meal is not considered complete unless served with rice. The cereal figures importantly in cultural traditions and ritual, and its pounding for consumption even marks the passage of time, as women's rhythmic striking of a pestle against a mortar full of rice grains heralds the beginning of a new day in countless villages of the region. But woven in complex ways with issues of identity is a deep understanding of how to grow rice in diverse habitats and to adapt the crop to challenging environmental circumstances. Rice is a knowledge system that represents ingenuity as well as enormous toil. In at least two important areas of New World slavery, South Carolina and the eastern Amazon in Brazil, planters adopted African expertise in rice farming to develop plantations based on the crop. In South Carolina where slaves' endeavors succeeded, knowledge of rice cultivation likely afforded them some leverage to negotiate the conditions of their labor. This book seeks to move beyond the imagery of the black Uncle Ben promoting the converted rice sold in U.S. markets to place that rice and his ancestors in their rightful historical context.

As we contend with a historical record that is too often mute on African slave contributions to the agricultural history of the Americas, an examination of rice systems across geographic space and within the context of specific regions and ethnic groups provides a way forward for historical recovery. The critical relationship between culture, technology, and the environment, at the center of this analysis, reveals how one of the world's key dietary staples developed across landscapes of the American colonies. The twentieth century began with questions about the African legacy in the Americas and it ended with so much more yet to learn. My hope is that *Black Rice* represents one more step in that crucial endeavor.

1

Encounters

Yet these populations, whose history is scarcely known, are often
bearers of a remarkable material civilization. In agriculture in
particular they perfected with their farming implements different
hydraulic systems.

—Roland Portères, "Vieilles agricultures
de l'Afrique intertropicale" (1950)

$\mathcal{T}$HE EMBARKATION of the Portuguese into the Atlantic in
the fourteenth century led to social and ecological transformations that
brought sub-Saharan Africa within the orbit of European navigation.
With the discovery of the Canary Islands in 1336, just one hundred
kilometers from Morocco off the West African coast, the Portuguese
found an Atlantic island archipelago inhabited by a people they called
the Guanche. The Guanche, whose ancestors left the African mainland
in repeated migrations between the second millennium B.C. and the
first centuries A.D., were farmers and herders. They tended crops and
animals originally domesticated in the Near East, which included
wheat, barley, peas, and sheep and goats. But contact with Renaissance
Europeans brought military defeat and enslavement. By 1496 the
Guanche had ceased to exist, the first indigenous people to become ex-
tinct as a consequence of European maritime expansion. Heralding the
fate that would await other peoples over the next 350 years, the islands
of the Guanche became stepping stones for the diffusion of sugarcane
plantations and African slavery throughout the Atlantic, a process that
radically recast the relationship between Africa, Europe, and the Americas.[1]

With the seizure in 1415 of Ceuta, located on the African side of the
Straits of Gibraltar, the Portuguese established a foothold on the mainland, from where they launched reconnaissance voyages, sponsored by

Prince Henry the Navigator. Over the next five years Portuguese mariners established two navigational routes for exploring West Africa, one along the coast from the mainland outpost at Ceuta, the other following the chain of Atlantic islands south from the Madeiras and the Canary Islands to the Cape Verdes, São Tomé, and Príncipe. The discovery of the Madeira Islands in 1420, named for their abundant forests, provided the fuelwood necessary to carry the expansion of sugarcane into the Atlantic, while the enclave established at Ceuta contributed to the growing familiarity of Portuguese mariners with the African coastline south from Morocco.

This was a barren coast that provided few terrestrial resources, albeit one whose offshore currents abounded in fisheries. Progress southward along this parched coastline over the next two decades as a consequence proved especially slow, but advanced rapidly when two Portuguese, Nuno Tristão and Dinis Dias, independently reached the Senegal and Gambia Rivers in the years 1444 and 1446. After hundreds of kilometers of barren coastline, the Senegal River presented a striking ecological divide, for at this point rainfall becomes just sufficient to support agriculture. One fifteenth-century Venetian chronicler, Cadamosto, memorialized the dramatic social and ecological transformation wrought by the Senegal River on the crews of Portuguese caravels: "It appears to me a very marvellous thing that beyond the [Senegal] river all men are very black, tall and big, their bodies well formed; and the whole country green, full of trees, and fertile; while on this side [Mauritania], the men are brownish, small, lean, ill-nourished, and small in stature; the country sterile and arid."[2]

Taking advantage of abundant marine resources for food supplies, the Portuguese established a trading fort north of the Senegal River on Arguim Island off the coast of Mauritania in 1448. The location served to provision the quickening number of Portuguese forays southward along the coast. This resulted in the discovery of the uninhabited Cape Verde archipelago, fourteen small volcanic islands some five hundred kilometers west of Senegal, on one return voyage in 1455. By 1460 the Portuguese had completed reconnaissance of the Upper Guinea Coast, the densely populated region from Senegal to Liberia that would serve as a major focus for the Atlantic slave trade.[3]

Over the next centuries European mariners would call this region the Grain or Rice Coast after its specialized production of cereals. Fol-

lowing the lead of the Portuguese, others too would depend upon surplus grain production for provisions. Thus for European ships voyaging along the West African coast, passage south beyond the Senegal
River brought them to a region abundant in cereals. East of Liberia,
grain cultivation gradually gave way to root crops like yams. Low in
protein and perishable on long voyages, these crops proved far less significant as food staples on ships than cereals.[4] While reference to the
Upper Guinea Coast conjures up images of the Atlantic slave trade, the
term "Grain or Rice Coast" does not. Yet the two reveal the Janus-
faced relationship of food surpluses to the dense populations that Europeans enslaved in the region from Senegal to Liberia. Widespread
cereal availability resulted from the sophisticated level indigenous agriculture had already attained in Africa in the early modern period.

Despite the significance of these agricultural systems in the regional
economy and commerce with Portuguese caravels, the cereals produced along the Upper Guinea Coast have received little attention in
historical scholarship. More research has focused on the food staples of
New World provenance introduced into Africa, such as maize, manioc,
and peanuts, than on those the Portuguese found in West Africa during
the first century of exploration. Yet increased scholarly attention to the
Grain or Rice Coast reveals a hidden narrative of the Atlantic slave
trade, one that contributes significantly to the historical recovery of the
African experience in the Americas.

Dependent upon the surpluses produced and marketed by African
societies, Portuguese caravels voyaging along the sub-Saharan coast
took note of the agricultural systems they encountered. The indigenous African cereals, millet and sorghum, were among the first crops
described in the region between the Senegal and Gambia Rivers.
When mariners proceeded to the wetter areas of the Upper Guinea
Coast south of the embouchure of the Gambia River, their accounts
mention the cultivation of rice. Thus rice, millet, and sorghum were
the three cereals grown along the Grain or Rice Coast reported in the
earliest European accounts.

The societies of the Upper Guinea Coast had a rich and varied food
supply. The Portuguese, and other seafaring Europeans who followed,
contributed to the complexity of the agricultural systems found along
the Guinea Coast and the surpluses available for sale to slave ships
crossing the Middle Passage. Africans readily adopted imported food

staples such as maize, peanuts, tomatoes, and manioc and frequently experimented with these American introductions long before they became established in Europe.[5] The introduced seeds rapidly became part of African cropping systems, and they were cultivated and prepared in the same manner as the indigenous food staples. A similar process characterized the European adoption of imported American seeds, although dependence on one crop out of a cropping complex, as with maize and potatoes, could result in malnutrition, even starvation.[6]

During the Atlantic slave trade, Europeans knew where cereals were grown in West Africa as well as where to find food surpluses. But over the ensuing centuries of slavery, this knowledge was overlooked and seemingly lost; the enslavement of Africans dehumanized its victims and disparaged their achievements in agriculture and technology.[7] The indigenous African cereals were viewed as nothing more than a few "inferior and miserable food staples."[8]

Since the undermining of African agricultural accomplishments proved a legacy of the Atlantic slave trade, it was also assumed, incorrectly, that the Portuguese must have introduced rice from Asia. The discovery of a maritime route to Asia at the end of the fifteenth century had brought Europeans into contact with hierarchical Asian societies based on rice. When Europeans encountered irrigated rice along the West African coast, they believed those systems represented a transfer of technology from Asian societies.[9] Certainly, it could not be the product of the nonstratified societies that Europeans found growing irrigated rice along the Upper Guinea Coast.[10] Credit to the Portuguese for bringing rice and irrigated culture to West Africa persisted without question well into the twentieth century despite the fact that accounts of Portuguese introduction of the crop to West Africa seldom addressed how mariners might have transferred knowledge of irrigated rice to Africans.[11]

To begin the process of the historical recovery of African agricultural achievements and their linkage to the Americas, we need to examine early accounts of rice cultivation along the West African coast. Conventional scholarship has placed the knowledge and extent of African rice cultivation in the context of Portuguese exploration and the transoceanic crop exchanges that subsequently became known as the "Columbian Exchange." Highlighting the Columbian Exchange usually emphasizes seed transfers, a process that assigns Europeans the principal role in global agricultural history. Instead we will explore the indigenous knowledge systems in which crops developed, a process which brings a West African rather than a European protagonist to the history of rice cultivation and its dissemination.

Early accounts of rice in West Africa should provide answers to three primary questions on the crop's cultural origins, beginning with whether the historical record suggests that the cultivation of rice was already established along the West African coast prior to the arrival of the Portuguese. The second concern is to determine whether descriptions of rice culture from the initial period of contact with Europeans indicate a sophisticated system of production. These would include methods of water control associated with irrigated rice, such as growing the crop under submergence, transplanting, and constructing dikes and embankments for flooding and drainage. A final, and related, consideration aims to determine to what extent the ecological and social factors that characterize the cultivation of rice in the contemporary period are evident in the past.

Early Descriptions of Rice Culture

Senegambia, the name given to the region encompassed between the Senegal and Gambia Rivers, was the first section of the Grain or Rice Coast reached by Europeans (Figure 1.1).[12] South of the Senegal River along the Upper Guinea Coast, precipitation increases steadily. The dominant cereals adapted to semiarid conditions, sorghum and millet, grade into rice over the broad region extending down the Atlantic coast from the Gambia River to Liberia, the area that would become known as the Grain or Rice Coast. Decades before ships would reach India, the Portuguese chronicler Gomes Eanes de Azurara recorded the first European mention of rice in West Africa. In 1446 Stevam Alfonso reached the mouth of a large river—possibly the Gambia—where he encountered the cultivation of wetland rice on floodplains: "They arrived sixty leagues beyond Cape Verde, where they met with a river which was of good width, and into it they entered with their caravels . . . they found much of the land sown, and many fields sown with rice . . . And he said that land . . . seemed like marsh."[13]

Alvise da Cadamosto, who visited the Gambia River in 1455 and again the following year, remarked upon the significance of rice as a di-

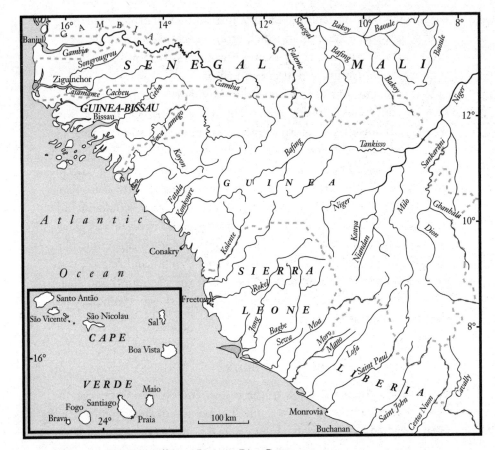

Figure 1.1 The West African Grain or Rice Coast

etary staple: "In this way of life they conduct themselves in almost all respects similarly to the negroes of the kingdom of Senega [Senegal]; they eat the same foods except they have more varieties of rice than grow in the country of Senega."[14]

By 1460, less than twenty years after the first caravel sailed past the Senegal River, Portuguese ships had completed reconnaissance of the one thousand kilometers spanning the Upper Guinea Coast as well as the Cape Verde Islands. From this period commentaries on rice become even more abundant. Journeying along the West African coast in 1479–80, Eustache de la Fosse observed the cultivation of rice along coastal estuaries as well as the active purchase of surpluses by Portuguese vessels. Duarte Pacheco Pereira similarly noted during travels in 1505–1508 that rice and meat were in great abundance in the region of

Guinea-Bissau.[15] Valentim Fernandes, a German of Moravian birth who worked in Lisbon with early Portuguese mariner accounts, recorded in the period 1506–1510 the active trade in rice, millet, milk, and meat among the Gambian Mandinka: "They eat rice, milk, and millet . . . Poor people who don't have sweet potatoes, have rice . . . Their food is like that of the Wolof [of Senegal] except that they eat more rice and they have so much that they take it to sell and exchange, also [palm] wine, oil, and meat and other foodstuffs. Because this Mandinka land is very rich in food like rice and millet, etc."[16]

For most of the fifteenth century trading was confined to ships, but by the end of the century Portuguese and Cape Verdean traders were being admitted to some West African communities.[17] Subsequent European scholarship assumed these same Portuguese navigators and traders introduced irrigated rice cultivation to Africans along the Upper Guinea Coast. Yet in this early period, the Portuguese were attempting to understand this form of rice cultivation. Attributing the sophisticated irrigated system to Portuguese tutelage in later centuries failed to question how they came by this presumed knowledge, nor did it accord with mariner accounts.

Along the coast south of the Gambia River to Sierra Leone, a distance of about five hundred miles, rice proved so abundant that Portuguese ships routinely purchased it for provisions, often from the non-stratified rice-growing ethnic groups like the Baga, with whom they initiated an early trade in indigo. When English privateer, buccaneer, and slaver John Hawkins raided an island offshore Sierra Leone in 1562 and 1564, one chronicler recounted: "The Samboses had inhabited there 3 yeeres before our coming thither, and in so short space have so planted the ground, that they had great plentie of mill [millet], rise [*sic*], rootes, pompions, pullin, goates . . . In addition to seizing all the captives they could, the English stole all the inhabitants' grains and fruits they could conveniently transport."[18]

The trade in rice along the African coast was extensive; ships increasingly depended on African cereal surpluses for their voyages.[19] Rice sales were frequently brokered with female traders, as the Portuguese-African (Luso-African) trader André Donelha observed around 1625 in Guinea-Bissau, "and here the black women hold a market when ships are in port; they bring for sale rice."[20]

Settlement of the Cape Verde Islands involved the import of slaves amid an active trade with the mainland that included a diverse array of commodities: gold, ivory, kola nut, melegueta pepper, cowhides, animal pelts, cotton, iron, dye wood, beeswax, and food staples.[21] The Cape Verdes were a crucial trading entrepôt for the expanding commerce with Portugal; ships bound for long Atlantic voyages in the fall and winter headed there with the prevailing northeast winds and followed the southward flow of the Canary Current before continuing on to Brazil, the West African coast, or India.

As the slave population on the islands grew, African agricultural staples became the basis for subsistence, with surpluses often sold to ships. By the early 1500s rice was being planted on the Cape Verde island most propitious for agriculture, Santiago, along with other key African domesticates such as yams, sorghum, and millet.[22] In 1514 rice appears on cargo lists of ships departing the Cape Verde Islands, and one record from 1530 mentions the deliberate export of rice seed to Brazil.[23] Portuguese vessels carried nearly all the slaves that made the trip to the Cape Verde Islands and the Americas prior to the 1620s, and they left the region with provisions on board. After crossing the Middle Passage, these vessels routinely stopped in Spanish Jamaica and Portuguese Maranhão to replenish victuals before continuing on to slave markets elsewhere.[24] With the arrival in Cape Verde of ships from other European nations in the last decades of the sixteenth century and the growing number of trading forts established along the coast, references to rice increase; both settlement and trade relied upon African cereals for food.[25]

Because of their proximity to navigation routes, the first African rice systems to receive mention were the ones located in coastal estuaries as well as upstream along the river floodplains of Senegambia. These rivers are low-lying and affected by marine water in the lower seventy to one hundred kilometers. Venturing upstream in search of potable water and safe anchorage, the Portuguese came across tidal floodplain cultivation. Valentim Fernandes (c. 1506–1510) recorded the first description of rice cultivation along tidal floodplains: "From Cape Vert until here there are two rainy seasons and two rains each year. Twice they sow and twice they harvest rice and millet etc., knowing they will harvest in April and in September, and when they gather in the rice then they sow yams and these they cultivate year round."[26]

Here rice was submerged by tidal flow. Fernandes's account confuses the presence of two harvests with two rainy seasons; the climatological and historical record shows that this part of Senegal, then as now, only experiences a single rainy season in the months from May/June to September/October. What his description alludes to, however, is the practice of flood-recession agriculture, sometimes known by its French name, *décrue*, which likely accounts for the two harvests he mentions. Flood-recession cultivation is a system of planting on the floodplain after the onset of the dry season, when the reduced volume in river water has caused available fresh water to retreat. As the account of Fernandes indicates, *décrue* planting on soils with stored moisture reserves occurred in late fall or early winter, with harvesting taking place at the height of the dry season in April or May. Flood-recession agriculture remains to this day extremely important in the Sahel, the region south of the Sahara Desert, and especially along the Senegal and Niger Rivers.[27]

Richard Jobson, an English trader and explorer who navigated upstream along the Gambia River in 1620–21, also described the tidal floodplain system. Jobson's ship traveled up the Gambia, where permanently saline water grades into seasonally fresh water in the section of the river from 70 to about 240 kilometers. In the interval between the first rains and the shift in the river from brackish to sweet water, farmers established rice seedbeds on inland swamps near their villages for later transplanting to the floodplain. Jobson's account provides an early indication of a second environment planted to rice, namely inland swamps, where seedlings were established for later transplanting once freshwater conditions returned to the floodplain: "But in Rice they do set it first in smal [*sic*] patches of low marish grounds, and after it doth come up, disperse the plants, and set them in more spacious places, which they prepare for it, and it doth yield a great increase."[28]

No rice production system, however, received as much attention and interest as that practiced in the estuaries along the coast, known as mangrove rice. This system of production involved the creation of irrigated perimeters from coastal mangrove swamps. Its proximity to maritime routes along the coast as well as the sophisticated transformation it wrought upon the landscape elicited considerable European commentary, even when salinity forced abandonment of the paddies. When a prolonged cycle of drought prevented mangrove rice cultivation in the Sine-Saloum estuary north of the Gambia River, land use shifted to collecting the accumulated salt deposits. Diogo Gomes, in 1456 the first Portuguese captain to enter the estuaries of the Geba (Guinea-Bissau) and Gambia Rivers, observed that the regional trade in a red salt originated on such abandoned rice fields.[29]

The mangrove system, unlike tidal floodplain production, required building huge embankments to prevent overspill from marine tides, ridging for soil aeration, and the construction of canals and dikes for miles along the coast. In 1594, almost a century before the colonization of South Carolina where similar systems would eventually predominate, André Alvares de Almada, a Luso-African trader based in Santiago, Cape Verde, provided a detailed description of this irrigated rice system found in estuaries along the coast from the Gambia River south to Guinea Conakry. He noted that "the residents were growing their crops on the riverain deposits, and by a system of dikes had harnessed the tides to their own advantage."[30] This was the same system European scholarship would subsequently attribute to Portuguese introduction. De Almada noted the use of dikes to impound rainwater for seedling submergence, ridging, and the embankment of plots to capture water. His account establishes the technique of transplanting nearly twenty-five years before Jobson described it along the Gambia, and in an entirely different environment sown to rice: "The Blacks make rice fields in these plains; they make ridges from the earth because of the river, but in spite of that the river breaks them and inundates many a time. Once the rice has sprouted they pull it up and transplant it in other lands better drained where then it becomes grain."[31] Despite errors in interpreting the function of ridges and canals, de Almada's description leaves no doubt that West Africans were quite familiar with planting irrigated rice, as in Asia, and possessed the sophisticated knowledge that is emblematic of a fully evolved wet rice culture.

An independent confirmation of de Almada's description of mangrove rice cultivation in coastal estuaries came in 1685, when Sieur de la Courbe journeyed overland through Diola settlements from the Gambia to the Geba River in Guinea-Bissau. He remarked that "there was no house which did not have a rice nursery nearby, while along the river banks the landscape had been transformed into a pattern of causeways with rice plants appearing above the flooded fields" and described the extensive system of dikes and rice paddies developed along river estuaries: "It had already begun to rain and I saw the rice fields which are all along the river. They are crossed by small embankments . . . to prevent the water from running off."[32] André Brüe, traveling through Senegambia in 1694 and 1724, observed other ethnic groups involved in irrigated rice alongside coastal estuaries. The Baïnouks of Casamance also constructed small canals to irrigate their polders.[33]

As the Atlantic slave trade deepened and seized many of the coastal peoples involved in growing wet rice, the mangrove system became associated with the expertise of one group of its practitioners, the Baga, who survived the earliest wave of Atlantic slavery. The Baga system of irrigated rice production so captured the interest of one slave captain, Samuel Gamble, that he depicted and described their cultivation practices in Guinea Conakry around 1793 (Figure 1.2):

> The Bagos are very expert in Cultivating rice and in quite a Different manner to any of the Nations on the Windward Coast [Sierra Leone]. The country they inhabit is chiefly loam and swampy. The rice they first sew [*sic*] on their dunghills and rising spots about their towns; when 8 or 10 Inches high [they] transplant it into Lugars [places/fields] made for that purpose which are flat low swamps, at one side . . . they have a reservoir that they can let in what water they please, [on the] other side . . . is a drain out so they can let off what they please . . . The instrument they use much resembles a Turf spade [*kayendo*] with which they turn the grass under in ridges just above the water which by being confined Stagnates and nourishes the root of the plant. Women & Girls transplant the rice and are so dextrous as to plant fifty roots singly in one minute. When the rice is ready for cutting they turn the water off till their Harvest is over then they let the Water over it and let it stand three or four Seasons it being so impoverished.[34]

Besides providing an excellent overview of irrigated rice cultivation in cleared mangrove swamps, Gamble's commentary reveals a significant feature of Baga production that would emerge in the crop's diffusion across the Atlantic: a division of labor by task that represented specialized, gendered systems of knowledge. Females transplanted the seedlings while males prepared the irrigated paddy with the flat-bladed shovel known as the *kayendo*. The latter was a long-handled specialized

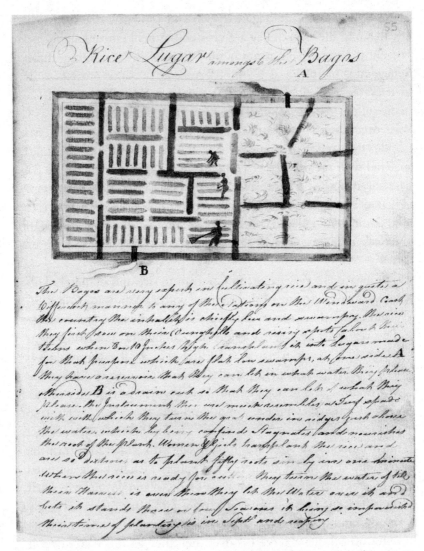

Figure 1.2 The slave captain Samuel Gamble's depiction of Baga rice cultivation, c. 1793

spadelike shovel used by men to lift and turn over the heavy clay soils planted to mangrove rice. Along the Upper Guinea Coast from Casamance, Senegal, into Guinea Conakry, where mangrove rice is planted, this specialized implement is synonymous with the labor involved in transforming the landscape into irrigated fields. Cadamosto describes its use in rice planting as early as 1455: "Their manner of farming is that four or five of them line up in the field with some paddles [shovels], throwing the earth ahead of them but not deeper than four fingers in the earth, which is heavy and sticky, yet enables the germination of all that which is sown."[35] This description of the key implement of mangrove rice, coming just ten years after the Portuguese encountered the Senegal River, clearly indicates the antiquity of irrigated rice cultivation and its development prior to their arrival.

As the Portuguese moved south along the Upper Guinea Coast along the littoral of Sierra Leone, a region known as the Windward Coast, they entered another major area of rice cultivation. From the late sixteenth century other European nations established trading enclaves along the Windward Coast, which brought traders into contact with rice systems not easily evident from shipboard. Their accounts take note of rain-fed rice cultivation in areas of moderate to heavy rainfall.[36]

Relying upon information supplied by Dutch merchants operating along the Windward Coast in the region between Sierra Leone and Liberia, Amsterdam geographer Olfert Dapper provided a clear exposition of the rice farming system around 1640. His account captured a fundamental principle of West African rice production, the importance of planting along a landscape gradient in distinct environments that include floodplains, inland swamps, and uplands:

Those who are hard-working can cultivate three rice-fields in one summer; they sow the first rice on low ground, the second a little higher and the third . . . on the high ground, each a month after the previous one, in order not to have all the rice ripe at the same time; this would bring them into difficulty with regard to cutting the rice, since it is cut ear by ear or stalk by stalk—a very wearisome task. This is the commonest practice throughout the country . . . The first or early rice, sown in low and damp areas . . . the second, sown on somewhat higher ground . . . the third, sown on the high ground . . .[37]

Dapper's remarks reveal a comprehensive understanding that a West African rice landscape represents a production system of distinct environmental components, which are planted at different times in relation to elevation and type of water regime available for cultivation.[38] Early commentaries on rice, made from shipboard or brief sojourns on the mainland, usually described just the lowland portion of this rice gradient, the section within easy sight of mariners such as the tidal floodplain or mangrove systems. But as Europeans set up forts and entrepôts along the coast of Sierra Leone during the seventeenth century, they came into contact with rain-fed environments planted to rice. The landscapes they observed were fashioned to achieve a broader agricultural strategy designed to respond to two key principles. The first was to minimize the risk of crop loss should production in one environment fail; the second aimed to reduce labor bottlenecks in the cultivation cycle by planting distinct environments at different times, thereby spreading out labor demands. These principles characterize West African rice culture to this day.

With increasing European knowledge of the African hinterland during the eighteenth century, comments proliferate on the inland swamp and rain-fed production environments. In the 1730s Francis Moore described the common practice of growing rice on ridges in inland swamps without transplanting: "The Rice, which is the second Kind and esteem'd their choicest Food, they set in Rills, as we do Pease; it grows in wet grounds, the Ears like Oats."[39]

During his travels through Senegambia from 1749 to 1753 one correspondent of the Royal Academy of Sciences, Michael Adanson, noted the widespread technique of placing earthen embankments, or bunds, around the perimeters of inland swamps to retain water: "Rice is almost the only grain sown at Gambia in the lands overflown by the rains of the high season. The negroes cut all these lands with small causeys [causeways] which with-hold the waters in such a manner, that their rice is always moistened. They had got in their crop long before my arrival; so that the rice fields in the month of February were a sort of drained morasses on which they grew a few wild herbs."[40]

These water management techniques also caught the eye of René Caillié in Senegal during the early nineteenth century: "As the country is flat, they take care to form channels to drain off the water. When the inundation is very great, they take advantage of it and fill their little reservoirs, that they may provide against the drought and supply the rice with the moisture which it requires."[41]

The comments by Moore, Adanson, and Caillié reveal several features of inland swamps that indicate a profound African understanding of rice culture. Along a landscape gradient that might include swamps beside seasonally saline or freshwater rivers, seedlings are often first established in inland swamps. They are transplanted to floodplains with the return of fresh water once their height can withstand tidal submergence. Jobson noted this use of inland swamps for seedling establishment in the Gambia in the early seventeenth century. But inland swamps were also an important production area for rice growing, especially since they obtain supplemental water from a high groundwater table or underground springs. The availability of other forms of water than rainfall alone meant that inland swamps retained water into the dry season, and therefore could be directly planted to rice, harvested, and then replanted to vegetables. Many inland swamp environments consequently enabled production of a second crop, with methods similar to flood-recession cultivation on tidal floodplains.

Complementing the description of the rice cultivation system provided by Olfert Dapper for Sierra Leone around 1640, S. M. X. Golberry, who traveled through this region from 1785 to 1787, drew attention to the short-handled hoes employed by women in field preparation and noted the use of female labor in hoeing and harvesting rice:

> The ground having been prepared, they begin to sow the rice towards the commencement of the rainy season. Some days after it has been sown, they break the ground slightly with pick-axes, about two inches in extent, and just deep enough as that the seed be properly covered. The rice is then left to grow, and when it is about a foot in height, the women proceed to hoe it, and this operation is performed with great care, and many times successively. Two months after it has been sown, the rice becomes matured, and the women then also proceed to collect it; they cut it with small knives, which they purchase from the Europeans, tie it into sheaves, and carry it away in baskets.[42]

Other key land-use features of West African rice culture also received attention by Europeans, such as the seasonal rotation of land from rice field to cattle pasture. One diagnostic feature of the African rice production system is its deep relationship to cattle herding, especially in the northern geographic limit of mangrove rice cultivation, located just above the area where trypanosomiasis ("sleeping sickness") occurs. Usually fatal to most large animals, the parasite is found in areas of dense vegetation where rainfall exceeds forty inches.[43] Francis Moore, who worked along the Gambia River during the 1730s as a factor for an English trading company, remarked upon the seasonal shift in land use between farmers and pastoralists on the river's floodplains. Evident throughout the region, the system provided farmers with manured agricultural land and herders with fields for dry-season grazing: "The sides of the River are for the most part flat and woody, for about a quarter of a Mile inland, in some Places not so much, and within that are pleasant open Grounds, which they use for their Rice, and in the dry Season it serves the cattle for Pasture."[44]

The extent of rain-fed cultivation and, particularly, the burning of forested tracts for agro-pastoral rotations in Sierra Leone would also attract the attention of Thomas Winterbottom in 1803.[45] The shift in land use from rice cultivation in the wet season to cattle pasture on the stubble during the dry season occurs to this day throughout West Africa, whether with zebu cattle or the trypanosome-resistant ndama breed. The experience of African ethnic groups such as the Fulani with systems of rotational land use that embraced both grazing and agriculture would contribute considerably to the development of numerous New World frontiers.

In addition to descriptions of the environments planted to rice, techniques of cultivation, and the key implements used in its production, Europeans journeying overland into the West African interior also commented on the types of rice found in West Africa. Writing in 1830, French explorer René Caillié noted the sowing of freshwater river floodplains to tall varieties that withstood tidal surges: "That rice grows to the height of four feet. The soil, which is composed of a very hard grey sand, is fertilized by the inundations of the Tankisso."[46]

These were, in fact, the floating varieties that French colonial botanists found widely grown along Sahelian rivers early in the twentieth century.[47] Even during the 1830s to 1850s, a period of increasing French interest in Senegal as the gateway to the western Sudan, there had been numerous references in Casamance Province south of the Gambia to the cultivation of long- and short-duration varieties of rice of a red color.[48]

But in Sierra Leone, to the south, a more abundant rainfall cycle enabled the cultivation of rice over several months of the year and the sowing of many varieties with growing seasons of different durations, a point Dapper addressed in the 1640s:

> In the middle of January or at the beginning of February they be-
> gin to work on the rice fields, namely first of all on the low and
> muddy places, which they make into fields by cutting down the
> trees and other plants. In sowing, one man goes in front and scat-
> ters the seed on the field. Others scratch it into the ground with
> a curved iron scratching tool. Generally it has already sprouted
> three days later . . . The second rice-planting is begun while the
> first is becoming dry. The sowing season of this rice is the begin-
> ning of May, since this happens on high ground and it is at this
> time that the rainy season begins, making the soil suitable for
> bringing forth crops. Those who are hard-working can cultivate
> three rice-fields in one summer.[49]

Rice was planted along an upland to inland-swamp landscape gradient with varieties of different maturities. The same system was again
described 150 years later by a correspondent with an English ship captain, Nathaniel Cutting. A resident trader operating off the coast of Sierra Leone provided Cutting in 1790 with details on the varieties sown
in different parts of the landscape:

> Cutting regarded the local "Red Rice, as this kind is sometimes
> call'd, [as] a distinct species" not requiring "that the Fields . . . be
> laid under water, yet a great quantity of moisture's necessary to its
> producing a good crop." There was in addition ". . . a distinct spe-
> cies of rice . . . sometimes [sown] in [swamp] grounds."[50]

There were several varieties of rice, cultivated along a landscape in
distinct types of upland and wetland environments. One was planted
with rainfall as its sole water source, another in inland swamps, while a
third type developed for cultivation with submersion.

The Social Organization of Labor in African Rice Culture

Early European descriptions of rice culture in West Africa often commented on the social factors regulating the crop's production. While

discussing food purchases by Dutch traders at Cape Mount near the
Liberian border in Sierra Leone in 1624, Samuel Brun provided an
early indication that women were especially involved in rice culture,
noting "for the rice they wanted only glass corals for their wives, because rice is the ware of women."[51] Following years of residence along
the Gambia River, Francis Moore wrote in 1738 that "the Crops are
the Properties of those who have tilled the ground" and that rice was a
woman's crop: "For every Town almost having 2 common Fields of
cleared Ground, one for their Corn [millet and sorghum], and the
other for the Rice, the Alcalde [village headman] appoints the Labour
of all the People, he being in the Nature of a Governor. The Men work
the Corn Ground and Women and Girls the Rice Ground."[52]

To this day rice remains a woman's crop in The Gambia, as it does
among the Mandinka ethnic groups of neighboring countries. The
Mandinka tidal floodplain system contrasts with that of the Baga,
where men and women grow irrigated rice, but both forms of rice
farming underscore the importance of women in the crop's cultivation.

Recognition of this gendered knowledge perhaps provides additional
insight into Francis Moore's observation that women possessed important individual rights in rice cultivation. Each female rice farmer could
lay claim to a portion of the harvest as her own property: "And the
Women [are] busy in cutting their Rice, which I must remark, is their
own Property, for, after they have set by a sufficient Quantity for Family Use, they sell the Remainder, and take the Money themselves, the
husband not interfering. The same Custom they observe too in regard
to Fowls, which they breed up in great Quantities when they can get
Markets for them."[53]

This system described by Moore for Gambia is typical of rice cultivation over much of the interior of the Sahel and is especially evident
among speakers of the Mande linguistic family, to which Mandinka be-
longs. Along the coast ethnic groups affiliated with the West Atlantic language family grow rice in cleared mangrove swamps; both men
and women participate in planting the crop. The mangrove rice area
involved a gender division of labor by task, with women in charge of
sowing the seeds, transplanting, weeding, and sometimes harvesting,
and men in charge of field preparation and maintenance. Captain Samuel Gamble described the role of Baga women in transplanting rice in
the mangrove system while Golberry similarly noted a division of labor

by sex among rice growers in Sierra Leone, with women involved in hoeing and harvesting the crop.[54]

Women thus played a crucial role in African rice culture regardless of the system. Their labor with rice, moreover, extended beyond the field to the crop's processing, preparation, and cooking. Over the period of the Atlantic slave trade, the importance of female labor in food preparation drew repeated comment from Europeans. Olfert Dapper (c. 1640) mentioned that men provided women no assistance with milling cereals in Sierra Leone; Jean-Baptiste Labat (c. 1728) noted in Senegambia that the crucial duties of pounding rice and food preparation fell upon females.[55] In Africa the standard device for preparing all cereals is the mortar, formed from a hollowed-out tree trunk. Grain is placed into the cavity of the mortar, where the hulls are removed by striking them with a wooden pestle. The removal of rice hulls and the underlying bran, a skilled operation like all other facets of food preparation, was already women's work in the initial period of the Atlantic slave trade. From along the Gambia River, Jobson provided the earliest (c. 1620–21) and most detailed description of the female role in rice milling: "I am sure there is no woman can be under more servitude, with such great staves wee call Coole-Staves [pestles], beate and cleanse both the Rice, all manner of other graine they eate, which is onely womens worke, and very painefull: next, they dresse both that and all other manner of victuall the men doe eate; and it is so ordered, they do bring and set it downe upon the Matte before them presently withdrawing themselves, and are never admitted to sit and eate with them."[56]

The deep association of African women with rice culture throughout West Africa extended to both cultivation and processing. Women's labor proved crucial to the rice-cropping system in ways that were not the case with other cereals such as sorghum and millet. This labor embodied specialized forms of knowledge that would make a significant contribution to rice history in the Americas.

DESCRIPTIONS of West African agriculture in the early period of contact indicate that rice cultivation was well established along the Upper Guinea Coast prior to the arrival of Portuguese mariners in the mid-fifteenth century. One reference to the specialized instrument of irrigated rice cultivation, the *kayendo*, appears in the historical record in

1455, so early as to provide indirect proof for the development of irrigated rice cultivation in mangrove estuaries independently of Portuguese intercession. Other environments identified as being planted to rice in the earliest contact period include the use of tidal floodplains for both wet- and dry-season cultivation (flood recession), inland swamps, and the rain-fed uplands. Cultivation cycles involved varieties whose growing seasons ranged from three to six months' duration, including types adapted to deep flooding. Several accounts refer to the red color of this African rice.

During this early period rice culture was already deeply associated with women's labor. In Senegambia and other areas settled by the Mandinka, rice was strictly a woman's crop, while a gender division of labor by task characterized the social organization of rice cultivation in the mangrove irrigation system. While men did not participate in rice cultivation everywhere the crop was planted, women emerge centrally in the crop's planting, milling, and processing throughout the Upper Guinea Coast.

Early European accounts of West African rice culture additionally call attention to the range of techniques available to farmers and, crucially, to the cultivation of specific environments along a landscape gradient. Such techniques included direct seeding, broadcasting, and transplanting; ridging, the making of earthen embankments, canals, and sluices; the use of tides, flood recession, and rainfall for planting; and specialized implements for preparing heavy soils; as well as the seasonal rotation in land use between rice field and cattle pasture.

Only by understanding West African rice cultivation as an assemblage of integrated component parts can one grasp the full complexity of the indigenous knowledge that enabled the crop's adaptation to so many different locales. In planting numerous lowland and upland environments along a landscape gradient, farmers had at their disposal a rich assortment of techniques that could be adjusted to specific soil and water conditions. Such techniques formed the corpus of a sophisticated knowledge system native to West Africa. Owing its origins to the achievements of African agriculture in the millennia prior to the Atlantic slave trade, indigenous knowledge of rice culture enabled the crop's cultivation over a broad area of the Grain or Rice Coast. During the sixteenth and the seventeenth centuries this African repository of knowledge would provide the principles and flexibility for adapting rice under new conditions in the Americas.

The eighteenth century witnessed the largest number of Africans seized for New World slavery. By the century's close the experience of the Atlantic slave trade had deeply prejudiced European perceptions of African people and their skills. The cultivation of rice in Africa along the Upper Guinea Coast no longer was viewed as autochthonous but as the outcome of European introduction. Meanwhile, the systematic breakdown of African societies from centuries of slave trading took its toll. Farmers, particularly those along the coast who planted irrigated rice, were especially vulnerable: their sedentary way of life and proximity to European navigational routes made them easy prey to slavers. Capture or flight contributed to the breakdown of these more labor-intensive rice systems, whose vestigial survival was increasingly confined to remote locales. Those rice systems that required less infrastructure and labor (like tidal cultivation) weathered the turmoil of 350 years of slavery with fewer consequences. As the availability of quinine in the nineteenth century afforded protection from the deadly ravages of malaria, Europeans began to explore the interior of Africa. The rice systems they observed along river floodplains and in inland swamps did not appear so sophisticated, for they involved little landscape manipulation. Encountering such systems of rice cultivation throughout the interior undoubtedly reinforced the belief that Africans could not have managed more complex forms of irrigated rice.

The mosaic of rice systems Europeans witnessed at the end of the eighteenth century consequently appeared considerably different from its antecedents centuries earlier. The extensive range of irrigated rice Gamble described as the Baga system, for instance, had contracted along the coast to less accessible estuaries in Guinea-Bissau and Guinea Conakry. The Rice Coast now centered on the region around Sierra Leone. Centuries of the Atlantic slave trade had profoundly disrupted indigenous African agricultural systems while selecting for less labor-intensive tidal cultivation over mangrove rice. The retreat of irrigated rice to remote enclaves along the coast, in tandem with racial prejudice that could not imagine an indigenous origin for such a complex system of production, contributed to the unquestioned belief that Portuguese traders and mariners introduced irrigated rice with seeds from

Asia. At the end of an especially brutal century of slavery, rain-fed and tidal production dominated the West African rice landscape. Produced with less labor and landscape manipulation, these rice systems confirmed long-standing beliefs that disparaged African achievements in agriculture and technology.

Over this same century, rice emerged in North America as the leading export crop of coastal South Carolina and Georgia. Prized in European markets for its high quality, Carolina rice served as the global standard for evaluating the types of rice systems encountered in different parts of the world at the end of the eighteenth century. Thus one French commandant based in the tidal rice region of Senegambia around 1770 could predict, "Rice may be produced here as much as in the Provinces of Carolina and Georgia."[57] What he failed to know was that it had been, and since ancient times.

2

Rice Origins and Indigenous Knowledge

Rice cultivation by irrigation and rice cultivation by submersion—
this is the difference between Asian and African civilizations.
—Pierre Viguier, *La riziculture indigène au Soudan français* (1939)

$\mathcal{R}$ICE CULTIVATION is essential to cultural identity
throughout much of West Africa. Among those ethnic groups for
whom the crop is the dietary staple, unless a meal includes rice, they
claim not to have eaten. Its cultural importance is evident in village cel-
ebrations and even in the funerary customs of some groups, where spir-
its of the dead are propitiated by an offering of rice.[1] Female labor is
central to the cultivation of rice throughout West Africa, either as a
crop that women alone grow or through the specialized agricultural
tasks that they alone perform. The Diola of Casamance, Senegal, refer
to rice cultivation as a "woman's sweat" while the Serer of Senegambia
note the importance of female labor in all foodstuff processing by placing the deceased's mortar and pestle on her grave.[2] With the dawn of
each day women's pounding of rice awakens millions of African villagers, the rhythmic striking of rice grains by the pestle providing the
steady heartbeat of community life. Rice is central to subsistence and
cultural identity over a broad area of West Africa; it was to become
equally so in communities of the Americas settled by enslaved persons
from the rice region and their descendants.

The cultivation of rice contributed to the dense populations of the
Upper Guinea Coast that Europeans plundered during the 350 years of
the Atlantic slave trade. An examination of the history of rice in West
Africa and its forms of production reveals the significance of agriculture

to culture in centuries past and the role of rice in the complex knowledge system that male and female slaves brought to the Americas.

Unlike the case of Africa, Asia has never been doubted as a center of
rice domestication, even though the exact area of the crop's origins and
its antiquity have been disputed. However, archaeological excavations
throughout Asia now indicate that the domestication of rice, *Oryza
sativa*, occurred some seven thousand years ago. The species likely
evolved independently yet concurrently in multiple sites over a broad
belt that extended from the Gangetic plain below the foothills of the
Himalayas near Assam, across upper Burma, northern Thailand, North
Vietnam, and into Southwest China near Yunnan.[3] Asian rice was first
domesticated on floodplains as a shallow- or deep-water crop, with cultivation later extended to the rain-fed uplands. By the second to third
century B.C. large-scale centrally managed irrigation systems were in
place, whereas plowing by water buffalo, manuring, and transplanting
developed early in the first centuries A.D.[4]

The beginnings of African rice history are just becoming known.
The reasons for this tardy awareness are multiple. The long-standing
research bias against Africa and its peoples and deep-seated views
within European and American culture that the development of technology was beyond the ken of Africans certainly have contributed. Belief that Africans failed to domesticate crops, a step crucial for the
emergence of civilization, and their presumed acquiescence to slavery,
impeded the advance of scholarship that would illuminate a different
vantage point. An examination of rice history and its underlying knowledge base in Africa reveals the depth of such erroneous yet enduring
legacies of the Atlantic slave trade.

A Shifting Paradigm on Rice

Despite observations of rice cultivation along the West African coast
from the earliest Portuguese voyages, remarkably, until the twentieth
century no scholar suggested the crop might have been established
prior to the arrival of Europeans. Prejudicial views toward Africans
precluded the consideration that rice farming might be indigenous or
Africans capable of developing the irrigated systems Europeans found
south along the coast from the Gambia River. Scholars routinely assigned the establishment of rice cultivation in West Africa to the Por-

tuguese, whom they credited with introducing the crop from Asia as well as the irrigation techniques needed for growing it.[5] No one questioned how or why Portuguese seafarers would be likely tutors for imparting this sophisticated knowledge.

Only twentieth-century botanical research raised questions about this long-standing interpretation. As Europe carved Africa into colonies during the 1880s and forced Africans to grow export crops desired in the metropole, whole systems of agricultural production were disrupted. Throughout the interior of the Upper Guinea Coast emphasis was placed on peanuts and cotton grown exclusively for metropole markets.[6] Food shortages became a persistent feature of colonialism as punitive tax structures forced farmers to cultivate cash crops at the expense of the traditional rain-fed staples, sorghum and millet. The cultivation of rice in lowlands received increasing emphasis for its ecological complementarity with cash crops on the uplands, and colonial botanists set out to improve the crop's performance.[7]

At the end of the nineteenth century a French botanical expedition (1898–1900) to the newly founded colonies of Senegal and Niger made an unanticipated and startling discovery. In 1899, in the region between the upper Senegal and upper Niger Rivers, they encountered a type of rice distinctly different from the Asian varieties familiar to them. South of Gambia in Casamance, Senegal, they found similar specimens: a red rice that grew on floodplains and in the water but bore little resemblance to any cultivated rice previously seen.[8] Their botanical collections revealed several wild relatives of this rice but none showing Asian parentage.[9] Its distinctive traits suggested an African origin.

Research on the distribution of this rice and its varietal diversity prompted French botanists to reexamine two collections of rice made in West Africa during the first half of the nineteenth century. Botanist Leprieur in Senegal collected the first specimens over the period 1824–1829, while Edelstan Jardin's collection came from islands off the coast of Guinea Conakry in 1845–1848. Both collectors identified their samples as *Oryza sativa* (Asian rice), the only species known in the Linnaean classification that had been established in the eighteenth century.[10] An early examination of the Jardin collection by German botanist Ernst Gottlieb Steudel in 1855, however, had led him to conclude that the samples represented a rice species distinct from Asian *sativa*, which he named *Oryza glaberrima* for its smooth hulls.[11] Nevertheless

his research did not suggest an African origin for this rice. The redis-
covery of Steudel's study in tandem with the botanical evidence led
French botanist August Chevalier and his colleagues in 1914 to advance the hypothesis for an indigenous African rice.[12] Their research
attributed the center of African rice domestication to the inland delta
of the Niger River in Mali, a center of *glaberrima* diversity.[13]

Thus began a debate on rice origins in Africa that would ensue over
many decades. The view that rice was grown prior to the arrival of Europeans and domesticated independently south of the Sahara met with
considerable skepticism. Only in the 1970s, with the accumulation of
overwhelming evidence from disparate fields of scholarship, was the
contention for an African origin universally accepted. The significance
of this research for views on Africa and its peoples is just being grasped.

Recognition of a Separate Species of Rice in West Africa

A great deal of intellectual capital was at stake in accepting the proposition that rice was domesticated separately in West Africa. When Lin-
naeus (1707–1778) classified rice, scientists recognized the domestication of only one species, *sativa*, in Asia. The view of a single Asian
origin for rice persisted and was championed by other scientific lumi-
naries such as Alphonse de Candolle, in his 1886 compendium on the
origin of cultivated plants.[14] For Chevalier and his colleagues to suggest otherwise was to go against a large body of European scholarship that attributed the emergence of agriculture and urbanism to one
place, the Near East, and its diffusion from there to Europe and Asia.[15]
Even the noted Russian geneticist N. I. Vavilov, whose pathbreaking
research in the 1920s on indigenous centers of plant domestication was
undermining the view of a single center for agricultural origins, failed
to dislodge this view. While recognizing plant domestication as having
developed in the Ethiopian highlands, Vavilov made no claim for rice
domestication in Africa.[16]

Meanwhile Chevalier pressed ahead with his contention that *glaberrima* represented a separate and African species of rice. The first challenges came from scholars who proposed instead that this rice was
probably of Asian origin and entered Africa at an earlier period, perhaps with the expansion of Islam between the eighth and fourteenth
centuries.[17] However, several problems emerged with this proposition.

A review of Muslim accounts did indeed establish the cultivation of rice prior to the arrival of Portuguese caravels along the West African coast. While rice is mentioned in Arabic accounts from the tenth century, Islamic scholar al-Bakri provided the first indication of its deliberate cultivation along the Niger River in 1068.[18] He described the planting of rice twice a year, once at the time of the Niger flood, and again when the ground was still wet, evidently a reference to flood-recession agriculture.[19] The adaptation of rice to different hydrological conditions suggested a production system that predated the relatively recent period of Islamic expansion. When Moroccan scholar Ibn Battuta journeyed along the Niger River to the Mali Kingdom during the fourteenth century he, too, noted the abundance of rice. But he claimed the consumption of rice harmful for nonblacks, revealing perhaps indirectly the association of rice cultivation with the black peoples south of the Sahara.[20] Leo Africanus, who traveled twice to the region, in 1511 and 1512, observed rice farming and sales along the Niger and Senegal Rivers at about the same period the diverse areas planted to the cereal were capturing the attention of Portuguese mariners.[21]

Translations of Muslim documents thus established the cultivation of rice prior to the arrival of the Portuguese and the existence of a production system older than the period of Islamic expansion into the region from the tenth century. But these references to rice also revealed another important point. Only in West Africa did Islamic scholars note a fully evolved rice culture. If Muslims had introduced the crop from Asia, a geographic link to East Africa or the Middle East should be evident. None has yet been discovered. Nor did an examination of other sources reveal an even earlier corridor of rice introduction along the Nile. There was no mention by Greek historians of its cultivation along Nile floodplains or reference to the cereal in ancient Egyptian hieroglyphics. The Greek geographer and historian Strabo (63 B.C. to A.D. 20), however, did record one instance of rice being planted (circa A.D. 12) in the oasis of Cyrenaica, located in Libya astride the caravan route to sub-Saharan Africa.[22] Polish scholar Tadeusz Lewicki, who translated so many of the early Arabic descriptions of West African food systems, has claimed Strabo's was the earliest reference to *glaberrima* rice.[23]

Linguistic evidence provided additional support for West Africa as an independent center of rice domestication. In regions of Africa where rice cultivation was unknown before the arrival of European traders, the local words borrow the names of those who introduced it, and thus the Arabic and European names *erruz, eruz, arroz, riz, rijst*, and *rice* are used. However, in the areas where rice cultivation was known or the crop formed part of an active trade in cereals, no borrowing of names occurs. Peoples throughout the Upper Guinea Coast of Africa use names for rice derived from African languages. For example, in Senegal and Gambia, reached by the Portuguese in the mid-fifteenth century, the terms *mano* (Mandinka) and *malo* (Wolof) or some derivative of *maro/maaro* are employed for the native African rice.[24] These same names were later extended to *sativa* rice, which Europeans introduced from Asia during the period of global seed transfers known as the Columbian Exchange.[25]

The areas of West Africa adopting Asian *sativa* varieties were the same ones that figured in early Portuguese commentaries on rice-growing societies, and Africans extended the native words for rice to these introduced varieties. Between the 1940s and 1960s French botanist Roland Portères determined two foci along the West African coast where Asian varieties initially took root in African rice farming systems: one located between the Casamance and Cacheu Rivers between Senegal and Guinea-Bissau, the other in the region between Conakry in Guinea and Buchanan in Liberia.[26] This includes the area where Europeans encountered irrigated rice farming in West Africa. In noting that *sativa* rice only became established in areas of Africa with a history of *glaberrima* cultivation, Portères underscores a crucial point: that the adoption of Asian varieties presupposed populations already skilled in the techniques and practices involved in growing rice.[27]

In the face of so much evidence, opposition to an independent African center of rice domestication finally gave way during the 1970s, even if its implication for perspectives on Africa was not widely appreciated. But the belief that Africans were incapable of sophisticated technological development remained tenacious. Even the French botanists conducting the pioneering research that established the independent domestication of rice along the buckle of the Niger River in Mali could not imagine Africans capable of developing the sophisticated irrigated rice system found south of the Casamance River along the coast. Constructed by speakers of the West Atlantic language group, the system proved the hallmark of African achievements in rice culture. The diversity of *glaberrima* seed collected from the area by Jardin in the 1820s failed to make botanists question whether the irrigated planting system where they were collected could in fact be of African origin. Instead, the mere presence of some Asian rice varieties in the region was enough to attribute a Portuguese origin to the system.

Africans were only credited with developing rice cultivation on tidal floodplains, those planted along the middle to upper reaches of the Niger, Senegal, and Gambia Rivers. Even the French botanist August Chevalier, who had done so much to substantiate an independent center of rice domestication in Africa, did not question the irrigated coastal systems as the product of Portuguese tutelage. He stressed this cultural distinction between the two primary concentrations of wetland rice cultivation in West Africa: "The coastal regions (the Southern Rivers) of West Africa, from Casamance [Senegal] to the frontier of Sierra Leone, where the Portuguese, established there for many centuries in the region, perfected [rice] culture by making a truly irrigated culture . . . [in addition to] the valley of the Niger where rice cultivation is quite ancient."[28]

Chevalier regarded this second African rice system as rudimentary, since farmers just let tides roll across the floodplain instead of canalizing their water for irrigation.[29] Colonial officials over the years echoed his view of the unrealized potential of irrigated rice on river floodplains, blaming Africans repeatedly for the failure of irrigated rice projects. The French did not understand the rationale of tidal rice farming, which formed part of a complex land-use system involving cattle herding, fishing, and rice cultivation. This land-use strategy strengthened regional subsistence security through diversified food supplies in an ethnically diverse region. Europeans never considered that the cultivation of rice by river tides might form part of a clever land-use strategy for a drought-prone region.

Nonetheless, the irrigated rice system along the coast suggested to the biased European perspective that Africans learned it through contact with the Portuguese. Arguments for a Portuguese origin for this most sophisticated of African rice systems failed to question the improbability of mariners, much less traders, teaching African farmers how to grow irrigated rice. Europeans simply could not imagine that the Africans themselves had experimented and adapted irrigation to their lands independently.[30] This prejudice extended even to historical scholarship, which did not survey fifteenth-century Portuguese accounts of Africans and their rice systems. Claims for Portuguese tutelage can at long last be dispelled. Africans along the coast adopted *sativa* rice just as they would other Asian and Amerindian crops of the Columbian Exchange. The successful establishment of Asian varieties occurred because a system of irrigated rice culture and methods to mill the cereal already existed.

By the 1970s the pioneering French botanical research on *glaberrima* had become widely known within the international scientific community, which accepted the conclusion that the species was indeed of independent African origin. Of the more than twenty species of rice found on the planet, only two were domesticated, one in Asia *(Oryza sativa)*, the other in West Africa *(Oryza glaberrima)*. Botanical research indicates that the cultivation of *O. glaberrima* occurred over a broad region of West Africa from Senegal southward to Liberia and inland for more than one thousand miles to the shores of Lake Chad (Figure 2.1). It is believed that *glaberrima* was originally domesticated in the freshwater wetlands of the inland delta of the middle Niger River in Mali, an area where rice is grown almost within reach of the Sahara Desert.[31] Genetic diversity in *glaberrima* also suggests two secondary centers of African rice innovation and development. One emerged on wetlands in the area north and south of the Gambia River between the rivers Sine and Casamance in Senegal, where salt water from marine tides flows over mangrove-covered floodplains. The other secondary center of *glaberrima* diversification developed in the Guinean highlands between Sierra Leone, Guinea Conakry, and Liberia in a region of abundant rainfall.[32] The diffusion of African rice cultivation appears then to have shifted from initial domestication in freshwater wetlands to marine estuaries and rain-fed, upland areas.

During the 1950s French botanist Roland Portères made the first attempt to speculate on the antiquity of African rice cultivation. On the basis of preliminary radiocarbon dates of megalithic stone sites located along former river courses in the rice region, he attributed the domestication of *glaberrima* to a period about 3,500 years ago.[33] Archaeological evidence from the postulated center of African rice domestication in the inland delta of the Niger River confirms a more recent date. In Jenné-jeno, located in the middle Niger along with Timbuktu and other early urban centers in Mali, archaeologists Susan and Roderick

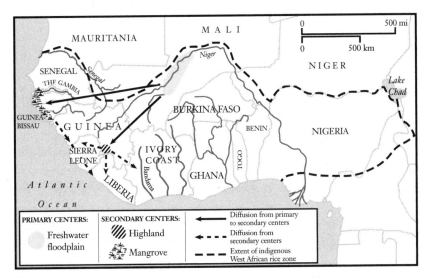

Figure 2.1 Centers of origin and diffusion of African rice

McIntosh have established the presence of *glaberrima* by A.D. 300.³⁴ The earliest occupation of Jenné-jeno dates from the second century B.C., not long after the appearance of iron smelting in the area. This enabled the making of metal tools that in turn allowed the exploitation of the Inland Delta's clay soils for rice cultivation.³⁵

The cereal's antiquity in the secondary centers of *glaberrima* diversification is not yet known, although its diffusion is often attributed to Mande speakers who migrated from the middle Niger River between the twelfth and sixteenth centuries. While they expanded rain-fed rice cultivation into the Guinean highlands, the mangrove or irrigated rice system found along the marine-influenced coastal estuaries developed among speakers of West Atlantic languages, a distinctly different linguistic family. These earliest inhabitants of the coastal littoral who grew rice included the Baga, Baïnouk, Manjak, Nalu, Balant, and Diola.³⁶ The Atlantic secondary center of rice diversification may well represent innovation from contact between two distinct farming systems—one Mande, based on freshwater floodplains; the other West Atlantic, located along marine estuaries influenced by salt water. Until paleobotanical research illuminates rice prehistory along West Africa's mangrove coast, current evidence establishes *glaberrima* cultivation along the middle Niger in Mali some two thousand years ago.³⁷

Rice Domestication and Empire Formation

It is no coincidence that the great West African empires emerged in the
region south of the Sahara following the domestication of rice. By the
final millennium B.C. there were already present numerous Mande-
speaking peoples adapted to wetlands, who lived between the water-
sheds of the Senegal and middle Niger Rivers. Their accomplishments
as fishers, aquatic hunters, metallurgists, collectors of wild grasses, and
farmers were already in place long before the region became linked to
the trans-Saharan trade in gold and empires formed.[38] At some point
over the six hundred years of severe regional desertification that
marked the period from 300 B.C. to A.D. 300, these Mande speakers
turned the region into a cradle of agricultural innovation by domesticating rice. Their wetland resource strategies, so vital to cultural survival in an increasingly drought-prone area, would make the fertile
middle Niger contested territory for successive empires.

By the period when rice was domesticated, the Mande language family had divided into a northern and southern branch. In the north the
Soninké branch included the Nono, who were settled to the east along
the western edge of the middle Niger (Figure 2.2). Oral traditions
claim them as the earliest farmers of *glaberrima* rice.[39] Under pressure
from a drying climate, the development of rice culture along floodplains provided the Nono and other Mande speakers a vital food security strategy to complement the increasingly riskier regional production of rain-fed millet and sorghum.

From the eighth century A.D. the Ghana Empire arose in the
Soninké area between the mid-Senegal and middle Niger Rivers.[40]
Gold, ivory, kola, and slaves from lands to the south were exchanged
by Mande speakers for the salt, copper, and luxury goods transported
across the Sahara by Berber caravans. Following another period of de-
clining rainfall the Ghana Empire was eclipsed by the territorial expansion of speakers from the Mande linguistic heartland. This southern
branch of the language family, located in the wetter lands to the south
and in proximity to the headwaters of the upper Senegal and Niger
Rivers, originated close to the contemporary border of Mali and
Guinea Conakry. By A.D. 1100 these Mande speakers were laying the
foundation for the Mali Empire, which extended in a northeast direc-

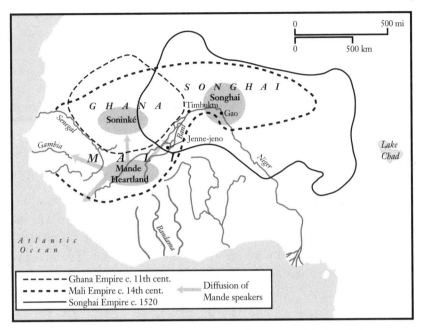

Figure 2.2 Source areas of empire formation in the western Sahel, eighth to sixteenth centuries

tion along the Niger River, absorbing the kingdom of Songhai centered near Gao in the Inland Delta.

This southern branch of Mande speakers fanned out from the middle Niger River over a vast region of West Africa. They diffused the cultivation of rice in two principal directions. One migratory wave proceeded southwest into the highlands and forests of Guinea, Ivory Coast, Sierra Leone, and Liberia.[41] The other path of Mande expansion followed the floodplains of the Gambia River and its tributaries nearly to the coastal settlements of West Atlantic speakers. Even though the linkage of the mangrove rice system they developed is poorly understood in relationship to the crop's diffusion by Mande migrations from the middle Niger, these rice growers on floodplains inundated with salt water forged a remarkable material civilization. On land seemingly ill disposed for the cultivation of rice, they developed three principles that would make theirs the most productive of all African rice systems. In contrast to the practice in the Inland Niger Delta of planting along freshwater floodplains, mangrove rice growers turned over their soils for aeration and cultivated the cereal atop ridges in estuaries within reach of the forceful marine tides. Rather than sowing seeds directly into the floodplain, mangrove growers transplanted their rice. And for lifting and aerating the heavy clay soils, they invented a specialized agricultural implement, a long-handled shovel.[42]

Mande migrations resulted in the expansion of *glaberrima* cultivation over a considerable area of West Africa. But from the mid-fifteenth century, at about the time Portuguese explorations were reaching the Upper Guinea Coast, the Mali Empire began losing its territorial grip. With the empire's fragmentation, Nilo-Saharan-speaking Songhai established an empire in the Inland Delta centered on Timbuktu, which had become a fabled center of Islamic learning. The Songhai was the last of the great empires in the western Sahel. After the seventeenth century, empires would never again form in the region. The onset of the Atlantic slave trade over the following hundreds of years would bring increasing political fragmentation, unparalleled social disruption, and depopulation as millions were enslaved for New World plantations.

From the eighth to the sixteenth centuries the fertile wetlands located between the Senegal and middle Niger Rivers witnessed repeated empire formation. The Sahel's first cities emerged in the region where Mande speakers planted, and likely domesticated, rice. This was a region where fishing and animal husbandry complemented the collection of wild grasses, while the growing of rice on river floodplains minimized the risks to food security involved with planting rain-fed cereals. As the climate grew steadily more arid, the wetlands became a vital repository of cumulative indigenous knowledge. Groups specialized in fishing, livestock management, and farming became interdependent through the diverse ways they cohabited the landscape. Wetland cultivation contributed to the region's emergence as an ecological crossroads at the nexus of long-distance trade routes to the north and the south. In the western Sahel, located between the Sahara and the forested regions to the south, traders converged to restock caravan food supplies.

Since ancient times the fertile wetlands along the rivers Niger, Senegal, and Bani supplied grain, smoked fish, and meat for caravans traversing the Sahel, as they also must have for those journeying to gold fields in the south. Muslim accounts provide a glimpse of the significance of the area's food surpluses for long-distance traders. When Ibn Battuta followed one route through the Mali Empire in the mid-fourteenth century, he observed the abundance of rice being cultivated and marketed.[43] An account by an Algeria-based Italian merchant, Antonio Malfante, in 1447, similarly noted the surplus of food, with one Muslim trader informing him of the widespread availability of rice in Gao, Timbuktu, Jenné, and Mali: "They have an abundance of flesh, milk, and rice, but no corn or barley. Through these lands flows a very large river, which at certain times of the year inundates all these lands . . . There are many boats on it, by which they carry on trade."[44]

The domestication and diffusion of rice resulted in an indigenous knowledge system that sustained human settlement over a broad and geographically diverse region of West Africa. This process of learning to cope with climatic instability through the management of wetland resources unfolded against the dramatic climatic shifts of past millennia. Despite the significance of indigenous practices and technologies in providing for collective regional food needs, the ecological significance of the area of *glaberrima* domestication remains to this day unappreciated. Historical accounts routinely emphasize the influence of exogenous peoples, Muslims from North Africa and Portuguese from Europe, in the region, which has contributed to views of the western Sahel as a region marginal for human settlement. This was certainly not always the case. Only by understanding the adaptation of Mande-speaking peoples and their neighbors to this ecologically complex area can we begin to grasp what they accomplished and the legacy they left in the Americas.

The domestication of *glaberrima* rice in the geographic setting of the Inland Niger Delta was thus in place long before any navigator from Java or Arabia could have introduced rice to the African continent via Madagascar or the East African coast.[45] From the sixteenth century African rice crossed the Middle Passage of slavery to the Americas, not merely as food in ship cargoes but also as an indigenous knowledge system known to so many of the Atlantic slave trade's victims.

The Environmental Setting of the West African Rice Region

The traditional rice-growing region of West Africa extends south along the coast from northern Senegal to the Bandama River in the central Ivory Coast and eastward into the interior for some 1,800 kilometers all the way to Lake Chad in the country of that name (Figure 2.1).[46] A region of considerable ecological and climatic diversity, the West African rice area reaches from the parched margins of the Sahara to the humid tropical forests of the Guinea highlands. Precipitation increases dramatically over short distances in the direction north to south but remains fairly consistent over even greater distances from west to east. For example, in the northern part of the West African rice region, annual precipitation averages only ten to twenty inches, and this low rainfall pattern characterizes the enormous distance between Senegal on the coast and Chad in the interior.[47] A similar rainfall pattern prevails a short distance to the south in The Gambia, where precipitation reaches thirty to forty inches per annum over a broad savanna area to the east. Rainfall again increases in Guinea-Bissau, averaging between thirty-eight and forty-three inches. The pattern of gradual precipitation increase continues steadily southward to the Guinea highlands and forested regions of Sierra Leone, Liberia, and the Ivory Coast, where rainfall may exceed eighty inches (Figure 2.3).

One of the most remarkable features of the traditional rice-growing area of West Africa is the extent of the territory that falls within the drought-prone Sahel and savanna, where rainfall grades from ten to thirty inches.[48] Drought presents a constant specter over much of the Sahelian region traditionally planted to rice. The amount and pattern of rainfall, however, is a function of longer-term climatic cycles that cause the Sahara to advance and retreat as much as 180 kilometers, much like an ocean tide.[49] Comprising the Sahel and the area affected by its cyclical ebb and flow are many countries of the West African rice region: Senegal, Mali, Niger, Chad, The Gambia, Burkina Faso and the northern portions of Guinea-Bissau, Guinea Conakry, the Ivory Coast, and Nigeria. These are countries where rainfall can vary considerably from one year to the next, and even in relatively wet years, its poor distribution over an agricultural season may cause crops to fail.[50]

But the threat of famine acted as an incentive for developing one of the world's most ingenious cultivation systems. In an area where the cultivation by rainfall of other subsistence crops like millet and sorghum periodically results in failure, rice flourishes. Thousands of years ago Sahelian peoples responded to mounting aridity in the region by

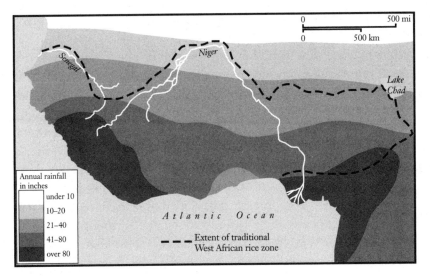

Figure 2.3 Rainfall patterns in the West African rice region

domesticating a grass of the *Oryza* species that they discovered grew well in surrounding wetland swamps. From then on their farming system would mitigate the vagaries of rainfall availability by the cultivation of rice in areas within reach of river tides and groundwater resources.

The diverse wetlands planted to rice in West Africa include river floodplains, coastal estuaries, inland swamps, hill slopes overlying subterranean streams, and bottomlands with high water tables. In the Sahel and savanna region, which forms the northern half of the West African rice region, rice is a wetland crop. Its cultivation is especially concentrated along the floodplains of the area's major rivers, the Senegal, Gambia, Niger, and Bani. The other great arc of wetland cultivation straddles the northern and southern halves of the West African rice region along the Atlantic coast south of Gambia to Sierra Leone. This is the mangrove system, where planting occurs in coastal estuaries. Rainfall is captured in enclosed plots to desalinate otherwise fertile alluvial soils, a practice that after a few years makes them optimal for rice farming.

The southern half of the West African rice region receives more than forty inches of rainfall, the ample precipitation favoring emphasis on rain-fed rice in upland areas. In the Ivory Coast, Sierra Leone, and Liberia, rice is grown along a landscape continuum that grades from its cultivation with rainfall atop a slope to planting the crop in lowland swamps.

The practice of wetland farming throughout the West African rice region represents an imaginative adaptive strategy to regional climatic and topographic differences, whether in the Sahel or as part of an up-land-lowland farming system in the Guinean highlands to the south. Growing rice in wetlands allows farmers to extend the agricultural calendar beyond the confines of the rainy season. Planting diverse microenvironments along a landscape gradient with distinctive water regimes minimizes the risk of crop failure while adding flexibility to farming practices. Rice in each microenvironment consequently ma-tures at different periods over a cultivation cycle, enabling agricultural practices to unfold in a sequence where labor is spread out over a farm-ing season. A diverse selection of seeds designed to flourish and mature under different conditions and duration periods aids in this land-use strategy.

Land Use in the West African Rice Region

The West African rice region bifurcates into a northern and southern portion at about thirty-five inches of annual precipitation. The result is two distinctive land-use systems for rice cultivation that informed the practices brought by enslaved West Africans to Carolina plantations. In the northern half, rice cultivation unfolds on wetlands in conjunction with cattle grazing. South of the area where annual rainfall exceeds thirty-five inches, animals figure less centrally as land use shifts from an agro-pastoral to a mostly agricultural system.

Ever since the period of the Mande expansions in the twelfth cen-tury, the forty-inch rainfall belt has roughly corresponded with the northern limit of the tsetse fly that carries the trypanosomes of sleeping sickness, a disease that is especially fatal to domesticated animals, as al-ready noted.[51] Extensive herds of domesticated herbivores, including the indigenous longhorn cattle and the introduced zebu breed, thus dominate the northern half of the West African rice region. Managed by pastoral Fulani, cattle form an integral part of the complex settle-ment history that characterizes the rice landscape. In the southern por-tion of the rice region, cattle are less significant. Within the transitional rainfall area, only the small ndama breed of cattle, resistant to trypanosome infection, survives. Here a landscape devoted to agriculture meets the eye.

The agro-pastoral system of the Inland Niger Delta unfolds on the vast expanse of wetlands fed by the Niger and Bani Rivers in the modern country of Mali. Annual flooding in the region inundates some fifty-five thousand square kilometers, the Delta's location within the arid Sahelian zone rendering it of vital importance for rice, fish, and livestock production.[52] This area of *glaberrima* domestication represents a crucial multipurpose resource for farmers as well as for more mobile fishing and herding peoples. Throughout the entire trypanosome-free zone of the rice region, land use shifts from rice farming during the rains to pasture in the dry season. Following the rice harvest in the fall and early winter, cattle enter the fields to graze upon the crop residue, their manure fertilizing the soil. This seasonal rotation between rice cultivation and pastoralism embraces a clever land-use strategy that satisfies both cereal and protein (especially milk) needs while improving crop yields through the addition of animal manure. Rice farmers south of the trypanosome belt do not have these advantages: in the absence of cattle they must rely upon other techniques to maintain soil fertility, such as rotating fields with nitrogen-fixing legumes and intercropping plants that add crucial nutrients to the soil. Meat and milk must be obtained elsewhere.

In the northern portion of the West African rice region, rice cultivation along freshwater floodplains does not involve landscape transformation with embankments and canals for drainage. The objective instead is to allow the unimpeded flow of water across the rice fields. While the annual rise and fall in river tides deposits fertile alluvium, the unencumbered landscape also facilitates the movement of both animal and fish populations.

Even when land use on the floodplain shifts to grazing during the dry season, an additional cropping cycle is sometimes established along the inner edge of Sahelian rivers with an ebbing tide. Farmers may plant a second rice crop, sorghum, or vegetables with flood recession. They wait for the retreat of floodwaters to plant in the moisture-holding soils.[53] The seasonal rotation of land use along floodplains, where rice cultivation and animal grazing is succeeded by cattle pasture and a flood-recession crop during the dry season, illuminates the ingenuity of West African farmers in adapting rice culture to existing environmental conditions.

Even though the African method of shifting land use between rice and cattle supports a complex land rotation and diversified nutritional base, the underlying rationale of the system eluded Europeans until well into this century. They viewed the wetlands of the Inland Delta, for example, as perfectly suited for the cultivation of two irrigated rice crops. That such a system had failed to develop autochthonously in an eminently appropriate environment confirmed for European colonial officials the supposed technological limits of African societies on the eve of the Atlantic slave trade. The land-use strategy developed by the region's farmers, herders, and fishers for coping with persistent drought served instead to bolster views of African cultural inferiority. In an era of scientific racism and colonialism, the denial of African accomplishment in rice systems provides a stunning example of how power relations mediate the production of history.[54] As a result, researchers ignored African rice history until well into the twentieth century.

European observers thus placed African farmers on a less evolved level within the hierarchy of agriculture, civilization, and progress. Formalizing the partition of Africa in the mid-1880s with colonial rule, Europeans saw themselves as bearers of a civilizing mission that would deliver technology and progress to the peoples of the Dark Continent. Eyeing the vast expanse of wetlands in the Inland Delta, colonial agricultural agents could only see before them a rice system of unrealized potential, one whose trajectory in Africa fell far short of the accomplishments of Asia, where the development of irrigated rice had led to cultural florescence and civilization. Armed with a cultural-evolutionary view of technology development, Europeans either outright denied African technological achievement in rice culture, as along the coast, or portrayed the systems in place along Sahelian rivers as examples of arrested technological development, thereby underscoring long-standing racial prejudices.

The floodplain cultivation system, such as existed along the inland delta of the Niger, symbolized then the limits of African technological accomplishments. Racial biases portrayed farmers as exerting little effort to subdue nature for food surpluses. Believing Africans lacked the acumen to develop more sophisticated double-cropping systems, officials denigrated floodplain cultivation along freshwater rivers for having failed to achieve the Asian trajectory of technology development toward irrigation systems with full water control. French irrigation specialist Pierre Viguier, who worked in the inland delta of the Niger in Mali, echoed prevalent European views in 1939. He attributed the presumed gulf between the levels of civilization attained by Asia and Africa to the technological gap between planting rice with irrigation and planting via tidal flow: "Rice cultivation by irrigation and rice cultivation by submersion," he noted, "this is the distance between Asian and African civilizations."[55]

The Atlantic slave trade and its legacy of racism, combined with the inherent sense of Western superiority during colonialism, conditioned European perceptions of African rice systems. In the years between the two world wars, colonial irrigation engineers and botanists aimed to bridge the perceived technology gap by developing large-scale irrigation projects along Sahelian rivers. In promoting rice cultivation year-round, these European-initiated projects radically disrupted the traditional balance achieved in alternating land use between farming and grazing systems. Despite the repeated failure of these irrigation schemes, the blame was always placed upon the presumed inability of Africans to comprehend the sophisticated concepts embodied in technology transfer rather than on the ill-conceived plans of outsiders.[56]

Rice and Women's Work

Throughout the West African rice region seed selection is the responsibility of females. Varieties exist for all the major problems encountered in landscapes planted to rice: deep or shallow flooding, seasonal salinity, cultivation with moisture reserves exposed by a falling river tide, acidity, drought, and high iron toxicity. The amount and timing of water availability also affects the growth period, with seeds selected to mature in periods that range from three to six months. Among the remarkable varieties cultivated by Sahelian rice growers are those planted with the annual flood of the Niger River, known as "floating rice" for the mats of vegetation they form along the river. This type of rice is harvested after 180 days of growth.[57] Seeds are additionally selected to repel predators, such as weaver birds, a pest in rice fields, whose dam-

age is minimized by varieties selected for spiky awns.[58] In just the Inland Delta alone, colonial officials in the early twentieth century recorded more than fifty distinct types of rice being grown, with another
thirty-five varieties collected in the mangrove rice area.[59]

The diversity of available seeds reflects women's keen awareness of
local environments and deep familiarity with rice culture. Throughout the Inland Delta, women are the harvesters of wild rice varieties;
women's enduring association with seed selection is in fact suggestive
that females may have initiated the process of rice domestication.[60] The
large number of varieties selected just for milling and cooking attest to
the traditional female role as plant breeders. Seeds are chosen for cooking properties, taste, ease in milling, and storage qualities.[61] In addition
to *glaberrima*, women farmers also plant Asian *(sativa)* rice. These two
types of rice do not readily intercross and are prized for their respective
properties, Asian varieties for their higher yields and African ones for
their productivity on problem soils.[62] *Glaberrima* grows better than
sativa in conditions of soil acidity, salinity, flooding, iron toxicity, and
phosphorous deficiency. Although generally lower yielding than *sativa*,
African rice develops quickly, making it more competitive with weeds
than Asian varieties. But its suitability for commercial purposes is
weakened by the tendency of African rice to shatter easily with mechanized milling.[63]

Another characteristic of African rice that distinguishes it from most
sativa varieties is the red color of its bran, which shifts between purple
and black tones in different varieties. Even in Figure 2.4, a black-and-
white photograph (where Mandinka women of Casamance, Senegal,
display bundles of *glaberrima* [left] and *sativa* [right] rice they have just
harvested in their fields), the color difference between African and
Asian rice is apparent. But the "great red rice of the hook of the Niger
River" is not the only red rice, making identification solely by color
problematic. Many wild *sativa* are also red in color, as is the bran of
some cultivated varieties found in subtropical Himalayan valleys.

Women's roles in rice culture, however, involve considerably more
than seed selection, hand milling, and cooking. From the earliest period of the Atlantic slave trade, Europeans had noted the crucial role of
females in African rice cultivation. Wherever rice is grown in West Africa, women continue working in the fields and their labor remains associated with the specialized tasks of hoeing, sowing, weeding, and

Figure 2.4 Mandinka women displaying bundles of African and Asian rice

transplanting. Central to the visual imagery of a West African rice landscape is a woman with her baby on her back, hoeing a field under unrelenting heat and humidity (Figure 2.5).

The centrality of the historical role of women in West African rice farming enables the identification of three broad production systems that illuminate gendered skills and work patterns long characteristic of the crop's cultivation. Each system is associated with the three major areas of *glaberrima* development—the primary center of domestication along the floodplains surrounding the buckle or inland delta of the Niger River and the two secondary centers of domestication, mangrove rice along the coast and the upland-inland swamp-planting system found in the area near the Guinea highlands. The role of female labor in each system varies in relationship to the significance of rice in the farming system, with male participation in cultivation more marked in

Figure 2.5 Diola woman hoeing rice field, Casamance, Senegal

cultures dependent on rice as the dietary staple. When rice assumes a less central role in the regional food system, the crop is often farmed solely by women.[64]

Along freshwater floodplains of the Sahel and especially where Mande languages are spoken, rice is usually a woman's crop, grown with little assistance from men. Women and their daughters carry out all the field operations involved in rice farming, from preparing the fields with hoes to harvest. A wholly different system of production characterizes rice growing in coastal mangrove swamps, planted by West Atlantic ethnic groups. Here, men and women grow rice in a system where gender differentiates responsibilities in farming. Males perform the heavy work of field preparation, while females are charged with sowing, weeding, and transplanting. Both sexes participate in the harvest.[65]

Yet another system characterizes the upland-inland swamp-planting system that typifies the southern portion of the West African rice area

Figure 2.6 Temne woman parboiling rice in Sierra Leone

reached by Mande linguistic groups between the twelfth and the six-teenth centuries.[66] In a system dominated by rain-fed cultivation along a landscape gradient, women carry out the specialized tasks of sowing and weeding rice in upland fields as well as the work associated with intercropping those fields with other subsistence staples such as cas-sava, maize, and vegetables. The cultivation of rice in the valley bot-toms of this upland-inland swamp system, however, usually remains the domain of women, perhaps indicative of the long-standing association of females of Mande language groups with wetland farming.[67]

While three types of gendered production systems are evident in the West African rice region, only women are involved in the processing and cooking of the cereal. After the crop is harvested females mill the rice with a mortar and pestle, winnow the grain in coiled baskets, and prepare the cereal for consumption. However, with newly harvested rice at the end of the cultivation cycle, when food is scarce and the grain not yet properly dried, the rice may be prepared by parboiling (Figure 2.6). Parboiling involves soaking the rice with its hulls still at-

Figure 2.7 Mandinka women using the long-handled hoe, the *baaro*

tached in cold water prior to cooking, steaming, and drying, a process that drives the oils into the bran, thereby facilitating hull removal.

The division of labor typical of West African rice cultivation extends to the specialized agricultural implements that developed over time for carrying out field tasks. This is especially evident in the great diversity of hoes for field preparation, which one researcher regards as "the best symbol that one can find of African agricultural systems."[68] Most hoes employed in rice cultivation are strictly associated with either female or male use.[69] For instance, use of the long-handled *baro/baaro* (Mandinka)—indispensable for preparing freshwater floodplains for cultivation—is exclusively the domain of women.[70] The handle of this iron-bladed implement often attains a woman's height because females work the *baaro* in a semi-upright position to break up clods of dirt and tear up roots (Figure 2.7). Weeding and transplanting, in contrast, demand a bent-over position, with women using the shorter hand hoe, the *daba* (Mandinka) (Figure 2.8).[71]

Men's work in rice cultivation also involves specialized implements

Figure 2.8 Mandinka women in inland swamp with the short-handled hoe, the *daba*

that women do not use. In the coastal mangrove area, preparation of the heavy clay soils demands lifting in order to improve aeration. Men perform this grueling task, turning over the soil with a long-handled, flat-bladed shovel that varies in length from 1.6 to 3.5 meters.[72] With this *kayendo* (Diola) men put up embankments, construct ridges and furrows, and overturn and bury weeds in a rice plot (Figure 2.9). In the upland-inland swamp system of the southern part of the rice region, men sometimes use a short-bladed hoe on a bent handle (known as the *donkontong* among Mande speakers) to ridge and furrow the fields.[73]

Rice Cultivation Systems in West Africa

West Africans plant rice in a complex system of production, which occurs in distinct environments along a landscape gradient.[74] In the Sahel this planting strategy unfolds along an undulating wetland landscape of microenvironments flooded with varying intensity and depth whose differences are only evident to the most practiced eye. The fact that cultivation occurs along a landscape gradient becomes far clearer south of the savannas, where the observer views rice being planted with rain-

Figure 2.9 Manjak man using the long-handled *kayendo* in field preparation,
Guinea-Bissau

fall on plateaus and in lowland swamps. Growing rice along an upland-
to lowland-swamp continuum enables farmers to utilize different forms
of water that may be available. Specific water regimes such as the onset
of rains, the amplitude of river tidal flow during the wet season, or the
depth of the groundwater table regulate sowing and harvesting dates.
Such considerations require a variety of seeds adapted to the growing
season of different environments, with shorter-duration (90–120 day)
varieties grading into longer-duration (140–160 day) ones as the cropping system shifts from upland to lowland cultivation.[75] The planting
of rice in different production zones along a landscape continuum extends the agricultural calendar so that cultivation precedes or extends
beyond the actual wet season, with harvests along the gradient occurring at different dates.

Even though the diverse microenvironments planted to rice are regulated by a similar precipitation and temperature regime, their location
along a landscape gradient means that water affects soils and cropping
in different ways. Rain-fed cultivation thrives on well-drained upland
fields at the upper end of the continuum, while midway down the slope
are a variety of inland swamps with drainage ranging from good to
poor. At the bottom of the landscape gradient are poorly drained
marshy lowlands with deep flooding.

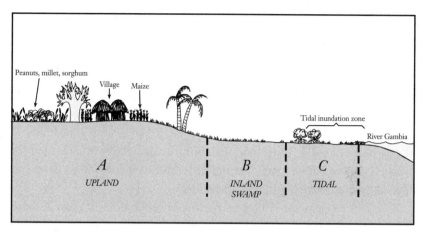

Figure 2.10 Rice cultivation along a landscape gradient: central Gambia

One overall classification of the diverse soil and water parameters that define different cultivation systems revealed more than twenty distinct microenvironments grown to rice in West Africa, including some that are not even planted in Asia.[76] However, position along a landscape gradient, principal water regime, and the key techniques that characterize cultivation can be generalized to provide a basis for comparison with the environments subsequently planted in South Carolina from the end of the seventeenth century. The principal environments of the upland to lowland landscape gradient fall into three broad categories of rice production: tidal floodplains; inland swamps using either high groundwater tables, subterranean streams, or moisture-holding soils; and rain-fed uplands (Figure 2.10).

Of the three forms of rice cultivation, the upland or rain-fed system occurs along the elevated position of a landscape gradient, where planting depends strictly upon precipitation. The upland system, which may actually rest only a mere hundred feet above sea level, is characterized by clearing forest for the planting of well-drained soils. Seed is planted in furrows, either by broadcasting or by dropping rice grains into a hole made by puncturing the soil with a special hoe. Then the shallow hole is covered with the heel of the foot, a technique that literally involves "sole on rice." Because the upland rice system is regulated by the length of the wet season, West African farmers usually plant seed varieties of short duration, grown over a three- to four-month period.

The productivity of upland rice cultivation varies considerably in relation to climatic factors and land use. Where rainfall is ample and cattle manure available, yields may exceed one ton per acre. In areas of variable precipitation, or where soil fertility is not adequately restored by fallowing or crop rotation with legumes, yields often only reach a few hundred pounds per acre. Generally upland rice cultivation occurs under favorable climatic, soil, and land-use systems, as in Sierra Leone and Liberia. There it dominates in a production system that includes the farming of valley bottoms. Although the initial effort expended for land clearance can be considerable, valley-bottom cultivation demands less labor than planting rice in wetlands.

The second principal rice system encountered along a West African landscape gradient is cultivation in inland swamps, where groundwater reaches the root zone for most of the growing period. The inland system overcomes the precipitation constraints of upland production by capturing water reserves from artesian springs, perched water tables, and catchment run-off. Soils are often poorly drained, which facilitates moisture retention. Inland swamps actually refer to an array of microenvironments which include valley bottoms, low-lying depressions, and areas of moisture-holding clay soils. The broad range of inland swamps sown to rice reflects a sophisticated knowledge of soils and their moisture-retention properties as well as methods to facilitate water impoundment for supplemental irrigation. Where high groundwater tables keep inland swamps saturated, rice planting may begin before the rains, continue beyond the wet season, and thrive despite low rainfall.

Cultivating rice in inland swamps requires careful observance of topography and water flow. Farmers construct earthen rims (bunds or berms) around the plot to form a reservoir for capturing rainfall to keep soils saturated through dry spells in the cropping season (Figure 2.11). Control over water inflow and outflow is achieved by piercing plot bunds with the hollowed trunks of palms, which are plugged with thatch (Figure 2.12). The practice keeps soils saturated during dry cycles within the cropping season. Farmers often improve drainage and aeration in inland swamp plots by mounding and ridging the soil.

Seedlings are then sown either directly atop the ridges or transplanted, the latter method being favored when waterlogging poses a risk to seedling development. In such cases, the young plant is established near the village and transplanted to the inland swamp about

Figure 2.11 Inland swamp system

three weeks later. Transplanting is the labor of women, who often do the work with nursing infants strapped to their back (Figure 2.13). Though labor intensive, transplanting confers many advantages, which include economy in the use of seeds and less work weeding. The process of pulling up the seedlings additionally strengthens the root system and promotes tillering, which causes the shoots at the base of the stem to multiply. Yields in transplanted rice plots increase by as much as 40 percent over direct-seeded ones.[77] Finally, in areas where water availability varies from one year to the next, transplanting provides a cushion against seed loss; hand-watered seedlings are established near a house and only moved into the swamp when conditions prove propitious. Such practices in inland swamp rice production result in rice yields that often reach over five hundred pounds per acre.

The remaining African production system is located downslope of a landscape gradient on floodplains of rivers and coastal estuaries. Dependent upon tides to flood and/or drain the fields, tidal cultivation involves techniques ranging from those requiring little or no environmental manipulation (such as planting freshwater Sahelian floodplains) to ones demanding considerable landscape modification for irrigated rice farming (coastal mangrove estuaries). The mangrove rice system embodies complex hydrological and land management principles that

Figure 2.12 Use of palms for sluices in water control, inland swamp

prove especially pertinent for examining the issue of African agency in the transfer of rice cultivation to the Americas.

These floodplain environments can be divided into three types: ones that occur along freshwater rivers, those where river water becomes seasonally saline, and those in coastal estuaries under marine influence. Techniques of cultivation in the first two involve similar methods of production, letting river tides irrigate the rice fields, while the third combines principles of each major rice system to enable irrigated cultivation under problematic soil and water conditions. All of these floodplain systems involve preparing land for cultivation with hoes designed for farming different types of wetland soils and for specialized use by males or females.

The riverine floodplain in the first two systems actually includes two flooding regimes, the deeply inundated area alongside a river irrigated by diurnal tides and the inner margin of the floodplain where the landscape gradient begins to rise. The inner floodplain, less deeply submerged, may only be reached by river water during full moon tides, so

Figure 2.13 Diola women transplanting rice in The Gambia

cultivation relies largely on moisture retention in the soil. The sowing of seeds in shallow flooded areas usually involves broadcasting, scattering them by the handful across the landscape. While this technique saves on labor, it requires a large amount of seed, and resultant losses to birds, insects, and microbes run high. To deter this problem farmers sometimes first envelop the seed in a film of mud or cow dung, which provides a protective casing. Once dried or pregerminated, the seed is then broadcast.[78] In areas where deep flooding might sweep away seed rice, a different technique is employed. Rice is usually first established on higher ground and then transplanted as seedlings.

Although the tidal flats adjoining freshwater rivers are sometimes cultivated year-round, the seasonally saline floodplain can only be planted after fresh water returns to the river, usually weeks to a month after the rains begin. Because rivers in West Africa follow a low gradient, with fresh water meeting marine water tides some distance upstream, salt water constantly menaces the downstream reaches of rivers. This effect wanes with the onset of the rainy season, which discharges a flood of fresh water that makes the saltwater interface retreat toward the river's lower reaches (Figure 2.14). The distance downstream reached by the seasonal freshwater flood is a function of rainfall

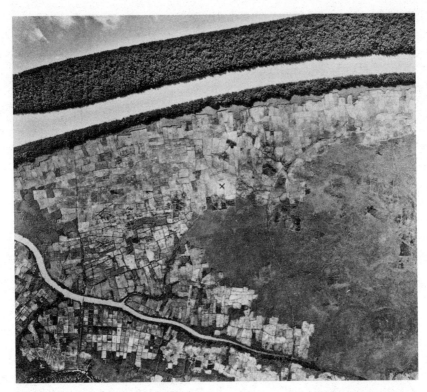

Figure 2.14 Tidal rice cultivation, seasonally saline river, The Gambia. Note the ribbon of mangroves, indicating brackish water.

regimes that regulate precipitation upstream along the river. Thus rivers of the northern part of the West African rice region, like the Senegal and the Gambia, remain permanently saline in the lower 100 kilometers and then grade seasonally to freshwater conditions for 250 kilometers upstream before reaching the point at which they remain fresh throughout the year.

The planting of rice along the middle stretches of floodplains seasonally covered by brackish water demands careful observation of salt- and freshwater dynamics during the rainy season in order to time the cultivation cycle to the availability of fresh water in the river. Rice can be planted along seasonally saline river floodplains which experience at least three months of fresh water, the length of the shortest-duration seed varieties. Growing rice on seasonally saline floodplains requires far less labor than planting freshwater areas, because brackish water depresses vegetation growth, thereby reducing the time spent on land preparation and weeding. The annual deposit of fertile alluvium along both types of floodplain results in similar yields, which routinely reach about one ton per acre.[79]

The third form of floodplain cultivation, mangrove rice, represents the most sophisticated production environment in West Africa. Located along the coast south from the Gambia River, this rice system developed in a region where rivers cut serpentine paths across the littoral. In a landscape mantled by mangrove thickets and swept by ocean tides that reach up to eighteen feet, there developed the most productive rice system of West Africa. An insalubrious environment that would seem inhospitable to all but mosquitoes, crabs, crocodiles, and birds served in fact as the locale for the hardworking and decentralized societies that created an ingenious system of irrigated rice.[80]

The principles underlying this system have not been sufficiently understood by historians of rice development in South Carolina who have looked to West Africa for potential influences. Their comparisons of rice production on both sides of the Atlantic basin single out for analysis the freshwater floodplain cultivation system, the production environment that sustained the antebellum Carolina rice economy. Because this environment is used for both rice and cattle production, it involves minimal landscape manipulation. Thus the irrigated rice system that appeared in South Carolina appears to bear little resemblance to the one that developed along African freshwater floodplains.

This type of comparison, however, actually distorts our understanding of rice history in the Americas. The analytical separation of one from several microenvironments typically planted along a landscape gradient obscures the full range of principles known and routinely used in African rice farming and does not accord proper attention to the rationale of the underlying land-use system. In the West African rice region the rationale is subsistence in a complex environmental setting and a cropping system that evens out labor demands over the agricultural calendar. In South Carolina, the land-use system was designed for profit, regardless of its demands on labor. This misunderstanding of the West African floodplain system contributed to obfuscating the African origins of American rice cultivation and the role of slaves in the crop's emergence in the Carolina colony.

The focus on one floodplain environment among the many planted in West Africa consequently misses the key insight of Olfert Dapper's

seventeenth-century informants—namely, rice as a complex production system with the crop simultaneously managed in distinct environments along a landscape gradient. In isolating for comparative
analysis just one among several floodplain environments—especially
the freshwater system the Europeans regarded as primitive—scholars
glimpse only a fraction of the agronomic techniques and specialized
knowledge that informed indigenous West African rice cultivation.
The case for African agency in introducing the sophisticated soil and
water management infrastructure to South Carolina floodplains shifts
considerably when detailing the mangrove rice system.

Floodplains of the lower reaches of West African rivers are located in
permanently saline water due to the influence of marine tides. Yet these
same tides also deliver fertile alluvium that becomes trapped by the ae-
rial roots of the mangroves found along the littoral. The deposited organic matter results in a heavy clay soil that is extremely fertile although waterlogged, known in Senegambia and Sierra Leone as *poto-
poto*.[81] Though rich in organic nutrients, these soils present the drawback of being quite acid, especially if they are drained for cultivation.
Poto-poto soils depend upon submersion to prevent them from oxidizing
and developing the acid-sulfate conditions that would render them too
acid for cultivation.[82]

This constraint failed to discourage West Africans from adapting
rice cultivation to an otherwise fertile floodplain environment, even
though the soils are difficult to lift and aerate for land preparation. Rice
farmers responded to the environmental challenges by developing cultivation on land cleared of mangroves, a system known as mangrove
rice. The most sophisticated and productive form of African floodplain
rice cultivation, mangrove rice is characterized by farming in saline estuaries. The abundant rainfall is captured in order to desalinate the
soils. Environmental constraints are overcome through the construction of an irrigation infrastructure, an elaborate network of embankments, dikes, canals, and sluice gates that serves to bar the entry of
marine water while retaining rainfall for field saturation and rice cultivation.

We now know that this indigenous form of irrigated rice cultivation
flourished in coastal estuaries south of the Gambia River. Eventually it
extended along the coast from Casamance, Senegal, south of Gambia
to Guinea Conakry, in areas of permanently saline water conditions

and where annual rainfall generally exceeds forty inches. In the nineteenth century, British colonial officials reported mangrove rice cultivation along the northern coast of Sierra Leone settled by the Temne.[83] By manipulating water regimes and developing a sophisticated irrigated infrastructure, generations of rice farmers had succeeded in putting a highly productive system in place. Indeed, mangrove rice is the highest-yielding crop in the West African rice region. Proper management avoids the formation of acid-sulfate conditions, while taking advantage of soil fertility from organic deposition along the floodplain.

During the Atlantic slave trade the mangrove rice system caught the attention of Europeans like Captain Sam Gamble, who described and sketched it among the Baga in Guinea Conakry around 1793 (see Figure 1.2). His drawing details embankments, sluices for irrigating and draining fields, and canals as well as field preparation with the *kayendo* shovel that men still use in lifting the heavy *poto-poto* soils for cultivation. Mangrove rice demands considerable landscape modification. It also requires cooperation among villagers and between villages to manage the extensive water control system.[84] This remarkable form of cultivation led Gamble to conclude: "The Bagos are very expert in Cultivating rice and in quite a Different manner to any of the Nations on the Windward Coast."[85]

Significantly, this irrigated system developed in relatively unstratified societies, disproving the overly deterministic contention of Karl Wittfogel that irrigated rice led inevitably to centralized water control and social hierarchy, as it had in Asia. The pattern in Africa followed a notably different trajectory. Instead of evolving along Wittfogel's model, the West African mangrove system thrived under decentralized water management and with a high level of intra- and intercommunity cooperation.[86] This cooperative effort barely survived the eighteenth-century slave trade, which sent ever more victims across the Middle Passage. Enslavement of the Baga, the Diola, and other mangrove rice practitioners profoundly disturbed the system, forcing many groups to flee to more remote locales. Their irrigated mangrove rice system managed to endure in less accessible locations in Senegal, Guinea-Bissau, and Guinea Conakry, where it continues in use to this day.

Preparation of a mangrove rice field begins with site selection and construction of an earthen embankment parallel with the coast or riverine arm of the sea. Frequently more than one meter in height and width (the dimensions needed to block the entry of marine tides onto the rice field), the embankment stretches for several kilometers, at times threading together rice fields of different villages. A stand of mangroves is often left in place between the estuary and the rice perimeter to reduce tidal force. The void left by soil removal for the embankment establishes the location of the principal drainage canal. A series of lower embankments (dikes) are then formed perpendicular to the main one in order to divide the perimeter into the individual rice fields. Men accomplish the earth-moving activities with the flat-bladed, long-handled *kayendo*. This hoe is unchanged in appearance from the one depicted in Gamble's drawing over two hundred years ago.

Water management in the mangrove rice system achieves a dual purpose. It captures rainfall for irrigation while storing water for the controlled flooding that drowns unwanted weeds. Sluices are usually made of palm or bamboo, which is plugged with thatch, to facilitate irrigation or drainage through the plot's canals. These smaller sluices drain into a more substantial one located in the principal embankment or exterior dike. One abandoned sluice constructed from a tree trunk is shown in Figure 2.15. The principal floodgate set into the field's embankment is sometimes fashioned from an old canoe with a board vertically positioned to control water flow, much like a ship's rudder.[87]

Once enclosed, rainwater is impounded and evacuated from the field at low tide. Rainfall (or in some cases seasonal freshwater springs) leaches out the salts, which low tides help evacuate into the estuary.[88] It takes two to three years to desalinate a mangrove field before cultivation ensues. Each season, as growers await the rains to rinse away residual dry season salts, women establish rice in nurseries near the village where the seedlings can be hand watered.[89] After about a month's growth they are transplanted atop the rice field's ridges, a practice that helps protect them from residual salinity. At this point the mangrove rice field reverts to rain-fed cultivation. Harvest occurs about four months later, the crop ripening from accumulated moisture reserves after the rains cease. The fields are turned over to cattle, whose manure enriches the soil, while compost and the burning of seashells also contribute to fertility. Mangrove rice soils can consequently be planted year after year without having to lie fallow.

Because the soil has often dried out at the beginning of a cultivation season, farmers open the sluices at high tide to facilitate the inflow of

Figure 2.15 Mangrove rice cultivation, permanently saline estuary: Casamance, Senegal

marine water. This action moistens the soil, thereby making it easier to lift and aerate, and reduces any process of soil acidification while enabling the deposition of organic matter. In the month or so preceding cultivation, the sluices once again are closed to block the entry of salt water. Farmers prepare the plot for the new cultivation cycle by layering the ridges with accumulated deposits of swamp mud; the first rains will eliminate the salt that accrued from opening the sluices to marine water.

The creation of an irrigated rice system from mangrove estuaries demands an extraordinary amount of labor over a period of several years. First, the mangrove vegetation must be cleared. Then, the salt-influenced soil needs repeated lifting and aeration in order to accomplish desalination. Embankments require construction and repair. Irrigation canals need to be cleaned of debris and silt to maintain their flow during the rainy season. The labor demands that men and women, households and communities, work together for the collective purpose of ensuring subsistence and cultural survival. Work of this nature, on such a monumental scale, rewards its practitioners with some of the highest yields in traditional rice cultivation, frequently exceeding one ton per acre. The mangrove system illustrates a preexisting West African familiarity with a sophisticated irrigated rice culture long associated with the South Carolina and Georgia tidal rice plantation.

THE COMPLEXITY of indigenous soil and water management is embodied in the practice of planting rice along a landscape gradient.[90] Such detailed knowledge systems permitted the cultivation of rice under differing climatic and microenvironmental conditions over a broad region of West Africa. Coming to understand the range of techniques, practices, and seed selection utilized by African rice farmers over centuries serves to restore rice to its proper historical-geographical location, as an important crop within a sophisticated African agricultural system already well in place at the dawn of the Atlantic slave trade. This assemblage of techniques and practices was to resurface in a radically different manner with slavery in the Americas, providing its bearers a means to negotiate the circumstances of bondage across the Middle Passage.

3

Out of Africa: Rice Culture and African Continuities

Particular know-how, rather than lack of it, was one factor that made black labor attractive to English colonists.

—Peter Wood, *Black Majority* (1974)

$\mathcal{T}$HE SOURCE of the food for the ships that left African shores with their human cargo reveals a crucial aspect of the Atlantic slave trade. Slavers arriving in Africa depended a great deal upon food surpluses produced there for provisions across the Middle Passage. The indigenous armies that sent captives into transatlantic slavery also made demands on food supplies. The growing need for surplus food in Africa was met by native African cereals as well as by crops introduced through the Columbian Exchange from the sixteenth century. The onset of the Atlantic slave trade was accompanied by the reorganization of African agriculture for surplus production. Although the ways in which this occurred have yet to be fully charted by scholars, they can be broadly outlined.[1]

By the sixteenth century the role of rice as a subsistence staple in West Africa was shifting. Warfare demanded a reorganization of agricultural systems to produce surpluses. Rulers of the Songhai state, located in the heart of African rice domestication in the interior of Mali, depended on rice plantations worked by slaves to provide cereal surpluses to chiefs and armies.[2] As the Atlantic slave trade intensified the growth of indigenous slavery during the seventeenth century, African nobles increasingly relied on servile agricultural labor to produce the food surpluses necessary to support the incessant wars that provided the trade's quarry. During the 1620s English trader Richard Jobson observed slaves organized for cereal production in agricultural villages along the Gambia River.[3]

Observations from the early eighteenth century report the widespread existence of slave villages throughout the Guinea region producing the food surpluses that provisioned rulers, armies, caravans, and slave ships.[4] Europeans visiting Senegal and Gambia mention *rumbdés*, villages where slaves cultivated the "plantations" of their owners.[5] Commenting at the end of the eighteenth century, which sent more Africans into slavery than any previous period, explorer Mungo Park reported that slaves nearly universally performed agricultural production throughout the western Sudan, the region where rice was widely grown.[6]

In its earliest phase indigenous slavery was more akin to European serfdom than the absolute control over a human being as property that became the distinguishing feature of chattel slavery.[7] Commentaries on the social organization of African agricultural production from the early period of the Atlantic slave trade suggest that a moral economy regulated the claims made on indigenous slaves working in agriculture. Europeans mention the use of indigenous slaves for cultivation but also refer to their rights. Alvise da Cadamosto, a crew member on a Portuguese caravel that traveled to the Senegal River between 1455 and 1456, reported a Wolof king turning war captives to agricultural production. A half century later Valentim Fernandes described Wolof domestic slaves having one day a week to work for themselves; André Alvares de Almada, writing in 1594, referred to "Fula slaves ruling the Wolofs."[8] Similar arrangements were in place on the sugar plantations of São Tomé in the period between 1520 and the 1540s.[9] Indigenous slaves in agriculture retained rights that specified days of the week or hours of the day for working on their own fields, and this apparently endured even into the 1820s.[10] René Caillié remarked that indigenous slaves in Guinea performed specific agricultural tasks five days a week, from early morning until early afternoon; but they "are allowed two days in the week to work in their own fields."[11] Slaves would later try to renegotiate such rights elsewhere in the Atlantic basin and occasionally succeeded, as on Carolina rice plantations, in a system that became known as task labor.

The earliest European references to indigenous sub-Saharan slavery indicate that those enslaved in Africa were not considered merely animate commodities; they retained rights within the social structure, and there were established limits on the hours or days their labor could be appropriated. The deepening of the Atlantic slave trade during the eighteenth century resulted in a loosening of the norms regulating those who could be sold to Europeans. No longer were they just captives taken in warfare, or individuals accused of capital crimes. Slavery was evidently shifting to facilitate European purchase.[12] Minor improprieties could designate someone as chattel for Europeans. Rural life grew increasingly insecure, and efforts to carry out daily activities became rife with danger. Many narratives of freed slaves reveal that they were captured while traveling to field, market, or home.[13] The breakdown of African societies was eroding the norms that had previously regulated those who could be sold to Europeans.

Those remaining as indigenous African slaves were disproportionately female because of the greater demand for male slaves on New World plantations. Over the course of 350 years, male slaves were shipped to the Americas in roughly a two-to-one ratio over females, leaving women particularly burdened with the crucial role of food production in Africa.[14] The slave trade favored adolescents to thirty-year-olds, and these males and females also contributed to African cereal production. They were often set to work in agricultural villages during the interlude between their capture and their deportation overseas.

Europeans aimed their slave ships to arrive in West Africa between the months of November and May, the dry season for much of the Upper Guinea Coast and the period of the year with favorable trade winds. Besides the dry season's navigational value, travel to the region during that time reduced the risk of death from malaria, rampant during the rains. Slaves captured in the off-season and awaiting transatlantic shipment were frequently set to work growing crops under strict supervision. This meant that captives held for later shipment could be made self-sustaining, perhaps even producing a small surplus for sale to slave ships over the food requirements for their own subsistence.[15] The pattern of using indigenous slaves for surplus food production endured even beyond the British abolition of slavery from Africa in 1807.[16] For instance, several members of the 1839 slave uprising on the *Amistad* recalled being forced to grow rice in Sierra Leone during the interlude between their captivity and shipment across the Middle Passage.[17]

Following the precedent established by Portuguese caravels, Europeans continued to depend upon African food surpluses during the Atlantic slave trade. Journals kept by ship captains make abundantly clear the extent of their demand for cereals to provision slaves across the Middle Passage. Their accounts record purchases of rice, especially along the Rice Coast, from Senegambia south to Liberia.[18] In the early eighteenth century rice, maize, millet, and manioc had become the primary cereals purchased by slave ships. The foods in demand, observed a ship's surgeon, John Atkins, in 1721, were vegetables, horse (fava) beans, rice, maize, and manioc meal, which provided the "common, cheapest, and most commodious Diet" for crossing the Middle Passage.[19] Alonso de Sandoval, an observer of the slave trade to Cartagena, Colombia, over the same period, noted that slave ships frequently purchased maize and millet for provisions.[20]

The Atlantic slave trade prompted an immense demand for cereals. Conservative estimates record that over the trade's 350-year duration more than twelve million persons left Africa as slaves. These are the numbers documented by surviving records, but figures may easily have reached twice that number given the fragmentary evidence and the high toll on life that characterized the trade. Mortality rates across the Middle Passage, a journey that could last from six weeks to three months, averaged 20 percent on slave ships.[21] It is difficult to grasp the magnitude of agricultural production that was required to meet the food demand of the Atlantic slave trade. Just to keep a human being alive as chattel in Africa required about a kilogram of grain a day. And even if the period from time of captivity in Africa to landing in the Americas proved swift, the aggregate food requirement would demand at least four months of food rations per person.[22] At the peak of the slave trade in the eighteenth century 100,000 slaves were being removed from West Africa annually. Some existing figures reveal the food demands on slave ships during this period. In 1750 John Newton bought nearly eight tons of rice for feeding 200 slaves, while John Matthews estimated that from 700 to 1,000 tons of rice would feed 3,000 to 3,500 slaves purchased along the Sierra Leone coast.[23] Those left in indigenous captivity were burdened with the need to produce surpluses that would sustain the enormous numbers sent across the Middle Passage. Women, children, and the old disproportionately shouldered this immense work burden.

In response to the demand for food surpluses, African societies swiftly adopted introduced crops, especially maize and manioc from the New World and some higher-yielding Asian rice varieties introduced to the irrigated systems along the coast. Maize, a plant of Amerindian origin, led the seed introductions in importance. Perhaps grown in West Africa within just a decade of the first voyage of Columbus, maize cultivation had become widespread in the Cape Verde Islands and along the Upper Guinea Coast by the mid-sixteenth century.[24] Several features of maize reveal the paramount importance of African-grown cereals, both indigenous and introduced, for the Atlantic slave trade. Adapted to the tropics, easily produced, storable, and cheaply transportable, maize became indelibly associated with slavery in Africa as well as on New World plantations. With yields generally higher than those of millet and sorghum, by 1729 maize was the staple food fed to slaves along the Senegal River.

Another New World domesticate, manioc, had also been introduced to West Africa by 1700 for provisioning slave ships. Unless converted into a meal or flour, root and tuber crops like manioc cannot compete with cereals for their ease in storage, transport, and cooking.[25] The staples of slave ships were cereals, chiefly ones adapted to the growing conditions of the African tropics, such as rice, maize, millet, and sorghum. The two most popular for their yields and taste, maize and rice, have long been claimed for the Columbian Exchange. But the attribution of Asia for rice diffusion has obscured the significance of African rice in global seed transfers. Between the sixteenth and the eighteenth centuries rice from Asia played a minor role in West Africa compared with that of indigenous African rice. We know this because accounts by colonial officials in the early twentieth century note the diversity of *glaberrima* varieties and the limited geographical distribution of *sativa*, confined principally to the two irrigated areas Portères identified along the coast. Even at the start of the twentieth century the West African rice region remained largely a zone of *glaberrima* cultivation.[26]

Rice Diffusion in the Atlantic Basin

The geographic pattern of the unfolding of the Atlantic slave trade along the West African coast in its first centuries influenced the diffusion of rice to the Americas. During the fifteenth and sixteenth centu-

ries the trade concentrated in the rice region between Senegal and Sierra Leone, within easy reach by European ships and the Cape Verde
Islands.[27] From the time of its settlement in the mid-fifteenth century,
Cape Verde emerged as a major entrepôt for the new trading relations
being established between Portugal and West Africa and, subsequently,
Latin America. The island chain lay west and southwest of the mouth
of the Senegal River, where the Sahara Desert grades into the Sahelian
savanna. In 1466 the Portuguese crown granted European colonists
settled there the right to trade along the western coast of Africa. The
island archipelago lay within easy reach of the region between Senegambia and Sierra Leone that the Portuguese called the "Guinea of
Cape Verde."[28]

This trade rested on slaves brought to the islands to grow crops for
subsistence and sale and to weave cotton into the cloth that was used as
a medium of exchange in the coastal trade.[29] Ships routinely stopped in
Cape Verde on voyages to Africa or Europe for food and repairs. The
islands quickly emerged as a major entrepôt for seed transfers and experimentation with the crops of the Columbian Exchange that then
diffused to the "Guinea of Cape Verde."[30] A major area where rice was
grown in West Africa served as the source for slaves in the Cape Verde
Islands.[31] And rice came to the islands with them.

At the beginning of the sixteenth century the German Valentim
Fernandes recorded earlier mariner accounts that mentioned the cultivation of rice on the principal island of Cape Verde, Santiago. He attributed its introduction, along with cotton, to the Upper Guinea
Coast.[32] Two types of rice cultivation are reported in subsequent records, one planted in inland swamps, the other grown by rainfall. The
cultivation of additional African plant domesticates is also recorded at
an early date: yams, sorghum, and millet.[33] The mortar and pestle
which women use to prepare all African cereals also transferred to the
islands in conjunction with these crops.[34] The commercial ties between
Cape Verde and the "Guinea of Cape Verde" involved enslaving numerous West Africans from a region where rice formed the dietary staple. Many would have been skilled in rice cultivation and growing the
crop in wetlands. In that this was a period in which Portuguese ships
had barely rounded the Cape of Good Hope, the subsequent claim for
this rice being of Asian, not African, origin is not very credible.

The initial crops of the Columbian Exchange, then, as the example of the Cape Verde Islands illustrates, were chiefly African. These African domesticates served as the primary food source for slaves and Portuguese alike prior to the voyages to the Americas that decades later resulted in the transfer of Amerindian crops like maize and manioc to the Cape Verde Islands and the African coast. The transfer of seeds, as noted, proved so important that it came to be known as the Columbian Exchange. The initial contact period between Portugal and Africa brought slaves and the plants they favored from West Africa to the previously uninhabited Cape Verde Islands. Within decades rice was accompanying Portuguese ships and the African exodus to the Americas.

The active trade in rice on Cape Verde is revealed through the cargo lists of ships departing during the years 1513–1515.[35] During the 1530s, within decades of Cabral's sighting of Brazil, Cape Verdean vessels bound for Portugal's new colony were supplied with seed rice, sugarcane cuttings, and African yams.[36] There is no need to look half a world away to Asia for the origins of this rice trade. The Columbian Exchange almost certainly involved *glaberrima* rice from West Africa. Just as the cereal and its cultivation accompanied slaves from the "Guinea of Cape Verde" to the island chain, so is it likely that African rice and slaves pioneered the crop's establishment in the sixteenth century across the Middle Passage to Latin America and the following century to North America.

Rice cultivation figured so early in the settlement history of Brazil that the German botanist F. C. Hoehne considered the possibility that its presence predated the arrival of the Portuguese.[37] Within one generation of the conquest of Peru, a report mentions that rice was being grown on wetlands there.[38] This observation occurs during a period when the first groups of slaves arriving in the New World originated in the region from Senegal to Sierra Leone. Although the historical record is meager, surviving records of slave imports to Peru from the mid-sixteenth century illuminate the geographic bias of the Atlantic slave trade during this period. Three-quarters of the slaves reported as Africa-born in Peru between the years 1548 and 1560 came from the rice-growing region of Senegambia and Guinea-Bissau. A second account from Mexico in 1549 shows that 88 percent originated from the same region.[39] Over most of the seventeenth century, the slave trade to South America shifted from dependence on Senegambia to an equally heavy dependence on the region around Angola as the principal source of supply.[40] The geographic pattern of the Atlantic slave trade for the sixteenth century in Latin America means that there were abundant numbers of slaves with the knowledge and skills to pioneer the cultivation of their principal food staple.

In subsequent decades other vessels delivered seed rice to the state of Bahia, which from the 1540s became the locus for the emerging sugar plantation system in Brazil's Northeast.[41] In recounting the crucial role of the Cape Verde Islands for animal and crop introductions to Brazil, Bahian planter Gabriel Soares de Sousa noted in 1587 the cultivation of both rain-fed and swamp rice, the use of the mortar and pestle for milling, and the triumph of African dietary preferences among the slave population.[42] French historian Jean Suret-Canale would later claim this wholesale export of crops and food-processing techniques from Africa to tropical Brazil as the cornerstone of the civilization that Africans brought under bondage to the Americas:

> The blacks had an agricultural civilisation already well adapted . . . and it was in just this sense that in Brazil in 1827 Brigadeiro da Cunha Matos, a convinced slaver, affirmed the civilising character of Africa in relation to America. It was even said in the Brazilian Chamber of Deputies by Bernardo Pereira de Vasconcelos in 1843: "It is Africa that has civilised Brazil." In effect, a whole material civilisation, including nutritional practices, was implanted in tropical America, not only in the African populations but in many areas among those of European origin. It was an imported African material civilisation.[43]

This imported African civilization, as Suret-Canale correctly observed, rested on agriculture as equally as it did on culture, because of the centrality of food for affirming cultural identity.

In 1637 the Dutch launched an expedition to northeast Brazil, where they took over an existing Portuguese settlement to establish a colony at Pernambuco.[44] This settlement proved among the more remarkable of all those established in the Americas because of its scientific objectives and promise of religious freedom for its settlers, who included some Jews displaced from the Iberian Peninsula.[45] Among the savants accompanying the governor-designate Count Johan Maurits of Nassau-Seigen was the Dutch physician Willem Piso, whose seven-

year stay resulted in the first truly scientific study of the geography and
botany of Brazil. Although rice interested Piso for its presumed medic-
inal properties, his account indicates that the crop was already present
in the area when the Dutch first settled there, as were okra and ginger,
which he claimed arrived in Brazil aboard ships from Angola.[46]

These crops were planted by slaves in provision gardens and maintained in communities of runaways, known in Portuguese as *quilombos*.
The largest maroon community of the Americas, the Palmares settlement in the adjoining state of Alagoas, included some twenty thousand
escaped slaves living in nine hamlets. Already in existence at the time of
Dutch settlement, it was located just two hundred miles southwest of
the Dutch colony at Recife, seventy kilometers inland from the coast in
the rainforest, extending from the Mundau river up a five-hundred-
meter escarpment. For most of the seventeenth century Palmares survived repeated Portuguese and Dutch military expeditions to destroy
it. It was an African nation in Brazil, with a well-organized system of
agriculture where blacks planted "extensive fields of cereals, excellently
irrigated."[47] While the crops are not mentioned, the description and
Piso's commentary suggest wetland rice may have been one of them.

Rice certainly figured prominently among the crops planted in
quilombo communities of runaway slaves throughout Brazil. In Maranhão and Amapá in the eastern Amazon where the Portuguese would establish cotton and rice plantations in the eighteenth century, maroons
grew manioc, rice, and maize for subsistence. In the archives of the state
of Bahia, historian Stuart Schwartz uncovered a remarkable document
from the eighteenth century—a peace proposal by rebel plantation
slaves setting forth the conditions under which they would return to
the fields. Among their demands was the right "to plant our rice wherever we wish, and in any marsh, without asking permission for this."[48]

After the Portuguese reestablished control of Pernambuco in the
middle of the seventeenth century, the Dutch moved their colony to
the Guianas, the region that today includes Suriname and part of Cayenne. During the eighteenth century this was one of the plantation
economies with the highest ratio of Africans to Europeans (65:1 compared with Jamaica's 10:1). Rice was among the crops slaves planted for
food. It also emerged a favored food staple among the maroons who
fled slavery for freedom in the rainforested hinterlands. When merce-
naries sought to capture these fugitives on expeditions to the interior of

the Guianas during the eighteenth century, they reported the cultivation of rice in forest clearings and inland swamps.[49] Maroons even named one of their rebel settlements after its suitability for the cultivation of rice. It was called Reisee Condre, after the quantity of rice it afforded.[50]

Publications written on areas of black settlement history along the Pacific lowlands of Ecuador and Colombia, eastern Nicaragua, Jamaica, and Cuba mention in passing the presence of rice from an early date.[51] But the historical research that might reveal its linkage to slavery, as historian Peter Wood meticulously undertook for South Carolina, has yet to be done. This is regrettable since the establishment of rice in Latin America dates more than one hundred years in advance of its cultivation in North America, making such recovery crucial for understanding the role of slaves and African rice in the agricultural history of the Americas.

An African Knowledge System in South Carolina

Nowhere in the Americas did rice play such an important economic role as in South Carolina. Rice and South Carolina share a history that led to the establishment of the crop early in its settlement and the colony's growing emphasis on rice as a plantation crop by the end of the seventeenth century. Within just twenty years of its founding, the crop was being cultivated for export. By the mid-eighteenth century the cultivation of rice extended along the Atlantic coast from North Carolina's Cape Fear River to the St. Johns River in Florida and inland for some thirty-five miles along tidal waterways (Figure 3.1).[52] On the eve of the American Revolution, over the years 1768–1772, rice exports from South Carolina exceeded sixty million pounds annually. Already rice had become the first cereal to be globally traded.

Production steadily increased during the antebellum period, and before the outbreak of the Civil War, an estimated 100,000 slaves were planting between 168,000 and 187,000 acres of wetlands to rice.[53] The antebellum rice economy included the richest planters of the U.S. South, and the region's capital, Charleston, gloried in one of the greatest concentrations of wealth in the world.

In 1860 large landholdings, prototypes of today's agribusiness complexes, characterized rice production with acreage concentrated in

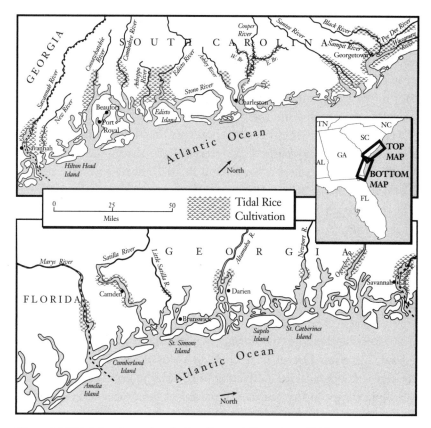

Figure 3.1 Tidal rice rivers, South Carolina and Georgia, c. 1800

about 1,600 plantations and farms.⁵⁴ Rice exports from the South reached about 182 million pounds per year, with South Carolina accounting for about two-thirds of the total, Georgia most of the rest.⁵⁵ The rice industry, growing phenomenally, relied exclusively upon slave labor to plant, harvest, and mill the crop for overseas markets.

Even though abolition doomed this slave labor system, a plantation economy that for over 150 years had delivered princely fortunes was not so easily extinguished in the memory of planter descendants. As blacks faced the failed promises of Reconstruction—second-class citizenship in the Jim Crow South of segregation and limited economic opportunities—planter descendants began their own reconstruction of historical facts to present slavery as a benign institution. Well into the twentieth century, memoirs written by descendants of rice planters nostalgically recounted the antebellum period, investing it with the kind paternalism that allegedly marked planter-slave relations. They celebrated the profitable landscape planters fashioned from malarial swamps and, especially, the ingenuity of their forebears in developing a crop so eminently suited to the region's tidal floodplains.[56] Their tributes to the rice plantation era never presented African slaves as having contributed anything but their unskilled labor.

Scholarship in recent decades, however, has told a different story. Peter Wood has established the presence of African slaves in South Carolina from the onset of settlement in 1670. Early accounts indicate that bondsmen produced their own subsistence crops and that the English and French planters had no prior rice-farming knowledge. Many of these early English-born planters had left land-scarce Barbados with their slaves in search of new plantation land. Displaced French Huguenots soon joined them in mainland North America. Neither European group had a history of rice cultivation. But this was not the case with some of their enslaved work force. The origin of Carolina rice agriculture, Wood argued, was likely African.[57]

Addressing the potential linkage of Carolina rice cultivation to West Africa, historian Daniel C. Littlefield focused on several issues. He looked at floodplain rice cultivation in Africa, the geographic origins of Carolina slaves during the crucial period of the crop's development in the eighteenth century, and archival sources that might reveal planter awareness of specific African ethnic groups with rice-farming skills. Littlefield established similarities between tidal cultivation in West Africa and its development in a similar environment in South Carolina and Georgia. He also noted that during the crucial period of rice development in the Carolina colony, more than 40 percent of its slaves originated in areas of West Africa with a tradition of farming rice. Additional documentation demonstrated planters' awareness of the African regions and ethnicities involved in rice cultivation as well as their requests for slaves of specific ethnic groups with this expertise. Whether or not planter requests were in fact ultimately met, the evidence reveals their awareness that certain African peoples possessed crucial knowledge and skills in rice cultivation.[58]

Although this scholarship has resulted in a revised view of the rice plantation economy as one influenced by slaves from Africa, the role of slaves in its evolution is still debated. The question is whether slaves from West Africa's Rice Coast were recruited as skilled laborers in a cropping system planters had already ingeniously developed, or whether slaves expert in rice cultivation showed Carolina planters how to adapt a preferred dietary staple to diverse lowland settings.[59] Addressing this question through documents is difficult: archival evidence for rice beginnings during the colonial period is fragmentary, as are any documents that reveal slaves' experience in their own voice. The paucity of records and the fact that racism over time institutionalized white denial of the intellectual or skilled capacity of bondsmen contribute to the problem of trying to determine whether slaves played a tutorial role in the Carolina rice beginnings. But there are other ways to give voice to the historical silences of slavery.

This examination of Carolina rice history and African agency in its diffusion across the Atlantic uses a geographical perspective focused on culture, technology, and environment to support the contention that the origin of rice cultivation in South Carolina is indeed African, and that slaves from West Africa's rice region tutored planters in growing the crop. In this approach the historical record is reconstructed to elucidate the environments planted to rice in the colonial period. This involves shifting research attention from rice as an export crop grown by slave labor to rice culture, the underlying knowledge system that informed both the cultivation and the milling of rice. Thinking about rice as a knowledge system reveals dynamics of agrarian diffusion, innovation, and the origins of specific agricultural practices that promote historical recovery. This perspective especially underscores the significance of wetland cultivation and how knowledge of growing rice by submersion provided slaves leverage to negotiate and alter some of the terms of their bondage.

The literature on the Columbian Exchange shows how seeds may diffuse independently of the people who domesticated them. Varieties of Asian rice transferred to the Americas long in advance of Asians. But the adoption and establishment of these varieties required the presence of human beings already familiar with rice culture, the knowledge to grow the crop in wetland environments and the means to mill the rice once it had been harvested. The only people in South Carolina possessing this familiarity were Carolina slaves who originated in the rice region of West Africa. To find the origins of rice cultivation one must thus look to Africans, who were among the earliest settlers in the Americas, for adapting the crop to challenging New World conditions.

The crucial period for examining these issues is the first century or so of settlement in South Carolina, from 1670 to the American Revolution, when coastal lowlands were transformed from woodlands and marsh into plantation landscapes based on the cultivation of irrigated rice. The period can be divided into two, with the Stono slave uprising in 1739 providing the demarcation. In the decades preceding Stono, rice emerged as the colony's principal export crop with its cultivation increasingly focused on productive inland swamps. The growing of rice on floodplains was at an incipient stage. In the period immediately following the Stono rebellion, slave imports into the colony declined. When they resumed in the 1750s the cultivation of rice was already shifting to floodplain irrigated systems.

In the initial decades of the Carolina rice economy, the work demand of shaping plantations from the wilderness placed the labor relations between black and white, slave and planter, in flux, because survival and success required mutual interdependence. Blacks' escape to establish maroon settlements in the interior or flight to Indian communities was a real possibility, as were alliances against white rule. As we shall see below, by 1712 conventions between slave and master were already in place over the permissible norms regulating work in the rice economy.[60] Slavery during this early frontier period involved a negotiated relationship.

By the decade of the 1730s, the relationship between black and white had profoundly altered. The Amerindian population had sharply declined due to warfare with colonists, slaving expeditions against them, and the introduction of diseases against which they had no immunity.[61] Their conquest was accompanied by an extension of white land ownership along the coastal lowlands of South Carolina. Slaves of African origin were in demand, and imports grew dramatically from 1720. In the decade preceding the 1739 Stono rebellion, over twenty thousand slaves were imported from Africa, a more than twofold increase over the twelve thousand present in the colony in 1720.[62] The work of clearing swamps for rice cultivation was arduous and accompanied by great loss of life.

White repression increased with the constant flow of new slaves into the colony and labor demands to clear swamps for cultivation, but the pattern of the slave trade in the decade prior to Stono presented new possibilities. Seventy percent of these slaves originated in Angola and its interior, giving the colony's black population a rare degree of cul-

tural and linguistic homogeneity among New World plantation societies. The result was their attempt to throw off the yoke of bondage,
known as the Stono rebellion. While the revolt was unsuccessful, fear
of what had been attempted resulted in a near ten-year moratorium on
further slave imports into the colony.[63] When imports resumed in mid-
century, the frontier had vanished and rice cultivation was spreading to
Georgia, closing avenues for escape from slavery. The institution of
bondage had deepened, diminishing the space for negotiation between
slave and master. The first century of black settlement in South Carolina and Georgia, the period that historian Ira Berlin terms the slaves'
charter generations, remains crucial for understanding the linkage of
rice cultivation to West African slaves.[64]

White and black settlement of South Carolina occurred at the same
historical moment. About a hundred slaves accompanied the first settlers arriving in South Carolina from Barbados in 1670; within two
years they formed one-fourth of the colony's population, and by 1708
blacks outnumbered whites.[65] From that period on South Carolina became a colony with a black majority. Documentation of rice cultivation
appears early in the colonial period. With food supplies limited before
1700, slaves raised their own subsistence crops. A pattern similar to the
Cape Verde Islands and South America probably resulted in rice's being grown as a preferential food among blacks in the earliest settlement
period.[66] No official document mentions the cultivation of rice before
1690, even though English officials from an early date considered the
cereal a potential export crop for South Carolina.

But several facts point to the likelihood that rice was grown from the
beginning of the colony's settlement. In 1674 several English indentured servants who ran away to Spanish St. Augustine, Florida, claimed
to Spanish officials that "some rice . . . grown on the soil was shipped to
Barbados."[67] In 1690 one plantation manager, John Stewart, claimed to
have successfully planted rice in twenty-two different locations.[68] His
occupation and nationality make it quite unlikely that he, a Scot, literally planted a crop that was not even grown in the country of his birth.
His slaves were the ones growing rice. Already present in the colony
and among Stewart's slaves were those skilled in rice cultivation who
were pioneering its establishment in diverse environments under both
rain-fed and wetland conditions. These fragmentary references indicate that the planting of rice in South Carolina was under way by 1690.

But to develop as an export crop, rice would have to be milled before shipment to overseas markets. The consumption of rice depends upon removing the indigestible hull and bran without damaging the grain they enclose. This was not so easily accomplished at the end of the seventeenth century with available forms of European milling. Unlike the cereals known to Europeans, which involve using a millstone to make flour, the objective of rice milling is to keep the grain whole as the husks are removed.[69] Until the advent of machinery around the time of the American Revolution to do this, the only method employed for milling rice was the mortar and pestle used by African women. A report from 1700 suggests the transfer of this knowledge had already taken place by the late 1600s. Edward Randolph, who visited the colony twice in 1697 and 1698, implied the African method of processing rice with a mortar and pestle was being used in South Carolina in his report to the Board of Trade, writing, "They have now found out the true way of raising and husking Rice."[70]

In 1690 John Stewart's correspondence mentioned the demand for Carolina rice in Jamaica, but the first record of its export is in 1695, with the shipment of one and one-fourth barrels to that island.[71] The shift of rice from a subsistence to an export crop over the decades from the 1690s to 1720s was indicative of the cereal's increasing economic importance in the colony. Exports reached 330 tons in 1699, and by the 1720s rice emerged as the colony's leading item of trade.[72] Years later, in 1748, Governor James Glen would underscore the significance of experimentation with rice during the 1690s for the development of the Carolina rice economy.[73]

Although experimentation with growing rice in diverse microenvironments would have revealed the higher yield potential of wetland forms of cultivation, the initial emphasis was on the rain-fed production system. As rice became established as a viable export crop in the early eighteenth century, its cultivation shifted to the higher-yielding inland swamps and from the 1750s, to the even more productive but labor-demanding tidal floodplain system that would dominate Carolina and Georgia rice plantations until the Civil War.[74] The historical record of the crop's development in South Carolina shows a changing economic emphasis on three main production systems over the first century of the colony's rice history, from rain-fed to inland swamp and then to tidal cultivation. While rice was planted in numerous locales during the period when the crop was becoming the leading export, these distinctive forms of production were evident at crucial historical junctures in the evolution of rice as a commodity. An overview of each of these reveals linkages to West African rice systems.

Upland or rain-fed rice production was emphasized into the early 1700s for its complementarity with forest clearance and stock raising. Slaves performed the labor of felling pine trees for wood and extracting the pitch, tar, and resin sold for boat caulking.[75] Beef also entered the export trade as salted meat for ship crews on transoceanic voyages. The clearing of forests resulted in a landscape devoted to raising cattle and subsistence farming. The rain-fed system of rice cultivation developed as part of a rotational land use with cattle, similar to what already existed in Africa.[76] Some of the slaves entering South Carolina possessed knowledge of both rice farming and cattle tending, since herding was widespread along the Upper Guinea Coast north of equatorial Africa's trypanosome-bearing tsetse fly belt. The South Carolina system, as in Africa, relied upon cattle grazing the stubble during the dry season, with their manure renewing soil fertility for the next cultivation period.

During the early colonial period planters in many regions of the Americas exhibited some preference for slaves with herding experience. In the mid-seventeenth century Cape Verdean mariner Lemos Coelho remarked upon the demand for slaves from the Senegambian area because of their skills with horses and cattle. African specialized knowledge of cattle-raising and equestrian skills were already valued on mid-sixteenth century Hispaniola estates, where nearly all the vaqueros and ganaderos (cowboys) were Africans from Fula, Wolof, and Mandinka areas of the Sahel, especially Senegambia.[77] These herders were from the rice region of West Africa, where grazing and the cultivation of rice figure prominently in land use. From the earliest settlement date in South Carolina, slaves were expanding the frontier for their owners through cattle grazing and by developing cow pens in remote areas. Their experience with livestock management led to South Carolina's emergence as an early center of the open-range cattle industry in the colonies.[78] Livestock production figured crucially in the colony's early economic history while experimentation with rice was under way. But for rice to become a feasible export crop, production would have to shift to higher-yielding but more labor-demanding wetland environments.

The export of salted beef, deerskins, and pine-tree byproducts for naval use generated by forest clearance and animal husbandry provided the funds for additional purchases of slaves, whose numbers dramatically increased in the first decades of the eighteenth century. In 1703 slaves numbered about three thousand, but over the short period from 1720 to 1739, the colony's black population rose from twelve thousand to twenty-nine thousand.[79] This vast increase in slaves gave planters the labor force to clear swamps and construct the infrastructure necessary for relocating rice cultivation to the higher-yielding inland swamps.

Cultivation in inland swamps illustrated mastery of key principles of water control that could only be realized by a considerable exertion of labor. Trees like bald cypress *(Taxodium distichum)*, tupelo *(Nyssa aquatica)*, and sweet gum *(Liquidambar styraciflua)* needed to be cleared from swamps infested by venomous snakes and biting insects. Following removal of the vegetation, the land was leveled and enclosed by earthen banks that retained or released water through a network of bunds and sluices. Rice cultivation in inland swamps involved impounding water from rainfall, subterranean springs, high water tables, or creeks for soil saturation. In some places this system of rice farming enabled the release of reserve water on demand for controlled flooding at critical stages of the cropping cycle, the objective being to drown unwanted weeds and thereby reduce the labor spent weeding.[80] The principle of controlled field flooding was identical to the one found in the West African mangrove rice system.

Because there were different types of inland swamps, field flooding for irrigation and weed control occurred in a variety of ways. For instance, swamps located within reach of streams or creeks often used the landscape gradient for supplemental water delivery. Placement of an embankment at the low end of an undulating terrain kept water on the field while the upper embankment dammed the stream for occasional release. Sluices positioned in each earthen embankment facilitated field drainage and irrigation as desired.[81] Similar principles were evident in the cultivation of rice in coastal marshes near the ocean.[82] Under special hydrological circumstances, like the location of a saltwater marsh near the terminus of a freshwater stream, rice was grown in inland depressions that were flooded by marine water. The conversion of a saline marsh to a rice field depended upon soil desalination, a process facilitated by a coastal rainfall regime that averaged between forty-eight and fifty-two inches annually, which is slightly above the range found in the mangrove system that developed under similar conditions in West Africa.

Often a creek or stream served the purpose of rinsing salts from the field. Once again the water control system relied upon proper placement of embankments and sluices. The lower embankment permanently blocked the inflow of salt water at high tides, while opening the sluice at low tides enabled water discharge from the plot. A sluice positioned in the upper embankment delivered stream water as needed for desalination, irrigation, and weed control. This type of inland swamp system functioned in the vicinity of the embouchure of the Cooper River, where "rice marshes tempted planters as far down the river as Marshlands [Plantation], nearly within sight of the ocean. Here they had to depend entirely on 'reserve' waters formed by damming up local streams."[83]

The principle of canalizing water for controlled flooding also extended to settings where subterranean springs flowed near the soil surface. In 1859 Edmund Ravenel described one system that was still functioning on the eve of the Civil War: "The water here issues from the marl which is about two or three feet below the surface at this spot. This water passes South and is carried under the Santee Canal in a Brick Acqueduct, to be used on the Rice-Fields of Wantoot Plantation."[84]

During the antebellum period another inland swamp system existed alongside tidewater rice cultivation. While its colonial antecedents remain uncertain, this system flourished where a landscape gradient sloped from rain-fed farming to the inner edge of a tidal swamp.[85] Enclosing a tract of land with earthen embankments on high ground created a reservoir for storing rainwater, the system's principal water source. The reservoir fed water by gravity flow to the inland rice field through a sluice gate and canal. Excess water flowed out of the plot through a drainage canal and sluice, placed along the lower end of the rice field. The water then drained into a nearby stream, creek, or river (Figure 3.2).[86]

Many of the techniques for water control evident in this inland swamp production are reminiscent of the mangrove system of West Africa. Desalinating fields with rainfall, employing a landscape gradient for rice farming, converting a swamp into a reservoir with earthen embankments, and using sluices and canals for water delivery were many

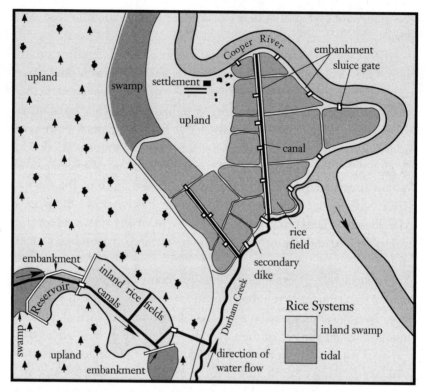

Figure 3.2 Inland and tidal river system, western branch of the Cooper River, South Carolina

of the practices that Europeans had described in rice cultivation along the West African coast. The development of a separate reservoir for water storage, however, suggests a South Carolina innovation. Only further research on the history of Atlantic basin rice systems can determine whether the creation of a supplementary reservoir for irrigating a swamp field is West African, European-American, or the hybridized contribution of both cultures.

Evidence from the early colonial period suggests that the principles of growing rice on tidal floodplains were known prior to the Stono slave uprising. One of the earliest references to tidewater rice, as it came to be known, appeared in 1738 with notice of a land sale by William Swinton of Winyah Bay, South Carolina: "Each [field] contains as much River Swamp, as will make two Fields for 20 Negroes, which is overflow'd with fresh Water, every high Tide, and of Consequence not subject to the Droughts."[87]

From the mid-eighteenth century rice production was steadily shifting from inland swamp systems to the even higher-yielding tidal river floodplains in South Carolina and then, just prior to repeal of its anti-slavery law in 1750, into Georgia.[88] By 1752 rich Carolina planters were commanding their slaves to convert inland swamps and tidal marshes along Georgia's Savannah and Ogeechee Rivers to rice fields, a process actively under way during the 1772 visit by the naturalist William Bartram.[89] The shift to production on alluvial floodplains remained the basis of the region's economic prominence until the demise of rice cultivation in the region by the 1920s.[90]

With the resumption of imports from the late 1740s, the swelling number of Africans entering South Carolina made possible the shift in rice cultivation from inland swamps to tidal floodplains. Crucial for the transition from the 1750s to the 1770s was the large number of slaves imported directly from the rice area of West Africa who possessed knowledge of the crop's cultivation. Over fifty-eight thousand slaves entered South Carolina in the twenty-five years between 1750 and 1775, making the colony the largest direct importer of African slaves on the North American mainland.[91] The share of slaves brought by British slavers into South Carolina from rice cultivation areas of Senegal, Gambia, and Sierra Leone grew during these crucial decades of tidewater development from 12 percent in the 1730s to 54 percent from 1749 to 1765 and then to 64 percent between 1769 and 1774.[92] By the American Revolution slaves from Senegambia and Sierra Leone formed the majority of forced migrants into South Carolina.

Planters knew such slaves grew rice; they also knew which ethnic groups specialized in its cultivation. This knowledge came from their sustained contact with slaves in shaping the Carolina frontier and growing food staples for mutual survival. The pattern of selecting ethnic groups experienced in cattle herding repeated with rice cultivation as planters in the early colonial period learned of the ethnic groups and geographical areas of West Africa specialized in growing rice on wetlands. Recognition of this knowledge held by some slaves was certainly evident in the initial period of settlement of Virginia, where experimentation with rice had also occurred. One surviving letter sent to England in 1648 records: "The Governor *Sir William* [Berkeley], caused half a bushel of Rice (which he had procured) to be sowen, and it prospered gallantly and he had fifteen bushels of it, excellent good

Rice, so that all those fifteen bushels will be sowen again this year; and we doubt not in a short time to have Rice so plentiful as to afford it at 2d a pound if not cheaper, for we perceive the ground and Climate is very proper for it [rice cultivation] as our *Negroes* affirme, which in their Country is most of their food."[93]

In South Carolina a century later, slaves from Gambia headed the list of planter preferences in the formative period of rice development.[94] The slave trade certainly was active in this region, and Francis Moore's 1738 account of his stay along the Gambia River as a trading factor between 1730 and 1735 provides ample testimony to the arrival of slave ships bound specifically for South Carolina.[95] Even though rice planters were not always able to obtain the slaves they desired because of availability and competition with other plantation areas, the records do demonstrate a demand by Carolina planters for bondsmen from specific regions where rice was grown. "Gold Coast or Gambias are best, next to them the Windward Coast are prefer'd to Angolas," wrote Henry Laurens, one of the leading slave importers in South Carolina, in 1755.[96]

As with the earlier demand for Fula cattle herders, planters sought the specific skills of slaves originating in the rice region. Newspapers advertised impending sales of slaves skilled in rice; one ad in Charleston boasted of 250 slaves "from the Windward and Rice Coast, valued for their knowledge of rice culture"; another on July 11, 1785, announced the arrival of a Danish ship with "a choice cargo of windward and gold coast negroes, who have been accustomed to the planting of rice."[97] Such prior awareness explains the stated preferences of planters for slaves from Gambia and the Windward Coast (Sierra Leone) during the crucial period of the eighteenth-century tidal rice development. Also evident is the pattern of direct imports to South Carolina of slaves from outposts of English slaving along the Gambia River and Bunce Island in Sierra Leone, where this knowledge was especially concentrated. Carolina-born, English-educated Henry Laurens, for example, had a special trading relationship with a wealthy British merchant, Richard Oswald, who owned the British slave factory on Bunce Island, located in the Sierra Leone River. From 1750 to 1787 Laurens and Oswald organized the slave trade from Sierra Leone, with Laurens importing Oswald's human cargoes directly to Charleston.[98]

Slave laborers skilled in tidal rice cultivation wrought the vast alteration of the lowland river floodplains of South Carolina and Georgia, which was nearly completed by the Revolutionary War. They created the irrigated landscapes that fed the international demand for the famed Carolina "gold" rice. But the demands on labor would brutalize the thousands of Africans who undertook the massive transformation of wetlands to irrigated rice fields.

The tidewater system, observed one South Carolina planter, was a "huge hydraulic machine" that rested on an "apparatus of levels, floodgates, trunks, canals, banks, and ditches requiring skill and unity of purpose to keep in order."[99] Although most of these elements were already present in inland swamp cultivation, on tidal floodplains they were employed on a much larger scale. Slaves from the West African rice area possessing this engineering knowledge became the preferred work force for transforming tidal swamps into productive rice fields. Even though the creation of a tidal plantation required enormous inputs of labor, once in operation the time spent weeding was greatly reduced over previous systems, due to controlled flooding. A slave was consequently able to manage five acres instead of the two typically planted to inland rice cultivation.[100] Tidewater cultivation, which came to dominate rice production until the Civil War, led to improved labor output and increased yields in turn, helping to create one of the world's most lucrative plantation economies.

This production system occurred on floodplains along a tidal river where the diurnal variation in sea level resulted in flooding or draining a rice field.[101] Four factors determined the siting of tidewater rice fields: tidal amplitude, saltwater encroachment, estuary size, and shape. A location too near the ocean risked saltwater incursion; one too far upstream removed a plantation from tidal influence. As with the West African floodplain rice system, a rising tide flooded the fields while a falling tide facilitated field drainage. Along South Carolina rivers the rise and fall of tides varied between one and three feet.[102] These conditions usually prevailed along riverine stretches ten to thirty-five miles upstream from the river's mouth.[103]

Estuary size and shape also proved important for the location of tidewater plantations, since these factors affected the degree of water mixing and thus salinity. The downstream extension of tidal rice cultivation in South Carolina and Georgia reflected differences in freshwater dynamics between rivers that drained extensive piedmont uplands (such as the Santee and the Savannah) and those with more limited inland drainage and extensive tidal flow from the sea (such as the Ashley and the Little Satilla). Because rivers of piedmont origin delivered fresh water within miles of the coast, tidal cultivation often occurred within a short distance from the ocean. But other coastal rivers are little more than arms of the sea, and the tide reaches further inland before encountering any significant influx of freshwater flows. Along such rivers the freshwater flow forms a pronounced layer on top of the heavier salt water, thereby enabling easy tapping of sweet water for tidal irrigation.[104] Suitable sites for cultivation relied on skilled observation of tidal flows and the manipulation of saline-freshwater interactions to achieve high productivity levels in the rice field, practices already known to West African tidal rice farmers.

Preparation of a tidal floodplain for rice cultivation followed principles remarkably similar to those of the mangrove rice system. Figure 3.3 presents the sequence of activities in the conversion of a floodplain to a rice paddy. First, slaves constructed levees, or rice banks, around rectangular-shaped plots on the mudflats. The rice field was embanked at sufficient height to prevent tidal spillover, with banks often reaching six feet in height. Earth removed in the process resulted in an adjacent canal, while openings in the rice bank admitted the inflow of tidal water onto the field. The next step involved dividing the area into quarter sections (of ten to thirty acres), with river water delivered through secondary ditches. This elaborate system of water control enabled the adjustment of land units to labor demands and allowed slaves to sow rice directly along the floodplain. Sluices built into the embankment and field sections operated as valves for flooding and drainage. When opened at high tide, the tide flooded the field. Closed at low tide, the water remained on the crop. Opened again on the ebb tide, excess water was drained away from the plot. The system functioned in the same manner as that of mangrove rice in Africa.

Tidewater cultivation required considerable landscape modification. It therefore demanded even greater numbers of laborers than the initial rice systems that featured prominently in the South Carolina economy. Slave laborers literally created the shape of rice cultivation in South Carolina through their presence and experience. The labor in transforming tidal swamps to rice fields involved a staggering effort, as his-

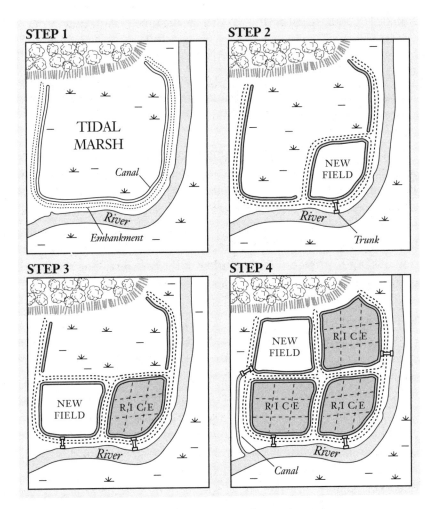

Figure 3.3 Tidal swamp conversion, South Carolina

torical archaeologist Leland Ferguson pointedly captures for one rice plantation in South Carolina:

> These fields are surrounded by more than a mile of earthen dikes or "banks" as they were called. Built by slaves, these banks . . . were taller than a person and up to 15 feet wide. By [1800], rice banks on the 12½ mile stretch of the East Branch of Cooper River measured more than 55 miles long and contained more than 6.4

million cubic feet of earth . . . This means that . . . working in the water and muck with no more than shovels, hoes, and baskets . . . by 1850 Carolina slaves . . . on [tidal] plantations like Middleburg throughout the rice growing district had built a system of banks and canals . . . nearly three times the volume of Cheops, the world's largest pyramid.[105]

Once in place, the irrigation infrastructure continued to make considerable demands on slave labor, as canals needed cleaning and constant vigilance to prevent their collapse. The labor involved in "mud work" was so grueling that it proved a consistent source of friction between slaves and their overseers.[106] Even after emancipation as hired laborers on tidal plantations, freedmen avoided mud work. Their aversion was not to growing rice but rather to the back-breaking mud work needed to maintain tidal plantations, since freedmen continued to cultivate rice on their own as a cash crop on unutilized inland swamps in South Carolina until the 1930s.[107]

With full water control from an adjacent tidal river, the rice crop could be flooded on demand for irrigation and weeding, and the field renewed annually by alluvial deposits. Historian Lewis Gray underscored the significance of tidal flow to the shift from the inland swamp rice system to tidewater cultivation: "Only two flowings were employed [in the inland swamp] as contrasted with the later period when systematic [tidal] flowings came to be largely employed for destroying weeds, a process which is said to have doubled the average area cultivated per laborer . . . The later introduction of water [tidal] culture consisted in the development of methods making possible a greater degree of reliance than formerly on systematic raising and lowering of the water."[108]

The systematic lifting and lowering of water noted by Gray was achieved by sluices, located in the embankment and secondary dikes (Figure 3.4). These crucial devices for water control assumed the form of hanging floodgates by the late colonial period. They were anchored into the embankment at a level above the usual low tide mark.[109] One archival photo taken in the 1920s of a Carolina rice plantation shows the relationship of the hanging trunks to the rice field (Figure 3.5). Gates placed at both ends of the trunk would swing when pulled up or loosened. The inner doors opened in response to river pressure as the

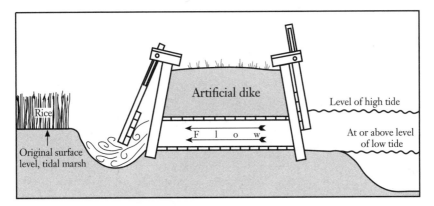

Figure 3.4 Sketch of a hanging trunk

water flowed through the raised outer door and then closed when the tide receded. Field draining reversed the arrangement, with the inner door raised, the outer door allowed to swing while water pressure in the field forced it open at low tide.[110]

On Carolina plantations these floodgates were called "trunks" even when they assumed a vertical structure. Curiosity about the origin of the term trunk for sluices or floodgates in the 1930s led one planter descendant, David Doar, to inadvertently stumble upon an issue that suggests the transfer of technology from West Africa:

> For years the origin of this name bothered me. I asked every old planter I knew, but no one could enlighten me. One day a friend of mine who planted on one of the lowest places . . . said to me with a smiling face: 'I have solved that little trunk question. In putting down another one, I unearthed the granddaddy of plug trunks made long before I was born.' It was simply a hollow cypress log with a large hole from top to bottom. When it was to be stopped up a large plug was put in tightly and it acted on the same principle as a wooden spigot to a beer keg.[111]

Such devices, constructed from hollowed tree trunks with a stopper at one end, preceded the innovative hanging gates of the late colonial period. Serving as a prototype, the plug trunks were placed in an embankment, which enabled control over the flow of fresh water for field flooding and the elimination of weeds. This is the exact water manage-

Figure 3.5 Floodgates on a Carolina tidal rice plantation, c. 1920

ment system still used in mangrove rice production in West Africa. The plug trunk served as the initial device for water control on Carolina inland swamp plantations, and the earliest systems functioned exactly like their African counterparts. Even when the hanging gate replaced the earlier plug form, Carolina planters and workers maintained the appellation "trunk" for the horizontal sluices and the vertical gates that regulated them. The continued use of this term throughout the antebellum period suggests that the technological expertise of Africans indeed proved significant for establishing rice cultivation in the earlier colonial era.

Recent archaeological research at Drayton Hall plantation (built between 1738 and 1742) in South Carolina shows an intermediate link in technology development, one that bears the imprint of both African and European technologies for water control. Over time the original plug trunk gave way to a modified form, before its culmination in the hanging gates that appeared by the American Revolution. In 1996 archaeologists excavated from beneath the former rice fields of Drayton Hall plantation a trunk intermediate in shape between the African plug form and the hanging gate sluices that characterized antebellum plantations. The uncovered device, which dates to the nineteenth century, was a sixteen-foot-long wooden box, two feet wide and about twelve inches high, with a groove at one end in which a rectangular gate was moved up and down to regulate water flow.[112] The evolution of trunks on Carolina plantations initially involved African experience, which later resulted in the hybridized product of both African and European inventiveness.

Long before millions were transported across the Middle Passage, West Africans had refined an elaborate food production system that displayed acute knowledge of landscape gradient, soil principles, moisture regimes, farming by submersion, hydrology, and tidal dynamics, and the mechanisms to impound water and to control its flow. The result was an array of rice production zones with a management portfolio more diverse than those occurring in Asia and more finely nuanced by microenvironmental soil and water parameters. This was a system that over millennia minimized subsistence risks, enhanced human survival in drought-prone environments, and contributed to the dense populations of the Upper Guinea Coast that were subsequently swept into the Atlantic slave trade.

The knowledge and the expertise to adapt cultivation of a preferred dietary staple to New World conditions proved among the scant "possessions" remaining to those pressed into slavery from rice-growing regions. For those arriving in frontier South Carolina, a similar geographic setting of diverse lowland habitats and climatic conditions optimized the transfer of a crucial African farming system to North America. But African ingenuity in Carolina rice cultivation, repeating a pattern established with irrigated rice in West Africa, would over time be attributed to Europeans. To the Portuguese who enslaved them in Africa and to the English and French slaveholders who relied on them to create Carolina's rice landscapes would go the credit for the inventive irrigated rice system Africans had developed under diverse wetland circumstances. Planter memoirs would celebrate the brilliant cultivation system invented by their forebears, while reducing the "savages" from the Guinea Coast to mere lackeys in their glorious schemes:

Rice culture reached a development and a degree of perfection in the Carolina lowlands which had not been attained in any other rice-growing country in two thousand years . . . Nothing but an ocular inspection . . . can give an adequate idea of the skilful [*sic*] engineering and patient, intelligent supervision that went to the successful result. The only labor at the disposal of the settlers who accomplished the feat was of the most unskilled character, African savages fresh from the Guinea coast. It was an achievement no less skilful than that which excites our wonder in viewing the works of the ancient Egyptians . . . The Southern planter who accomplished this result was a man who worked with his brains on an extended scale.[113]

No antebellum planters or, for that matter, their descendants considered the possible role of Africans in colonial rice development. The Africans were property and, as such, incapable of contributing valuable knowledge, skills, and experience. They were treated as mere animate commodities to be set into motion by others.

Task Labor: Knowledge, Resistance, and Negotiation

Plantation owners in South Carolina profited mightily from a farming system perfected over millennia by West Africans, which in turn was diffused to the Americas through slavery. But an important question remains. Why would West African slaves transfer to planters a sophisticated agricultural system, based on the cultivation of rice, that would in turn impose upon them unrelenting toil throughout the year? Why then cooperate in developing an agricultural system that would expose them to deadly malaria and life-threatening amoebic dysentery for decades to come? Why would they painstakingly work toward elaborating the infrastructure for tidewater cultivation, a system they later rejected as "mud work" following their emancipation?[114]

The answer to these questions can perhaps be sought by examining the definition of slavery as well as the changing lineaments of the social relations of production in South Carolina's rice economy. It is possible that the attempt to convey the meaning of slavery and bondage in an essential, clear, and forceful manner often obscures significant and complex details—details that reveal how slaves and their masters engaged in struggles marked by acceptance and resistance, coercion and consent.[115] By recognizing the complex ways in which social relations are challenged and transformed in slave societies, we may develop an alternative perspective toward the ways in which enslaved persons may have seized rare opportunities to negotiate and improve the conditions of their unfree labor.

By the Stono rebellion in 1739, all the major rice typologies were present in South Carolina. Also evident was an innovative form of labor organization, quite different from the pervasive "gang" form: the "task" labor system. The task labor system characterized work on coastal rice plantations from the early eighteenth century up to the Civil War. Under this "new" organizational form "the slave was assigned a certain amount of work for the day, and after completing the task he could use his time as he pleased."[116]

This was clearly different from the more pervasive gang system, where the laborer was compelled to work the entire day.[117] The task system represented a significant improvement in that it provided slaves the opportunity to allocate more time to cultivate their garden plots, hunt, fish, and gather products that could either go toward improving their nutritional status or be sold in local markets for small profits.[118] Tasks were measured in terms of an acre and on tidal floodplains, divided into units of work by irrigation ditches that demarcated boundaries.[119]

Without overstating the differences in workload between gang and task labor, the task system did set normative limits to the number of hours demanded. Expected work burdens on Carolina rice plantations were already established in customary practice by 1712. The earliest description of work practices in the rice economy reveals a sharp distinction between the time owed the master and the slaves' own time. In the first decade of the eighteenth century some South Carolina clergy complained of slaves planting "for themselves as much as will cloath [sic] and subsist them and their famil[ies]."[120] But Johan Bolzius observed in 1751 that slaves' own time counted for just a minor portion of each day: "If the Negroes are Skilful and industrious, they plant something for themselves after the day's work."[121] But even such seemingly minor gains over the permissible claims to slave labor were capable of delivering tangible improvements in their nutrition and health.

The task labor system appeared at the crucial juncture of the evolution of rice as a plantation crop in South Carolina and the shift to the more productive but labor-demanding inland swamp systems. Established conventions for the task changed considerably in the period following the Revolutionary War. During the antebellum era, the labor involved in growing rice under a task system differed little in the time to completion from that facing a slave laborer in other types of plantation economies.[122] The emergence of the task system in the early colonial period, however, may provide indirect evidence for African agency in Carolina rice cultivation.

The task labor system is probably of African origin, as it was already a feature of African slavery along the Upper Guinea Coast and its hinterland during the Atlantic slave trade. Task labor guaranteed those in indigenous servitude partial autonomy from claims on their labor through conventions that regulated the terms under which slavery could be exercised. With their social status reduced to that of chattel labor on European plantations, slaves would attempt to renegotiate these rights elsewhere in the Atlantic world during the charter generations of slavery.[123] But they would succeed in only a few places, and the most significant economy where they managed to do so was on South Carolina and Georgia rice plantations.[124] However, whether the task labor system mentioned by Bolzius in 1751 represented the transfer of an entire labor process from West Africa or the result of negotiation and struggle between master and slave over agronomic knowledge and the labor process cannot as yet be determined from the historical record.

Historian Clarence Ver Steeg, who has questioned conventional representations of white-black relations in colonial South Carolina, suggests that prior to the Stono uprising slaves were not considered incompetent and semihuman; they were, in fact, entrusted with considerable responsibility, even to the extent of bearing arms for the colony's defense.[125] Perhaps the basis for this initial esteem derived from slaves' vital role in transforming marshlands into swamps and the creativity they exercised in tailoring rice production to South Carolina's diverse lowland environments. From this perspective, the innovative task labor system—documented to have evolved in the United States first in South Carolina—may well have been forged from the complex process of resistance and negotiation between slaves and planters in which slaves provided critical expertise in exchange for a labor regime that would improve the conditions of their bondage. If so, West African bondsmen may have attempted to ameliorate European chattel slavery to the less brutal form they knew in their own lands of origin.[126] The historical juncture that marks the transition to wetland cultivation systems with the appearance of task labor in the decades prior to Carolina's Stono rebellion in 1739 argues in favor of such a hypothesis.

With the consolidation of slavery following the Revolutionary War, the task labor system lost much of its flexibility. During the antebellum period the tasks for planting, harvesting, and maintaining rice fields on Carolina and Georgia plantations required long days and sustained work that differed little in time from the labor demanded of slaves in other types of plantation systems.[127] The conventions that mediated the task labor system had eroded considerably by the end of the eighteenth century, probably as the result of massive imports of slaves from Africa. Between 1782 and 1810, South Carolina imported nearly ninety thousand slaves, thirty-five thousand entering in just the five years from 1803 to 1808, when the trade became illegal. This was more than twice as many as in any similar period in the colony's history. The result of this record-breaking influx meant that slaves born in Africa composed more than one-fifth of the bondsmen in South Carolina.[128]

Although the forced immigration of Africans contributed to the distinctive regional and Africanized Gullah culture of low-country South Carolina and Georgia, the increased importation of slaves adversely affected prevailing conventions regulating the task labor system. As historian Ira Berlin observes, "slaveholders used the occasion of the entry of new slaves to ratchet up labor demands, apply new standards of discipline, and create an order more to their liking."[129]

Thus in showing their masters the needed skills, enslaved persons were able to use their knowledge of rice cultivation to alter, albeit slightly, the social conditions of work through the task labor system. But the benefits received by the able and healthy during the charter generations of slavery would not endure after the institution's entrenchment during the antebellum period.

Ethnic Traditions and Farming Systems

A brief overview of the farming systems known to Europeans and Africans at the time of Carolina's settlement provides additional evidence for the agency of slaves in the establishment of rice in colonial South Carolina. Because rice was actively promoted as a potential cash crop for the English colonies as early as 1609, doubt exists as to African inventiveness in pioneering the cultivation of rice in the United States. Even earlier than South Carolina, Virginia colonists experimented with rice, their slaves informing them that the growing conditions were suitable for the crop's cultivation. A Virginia pamphleteer in 1648 praised the colony's agricultural potential, the "great Plains, fine and thick Grasse, Marshes . . . [and] rich black mounded countries for Tobacco, Flaxe, Rice, choice trees and Timber for Shipping."[130] But despite rice's potential, Virginia colonists tried and then abandoned its cultivation. In distinguishing the colony's marshes from the areas suitable for planting crops, the pamphlet's author perhaps reveals why. Rice experimentation took place on the uplands, alongside tobacco and flax, relying exclusively on rainfall.

Virginia colonists experimented with rice but grew it as a rain-fed crop in the manner of all the seeds they planted, in keeping with the tradition of farming they brought with them from Europe. As with tobacco, which soon emerged as the dominant export crop, the early experiments with growing rice in Virginia represented the addition of another crop of the Columbian Exchange to the farming system. This was a northern European system, where seeds were broadcast in plowed rows and grown with rainfall. Virginian colonists possessed no prior experience with growing crops under submersion in wetlands. Even though rice can be cultivated with rainfall, the yields are much lower than from planting the crop in wetlands. The feasibility of rice as an export crop would depend upon obtaining and mastering this knowledge.

From the end of the seventeenth century rice cultivation was under way in both North and South Carolina. The rice John Lawson described as being planted in North Carolina in 1709 was grown with rainfall.[131] Rain-fed rice also figured among the earliest varieties planted during the 1690s in South Carolina, where it was grown " 'as barley,' . . . broadcast" and in rows—that is, with rainfall in the manner Europeans traditionally sow their cereals.[132] But Africans also grow rice in this way. A focus on rain-fed rice does not illuminate which ethnic tradition should be credited with its establishment. The cultivation of rice in wetlands, however, is another matter, for its implementation depended upon the presence of ethnic groups skilled in growing the cereal in water.

By the end of the seventeenth century a new way of growing rice had appeared in South Carolina, cultivation in swamps. It caught the attention of one visitor to the colony, Mark Catesby, who wrote in 1731 that rice there was being grown "wholly in water."[133] This manner of growing rice depended not merely on an environment suitable for its cultivation but also on the presence of representatives of a farming system practiced in germinating seeds for growth in standing water. Such an agricultural system developed in just two areas of the world, Asia and West Africa.

Could wetland rice cultivation in South Carolina have been learned elsewhere through, for instance, the Dutch? A review of fenland cultivation in England during the seventeenth century reveals the role of Dutch engineers in teaching proper drainage techniques for reclaiming marshes, following the procedures they had mastered in marine land reclamation for agricultural expansion in Holland. But the Dutch system of draining waterlogged soils for reclamation always turned the reclaimed areas into new land for the production of cereals with rainfall, not for cultivation in water. Nor, by the founding of the colony of South Carolina in 1690, were such drainage and reclamation methods widely known in England.[134] There is no evidence for English or Dutch expertise in wet rice farming in South Carolina in the second half of the seventeenth century. Its origins lie elsewhere.

In 1650, just a few years after the report discussing rice cultivation in Virginia, a pamphleteer in England asked, since rice "groweth in the Fenny places of *Milan*, . . . why may it not grow in our Fens?"[135] The quote indicates English awareness that rice was being planted in the Piedmont area of northern Italy. Although it was not cultivated in England the crop had been grown in Italy since at least the fifteenth century, perhaps as the result of an earlier Muslim introduction via Spain or Sicily.[136] This system of rice cultivation was somewhat different from the one that developed on the Carolina wetlands. In the Mediterranean climate of Spain and Italy, with modest winter rains and dry summers, irrigation involved storing rainwater, lifting water, or diverting streams in order to irrigate lands that could be reached by gravity flow. Rainwater was often only a seasonal resource, which affected the amount of land that could be planted and crops grown. The expansion of rice farming in northern Italy during the Middle Ages involved adjusting the crop to summer cultivation and a system of canals to deliver river water through gravity flow. It resembled more the cultivation system on levees of the Mississippi River and its tributaries, where rice planting relocated in the United States after the 1880s.[137] Lying above flood levels, this land supports the weight of agricultural machinery and can be planted to crops other than rice, as it is in Italy where rice is grown in rotation with other rain-fed cereals.

Such principles, however, could serve as the basis for experimenting with wetland rice cultivation elsewhere. But there was no Italian immigration to South Carolina nor is there evidence that planters had studied the systems of southern Europe as the basis for developing tidal rice cultivation during the colonial period. Neither Italian rice nor its distinctive Italian and Spanish cooking styles, whose presence would suggest an influence on Carolina rice development, appeared in South Carolina. The small, round Italian rice—with its hard endosperm and resistance to breakage with mechanical milling—only arrived in South Carolina in 1787, when Thomas Jefferson experimented with growing the crop again on uplands. The experiment did not succeed, and rice failed to become established there.[138]

As for wild rice, *Zizania aquatica*, cultivated by some Native American groups, it could not have served as the basis for rice cultivation in Carolina. Not a true rice but a grass that is collected, *Zizania* was prepared by scorching or parching the rice, which in turn helped to remove the hulls, a different practice than that employed on Carolina plantations.[139]

At the time of settlement of the South Carolina colony, the tidal rice system existed in only two areas of the world, Asia and West Africa. Contact with Asia at the end of the seventeenth century, during the period of Carolina settlement, however, was indirect, mainly through the purchase of coveted trade goods such as tea, porcelain, and silk. The merchants and mariners who brokered this trade in Asia rarely ventured into the hinterlands beyond coastal ports and could hardly have mastered in a quick visit the complex principles of wet rice cultivation. There is no evidence during the crucial period of Carolina rice development that European migrants possessed the detailed understanding of Asian systems that involved techniques of transplanting, irrigation, and drainage for paddy cultivation.[140]

The origin of Carolina rice cultivation is most likely African, the product of an indigenous knowledge system introduced by West African slaves familiar with the crop's cultivation. Among the colony's settlers only slaves from the rice region of West Africa possessed a farming system that involved wetland cultivation. In South Carolina, as in Peru and Brazil, the planting of rice in wetlands was evident in the earliest frontier period and always in areas settled by slaves. The Carolina frontier presented to slaves a terrain more like what they knew in West Africa than anything previously familiar to the colony's European settlers. This was an environment ideally suited to the cultivation of a preferred cereal so central to cultural identity in many parts of West Africa.

To carve plantations from Carolina landscapes, Europeans depended upon slaves for labor. But they also relied on slaves to produce food for subsistence. Rice, a favored dietary staple among many of the colony's black settlers, could be easily grown in the abundant Carolina wetlands. The cultivation of rice proved ideally suited for the physical environment as well as the psychological terrain that shaped relations between master and slave during the frontier period. Mastery of wetland rice cultivation would deliver the high yields crucial to realizing its potential as an export crop. This accomplishment would eventually make planters rich and Carolina rice world famous, but it depended upon Africans familiar with rice culture showing the way to grow the crop in wetlands. Knowledge of rice cultivation resulted in African slaves' establishing a plantation sector that profited from a startlingly unusual form of technology transfer, one based on their own enslavement. The psychological environment between master and slave in the early colonial period thus involved the establishment of an African knowledge system for white purposes. This is a point Peter Wood succinctly captures: "the problem faced by white Carolinians during the first and second generations of settlement was less one of imparting knowledge to unskilled [slave] workers than of controlling for their own ends black expertise."[141]

THE EVIDENCE for the transfer of the technology of rice culture from West Africa to South Carolina shows dependence upon specific African ethnic groups familiar with the crop's cultivation. African experience with planting a whole range of interconnected environments along a landscape gradient, first mentioned by Dutch geographer Olfert Dapper around 1640, presaged the sequence of adaptations that marked the growth of the Carolina rice industry during the colonial period. For slaves, this knowledge of rice cultivation presented a rare opportunity to negotiate the terms of their bondage to a form resembling the indigenous servitude they knew in Africa. In reaffirming the claim for autonomy over their labor for part of the day, slaves were engaged in a struggle to humanize their degraded shift to chattel. Thus in frontier South Carolina, as Africans and Europeans faced each other in new territory under dramatically altered and unequal power relations, the outcome was agricultural diffusion, technological transfer, and novel forms of labor organization.

As involuntary immigrants, enslaved Africans constituted the largest number of settlers entering the Americas for much of the eighteenth century.[142] Their presence in the early settlement history of the Americas profoundly influenced the development of technology in ways yet to be examined by scholars. Across the Middle Passage slaves showed the way to plant and process new crops introduced from Africa, to herd cattle in open range, and to provide techniques of weaving and dyeing. The trend throughout the subsequent centuries of slavery was to erase the momentous African contribution, which scholarship is only recently beginning to uncover. This consideration of the complexities of rice culture draws attention to just one of the numerous knowledge systems that slaves introduced to the Americas in the face of staggering difficulties and loss of personal liberty.

4

This Was "Woman's Wuck"

It was work—work consistently sustained and ruthlessly enforced.
—Charles Joyner, *Down by the Riverside* (1984)

𝒯HE TENDENCY of the Atlantic slave trade to ship a greater percentage of females to South Carolina than to the Caribbean reveals the crucial role of African women in plantation rice culture. Female slaves bound for South Carolina received a higher purchase price than in other plantation economies, and their labor was valued more on a par with that of male bondsmen than in the slave markets of the West Indies. Indirect tribute to African women's expertise in rice culture probably underlies Thomas Nairne's observation in 1710 that female slaves in South Carolina received the same market price as males and performed equivalent tasks.[1] More than the labor of females would be valued on coastal plantations. Key aspects of rice culture embodied specialized knowledge systems, often the domain of African women.

Over much of the northern portion of the West African rice region, rice has long been a woman's crop. Only in mangrove cultivation along the coast have women and men participated equally in rice growing, although responsibilities are sharply demarcated by a gender division of labor. A similar division of labor has long characterized the crop's cultivation in the southern portion of the rice region, but when emphasis shifts to the bottomlands of a landscape gradient—the inland swamps—cultivation becomes chiefly the responsibility of women. Wherever rice is grown in West Africa, women are involved. They display sophisticated knowledge in recognizing soil fertility by plant indicators, which reveal, for instance, soil impoverishment or recovery. Females are responsible for seed selection, sowing, hoeing, and rice processing. Seed selection in particular requires a sophisticated under-

standing of the specific demands made by diverse rice microenvironments, such as water availability, the influence of salinity, flooding levels, and soil conditions.

Women's expertise in African rice culture extended beyond knowledge of the crop's cultivation to include the processing of rice. Given
the role of slaves familiar with rice culture in establishing the crop in
South Carolina, perhaps some female skills also transferred across the
Atlantic. To what extent did the gendered knowledge systems of African rice culture diffuse to South Carolina? Did the institution of slavery reproduce any of the gendered forms of African cultivation and
processing systems on Carolina rice plantations?

Specialized Knowledge and Technology Transfer

The hoe is the primary agricultural tool throughout the entire West
African rice region. Indispensable to women's work in rice culture are a
long- and short-handled version, the former used for field preparation
and the latter for detailed work and weeding. Several colonial-period
engravings and paintings of American rice plantations depict slaves,
often females, carrying or working with the long-handled hoe.[2] Its significance in field preparation continued after Emancipation (see Figure
4.1). Written accounts of Carolina rice culture also mention the use of
short-handled hoes, with handles four and eight inches in length, for
detailed plot work.[3]

During the colonial period the use of hand tools predominated in
southern agriculture. The clearing of forests resulted in fields full of
stumps and roots, which could not be worked by draft animal traction.
However, by the close of the period hoes were being replaced, as stump
removal and decay facilitated the use of horse- and ox-drawn plows.
The exception to this pattern occurred on Carolina rice plantations,
where the use of hand tools continued into the antebellum period. Historian Lewis Gray calls the use of hoes in Carolina low-country agriculture the "West Indian method," which he claimed to be fixed in local custom rather than technological necessity.[4] Gray's West Indian
method links the continuance of hoe agriculture in South Carolina to
the system of planting in islands of the West Indies, such as Barbados,
whence migrated some of the first European and black settlers to the
Carolina low country. The West Indian tradition of using hand tools,

Figure 4.1 Woman holding a long-handled hoe on former South Carolina rice plantation, c. 1900

however, likely has its roots in West Africa. Metal tools were unknown to the Amerindians whereas those being used for clearing and planting in the West Indies resemble the implements long employed for specialized agricultural activities in West Africa.[5]

As an agricultural implement the hoe actually played a minor role

in eighteenth-century European farming systems, which relied principally on draft animal traction. Hoes were typically used for work in the
corners of fields, on small parcels, or for specialized crops like grapes.[6]
In Africa, the hoe took on a preeminent role since much of the continent potentially favored for draft animal traction suffered adversely
from trypanosome infection lethal to cattle. On no other continent but
Africa does the hoe figure so centrally or take so many forms.[7]

   Three cultivation techniques on Carolina plantations suggest African antecedents. Throughout West Africa women are the sowers of
rice. On Carolina and Georgia rice plantations, sowing was typically
the work of female slaves. The method of planting additionally reveals
an African basis. Sowing usually involved dropping seeds onto the
trenched ground and covering them with the foot (Figure 4.2).[8] African
antecedents are also evident in a second, though less common, method
in which seeds are enveloped with marsh clay before planting. The
technique is similar to one long used in West Africa, where women
wrap seeds in cow dung and/or mud to protect them against birds, insects, and microbial parasites.[9] The documentary *Family across the Sea*,
which profiled many of the similarities in rice cultivation between
South Carolina and Sierra Leone, filmed African women dropping the
encased seeds in the soil for cultivation. In South Carolina and Georgia
this method of sowing became known as open-trench planting, and the
correspondence with the African system becomes clear from its description by planter descendant Theodore Ravenel:

   It is not commonly planted, not over 5 per cent of the entire acreage . . . Before sowing . . . it is necessary to cover the seed with clay
   water . . . made by mixing clay and water to about the consistency
   of thick whitewash . . . so that each seed is covered with a coating
   of clay. It is then spread out thin, so that it will dry . . . As soon as it
   is dry, proceed as in covered rice except . . . that the seed is sowed
   on top of the land. In open-trench rice, the water is held not only
   until the seeds germinate but until it has a leaf and a fork about
   three-fourths of an inch long. It is then dried for twenty-four or
   forty-eight hours to allow it to take root. After it has taken root,
   put the water on it again immediately, and proceed as with the
   other rice [covered or closed-trench method].[10]

Figure 4.2 Women sowing seeds on Carolina rice plantation

Although the dominant method of sowing seeds still involved drop-ping seed into a hole and covering it with the foot, specific circum-stances favored the open-trench planting method. In areas where bird or insect predation reduced seed survival, this method was used. It was also favored on irrigated fields that experienced drainage problems, where the standard planting method might cause the seed to rot.[11]

Another technique in Carolina rice cultivation that indicates the transfer of a gendered knowledge system across the Atlantic relates to the method used for cultivating freshwater river floodplains. Rice culti-vation in this environment is often a West African female farming system with transplanting practiced only in areas beset by high tides or when variability in the onset of precipitation delays the return of the flood. In fact, French colonial officials viewed the absence of trans-planting on floodplains of the Inland Delta of the Niger River as one of the features distinguishing African from Asian rice systems. Tidal rice cultivation in South Carolina and Georgia also developed on freshwa-ter rivers and seldom involved transplanted seedlings, relying instead upon direct seeding of floodplains, as in Africa.[12]

Another group of techniques that testify to the transfer of female knowledge systems to the Americas relates to the manner of milling and cooking rice. For most of the colonial period rice was milled with a wooden mortar and pestle, with winnowing accomplished with fanner baskets. Thus until the advent of water-driven mechanical devices during the second half of the eighteenth century, rice milling was performed in the African manner with an upright wooden mortar and pestle, the standard method women have used to process all food throughout the continent.

West Africa was not the only place to use the mortar and pestle for the processing of rice; Asian societies also used the device. But the processing of cereals traditionally is the work of women, in both Asia and Africa, and there was no Asian migration to South Carolina during the colonial period nor evidence to show that planters learned the skilled technique from Asia. There would have been no need to do so in the presence of female slaves who processed all crops in Africa with the mortar and pestle. But at the time that female slaves in South Carolina were transferring knowledge of the mortar and pestle, several innovative devices for rice processing had displaced its use in many areas of Asia. Chief among them was a foot-operated device involving a fulcrum to which a pestle was attached on one end. Raising the fulcrum with the foot allowed the pestle to fall into a mortar (often just a hole in the ground or floor), where the striking action removed the grain's hulls. This device for processing *sativa* rice was in use over a broad area of Asia from India to Japan. Its use in Japan is described in *The Tale of Genji*, written early in the eleventh century. Asian innovations in the mortar and pestle reflected in part significant differences between Asian and African rice. The fulcrum type of mortar and pestle works well on *sativa* varieties, whose grains do not shatter easily, but only the mortar-and-pestle method reduces breakage of *glaberrima* rice in milling.[13]

A focus on comparative rice processing devices additionally illuminates the linkage of technology to specific cultural funds of knowledge and the relationship between technology, the migration of specific populations, and rice history. For example, in a rice-growing area of Belize characterized by small landholdings and peasant farming systems, descendants of indentured laborers from India grow rice, as do their neighbors of African descent. Striking differences are evident in the way the two populations mill rice, the mortar and pestle the device of choice by the descendants of slaves, the fulcrum processing method favored by the Indian Belizeans whose forebears introduced it following their immigration in the first half of the nineteenth century. Where Indians went they brought the milling technology most familiar to them. Similarly, the African diaspora involved diffusing the mortar and pestle throughout areas of black settlement in the Americas. Thus one need not look to Asia for the origin of the milling technology or to planters for transferring the process from Asia to South Carolina. While Africans were not the only people to develop the mortar and pestle for rice milling, they were the first immigrants in the Americas to do so.

The processing of rice also involves the removal of the indigestible hulls or chaff, a process known as winnowing. In West Africa, winnowing occurs by placing the hand-milled rice, a mixture of grains and empty hulls, in circular and shallow straw baskets as much as two feet in diameter (Figure 4.3). During a breeze the grains and hulls are rotated inside and repeatedly tossed in the air. By tossing the grains and hulls up and down, the lighter chaff is carried off into the air, leaving the heavier husked grains inside the basket. Winnowing on South Carolina plantations followed the same method. The winnowing baskets, known on rice plantations as fanner baskets, were shallow disks with a raised lip about two feet across. They could hold about a pound of rice at a time (Figure 4.4).

Even the weaving style used in making fanner baskets displays an African origin, as anthropologist Dale Rosengarten has established. In a comparative analysis of African and Native American basket-weaving traditions, Rosengarten links the fanner baskets used for winnowing on Carolina and Georgia plantations to a tradition derived from the West African rice area. Rosengarten shows that the weaving style is not Native American, since the baskets of Southeast Indians employed a plaited or twilled design. Fanner baskets, in contrast, were always coiled. Those marketed as a folk craft by female African-American vendors in the Charleston area today are woven in the identical manner as the fanner baskets used for winnowing during the era of rice plantations. Rosengarten's exhaustive analysis of African weaving styles in museum basketry collections in Europe and North America locates the prototype of the fanner basket within Africa to the Senegambian region, a secondary center of *glaberrima* domestication. In the contemporary period women in the West African rice area continue weaving

Figure 4.3 Mandinka girl with rice-winnowing basket in The Gambia

coiled baskets for winnowing just as female basket weavers in South Carolina carry on that tradition through practices that date to the plantation rice era.[14]

Methods of cooking reveal additional linkages to Africa. The characteristic way of preparing rice in the Carolina plantation kitchen favored grain separation, the way African dishes based on *glaberrima* rice are typically cooked. In South Carolina and elsewhere in the Americas this culinary tradition could be achieved with *sativa* rice by using medium- to long-grained varieties that tended not to clump together. Then the plate of rice was prepared so that it appeared "white, dry, and every grain separate."[15] The method involves steaming and absorption, boiling rice first for 10–15 minutes, draining off excess water, re-

Figure 4.4 Rice winnowing with a fanner basket, South Carolina

moving the pan from direct heat so the grains can absorb the moisture, and leaving the pot covered for at least an hour before eating. Often the product was encased in a thick residue of crust on the inner edges of the pot: "[Rice is properly cooked only when it is] boiled till *done*, the water 'dreened' off, and set on the ashes to 'soak.' Around the pot there is a brown rice-cake, in the center of which are the snow-white grains, each thoroughly done and each separate. Unless one has eaten rice cooked in this way, he knows nothing about it. The stuff called rice—soft and gluey—may do to paper a wall, but not to feed civilized man."[16]

This is the same manner in which rice is traditionally prepared throughout the West African rice region, especially in the Sahelian area where wood for cooking is scarce and its procurement often the added responsibility of women. A similar method of cooking rice is found in other areas of the African diaspora—in Suriname, for example, among descendants of the Saramaka maroons. Women cook their rice in the manner just described, moistening the crust as a snack for children. Cuban rice cooking gives its own name to the delicious residue that forms at the bottom of the pot, *raspa*.[17]

The culinary method of cooking rice for grain separation rather than stickiness provides one way of distinguishing culinary traditions that are African from those that are East Asian. In a similar way, rice dishes prepared with water rather than with animal fat or vegetable oil suggest another way to identify African antecedents to the Carolina rice kitchen over putative influences from southern Europe.

Chinese and Japanese dishes, for instance, involve the use of short-grained varieties selected for the sticky endosperm trait which favors rice grains that adhere to each other and are easy to eat with chopsticks. Short- to medium-grained Asian varieties also typify Mediterranean rice dishes like pilaf and risotto. The Italian risotto aims for a sticky or gummy quality and achieves it by sautéing the rice in animal fat, then gradually adding liquid. The Spanish paella and pilafs, while less sticky than a risotto, also involve using oil or animal fat in rice preparation. Food historian Karen Hess attributes the use of oil or animal fat in rice dishes to Persia and India, whence the Arabs introduced the crop to the Mediterranean. African societies with a tradition of rice cultivation, in contrast, do not cook the cereal with animal fat, even though cattle herding is of considerable antiquity throughout West Africa and contributes to the system of land rotation in the rice region.[18] The signature of Mediterranean rice cooking, the use of animal fat, did not transfer to the Americas even in areas where the Arab/Spanish cooking tradition should have accompanied Spanish colonization. This suggests that the culinary tradition of cooking rice came via slaves rather than from their masters. Throughout the Americas the method of cooking rice followed the African style, favoring medium- to long-grained varieties whose grains separate with cooking.[19]

Despite the familiar logo of Uncle Ben on the converted rice marketed by that name in the United States, it was African women who perfected rice cooking in the distinctive manner that characterizes both African and Carolinian culinary traditions. They also developed the method of parboiling, another name for converted rice.[20] In newly harvested rice, which has not properly dried for milling, parboiling facilitates the removal of hulls. While the steaming of rice in its hull improves nutritional value by concentrating vitamins in the grain's center, parboiling causes the oils to migrate to the bran, a process that eases milling. As partial cooking reduces storage loss from mold, parboiled rice additionally confers superior keeping qualities.

For such reasons parboiling continued as a method of rice preparation in some rural southern communities well into this century. The method was undoubtedly known to the black Texas rice farmers symbolized by Uncle Ben, whose trademark was established when the process was industrialized during the 1940s.[21] Although the passage of time would divorce the image of Uncle Ben from its historical context to mere product icon, his representation on a well-known consumer product speaks to a deeper social and cultural memory of the early twentieth century, which associated black Americans with rice culture. The method of parboiling represents the diffusion of a female knowledge system from Africa, which survived slavery in the cooking practices of their free male and female descendants.

Thus more than the cultivation of rice took root in the Americas. Rice culture embodied a sophisticated knowledge system that spanned field and kitchen, one that demanded understanding the diverse soil and water conditions of seed survival along with cooking methods for consumption. The transformation of rice from field grain to food depended on yet another knowledge system perfected by African women, that of milling the cereal by hand. During the colonial period rice milling involved a skilled tapping motion for removing hulls without grain breakage. This female knowledge system served as the linchpin for the entire development of the Carolina rice economy. For without a means to mill rice, the crop could not be exported.

The issue of milling on Carolina plantations raises one remaining and pertinent question. To what degree, if any, did the gender division of labor characterizing African rice cultivation reappear under slavery in South Carolina? Since slavery could dissolve any preexisting pattern of work, what were the broader implications of the transfer of a knowledge system both African and gendered? An examination of the work cycle regulating life on rice plantations illuminates these issues while bringing attention to the colonial milling method, which involved use of the mortar and pestle. The brutality of slave labor during the colonial period vividly portrays the complexity of the demeaning shift of work that blacks experienced under slavery.

The Rice Calendar: Labor Patterns and Market Demand

Rice cultivation was arduous, requiring slaves to labor under strenuous and insalubrious conditions year-round. Slaves worked in knee-deep water, which exposed them to malaria, dysentery, and other water-borne diseases that in turn contributed to the high mortality rates on rice plantations during the nineteenth century.[22] During the hot and humid summers of South Carolina and Georgia, where temperatures average over 90 degrees Fahrenheit, slaves labored mightily to keep up with the demands made upon their bodies. Partly to avoid the summer heat, the slaves' day began at sunrise on rice plantations. The pernicious conditions of rice cultivation and slaves' presumed racial predisposition to working in heat and humidity were captured by one planter descendant, Duncan Heyward: "For there was at that time in the province no white labor which could perform the work of reclaiming the river swamps. The white man could not stand the summer heat, nor could he endure working in the water. Negroes alone had to be relied upon."[23]

The rice calendar involved year-round work, and most of it was done completely by hand. Only in the last decades of slavery were animals brought into use for plowing and transport of materials. Before that time even the harvest was carried out from the fields, typically in baskets placed on the head. Slaves began preparing for a new cycle of rice cultivation almost immediately after the harvest of the previous crop. The agricultural calendar got under way with land preparation from December to March. This involved burning the stubble from the previous harvest, digging out ditches, and fortifying the sides of canals that had slumped as well as removing excess mud from ditches. Slaves found especially odious the strenuous work involved in the digging, cleaning, and repair of ditches, where they were forced to labor over vast acreages with just their hands, buckets, and simple tools.[24] Then in the spring the fields were cleared, leveled, and clods were broken apart with hoes in preparation for cultivation.

In the tidewater system the sowing of seed was staggered in two planting periods, one from mid-March to early April and the other in late May through early June. The full moon regulated both sowing periods because its stronger tides facilitated germination by spreading water over the entire field.[25] Sowing was immediately followed by the first of four protracted floodings. The first or "sprout flow" aimed at seed germination, a period that lasted between three to six days. Then the water was drained off to allow the cleaning of debris, which was followed by hoeing and weeding. Next came the second irrigation flow, known as the "point or stretch" flow. Water remained on the field for another three to seven days, after which hoeing and weeding again took place.

Over the period from mid-July through August the field was once more flooded, the "deep flow" lasting for about three weeks. Hoeing and weeding again followed the draining off of water before the fourth and final period of field flooding, the "lay by or harvest flow." This referred to the irrigation phase when the plant began to joint so that the stalks supported clusters of rice. Water now stayed on the field until the rice crop reached maturity. The staggered sowings of rice enabled the cultivation of two rice crops and, as in Africa, reduced the labor bottlenecks in hoeing, weeding, and harvesting. The cycle of rice cultivation spanned a period from six to seven months. Once ripened, the crop was harvested with a sickle, usually over a six- to eight-week period from late August or early September into October.

Evidence from archival and historical sources yields clues on the division of labor underlying rice culture in South Carolina and Georgia. These include reminiscences by planter descendants and elderly ex-slaves of the Depression-era Federal Writers' Project, planter records on the division of plantation labor, and drawings that depict slave labor in rice cultivation, such as those of Alice Huger Smith for Elizabeth Allston Pringle's 1914 plantation memoir. Such evidence indicates that female slaves composed the majority of "prime hands" on Carolina and Georgia rice plantations.[26] Rice cultivation was characterized by a field labor force that was disproportionately female, with the less arduous artisanal "skilled" work such as making barrel staves for the crop's shipment, blacksmithing, and cooperage monopolized by male bondsmen.[27]

Although scholars in recent years have drawn attention to the necessity of revising conceptions of slavery that display a gender bias, such as those that undervalue agricultural and women's work by designating it as unskilled, there are other important considerations for examining the gender composition of field labor on Carolina rice plantations. Because women figure so centrally in rice culture in West Africa, the question arises whether the patterns of labor with slave-produced rice bear any resemblance to the gender division of labor found historically in West African rice cultivation. This objective goes beyond elucidating the central role of women in field labor in plantation economies throughout the Americas. Given the historical significance of women in African rice systems, the concern here is to illuminate whether patterns of rice development in colonial South Carolina and Georgia reveal the residue of a knowledge system transmitted by African women across the Middle Passage.

Any attempt to answer this question is somewhat equivocal, because the institution of slavery meant that the preexisting gender division of labor that characterized production of a crop in Africa could be disassembled in the Americas to accord with the dictates of the market and requirements of the plantation owner. Early accounts, however, do reveal the contours of a gendered system of production. Writing about rice cultivation in Georgia during the colonial period, Johan Martin Bolzius noted that with the exception of milling, there was no difference in the labor demanded of male and female slaves. However, men usually repaired rice embankments and ditches while the sowing of rice was principally performed by women.[28] The association of rice sowing with female labor continued throughout the antebellum period, as planter descendant Duncan Heyward remarked: "Women always did this work, for the men used to say this was 'woman's wuck,' and I do not recall seeing one of the men attempt it."[29] Another description of slaves planting rice in *Harper's New Monthly* from 1859 supports his contention. It notes: "Close upon the heels of the trenches come the sowers, generally women, who scatter the seed freely as they pass."[30] Women wielding long-handled hoes, the "human hoeing machine" as Frances Kemble described them at work in rice fields during the 1830s, provided crucial labor for land preparation and weeding.[31] Following patterns established in West African rice culture, women typically performed the tasks of sowing, hoeing, and weeding on Carolina plantations.

When examining the division of labor on low-country rice plantations, gender then emerges as an important aspect of the allocation of work. But the feminization of rice culture that characterized most plantations probably resulted from men's greater involvement in nonagricultural tasks, which left fieldwork disproportionately to women. The need for able-bodied workers in the fields was paramount, and plantations adjusted their work gangs to labor availability, demanding from women the same amount of labor in rice fields as required of men. However, as the principal growers of rice in West Africa—specialized in sowing, weeding, and cultivating freshwater floodplains—the expertise of female slaves in rice culture must have proved of value for adapting the crop to new conditions in the Americas.[32]

As the cultivation cycle drew to a close with harvest in late September or early October, rice milling got under way. The processing of rice dominated the agricultural calendar until the resumption of cultivation in March or April.[33] Although the actual period of farming was concentrated in the months from mid-March through October, production of rice for international markets in fact demanded work every month of the year. Nor was rice the only plantation crop cultivated. Its agricultural calendar was superimposed upon the planting, weeding, and harvest of subsistence crops like corn, beans, potatoes, and greens. The work of slaves on rice plantations intensified even more from the mid-eighteenth century with the cultivation of an additional export crop, indigo.[34] Over the same period plantation labor demands were increasing with the expansion of tidal rice cultivation, which necessitated swamp reclamation and the construction of irrigation infrastructure. Such factors strained the endurance of slaves on rice plantations and undoubtedly contributed to their abbreviated life expectancy.

But no work was as demanding as the toil of the postharvest period. Once the crop was harvested, rice stubble required plowing-under, then burning. Next the land was hoed to break up the soil. Field embankments, ditches, and fences needed repair, the canals cleaning and digging. But most important, the international market demanded a crop already milled. Once harvested, rice required threshing, winnowing, and pounding prior to shipment overseas. During the months from December to May work on a rice plantation intensified. In 1765 one Charleston visitor commented on the "active" work pace of slaves during winter and spring, when the "crops of rice and indigo [were] brought to town and shipped off."[35] But the activity involved a great deal more than harvesting and loading the ships. Millions of pounds of rice required processing before shipment and this fact set the pace for the season's activity. The work regime of a Carolina rice plantation was thus more rigorous and sustained throughout the year than that on comparable cotton or sugar plantations.[36]

The principal demand for the rice crop in the colonial era was in Catholic Europe, with peak market prices prevailing during Lent.[37]

Aiming production at this southern European market, planters sought
to complete rice milling by early winter in time for the transatlantic
voyage that would deliver the grain in February.[38] The market structure consequently acted as an impetus to further abbreviate the period
of time allocated for processing during the rice cultivation calendar.
But the goal of punctual delivery to Europe was often not met, as is
evident from one Charleston merchant's complaint in January 1726
about the shortage of milled grain for loading his waiting vessels:
"Here thirty seven barrels of Rice and two Chest of Deare Skin Ship
by me Richard Splatt on board the *Lovely Polly* Michael Bath Master
bound for London on my proper account and . . . goes Consigned to
Mr. William Crisp . . . that there is not rice to load the ½ of 'em."[39]

Market schedules somewhat improved in 1730 with changes in the
Navigation Acts that enabled the direct shipment of Carolina rice to
the Iberian Peninsula instead of via England. But changes in pattern
and time of shipment also acted as an incentive to expand rice cultivation in the colony. The growing demand for Carolina rice in European
markets, in addition to increased yields with the shift to tidal production, made ever greater demands on slave labor for processing the annual output. Sometimes it was far into winter before the entire crop
could be milled for market.[40]

A Carolina rice plantation during the colonial period represented a
stark departure in the work rhythms known to slaves who grew rice in
West Africa. Instead of signaling the end of an agricultural cycle, the
harvest marked the prelude to even more grueling work routines associated with milling. No wonder that cases of barn burnings as acts of
sabotage increased in the fall, when the huge rice harvest had been
gathered from thousands of acres and impatient planters were demanding that the crop be cleaned quickly and transported in heavy barrels to
waiting ships.[41] The intensified work effort required to process millions
of pounds of rice by hand during the postharvest period brutalized
slaves while transforming the colonial plantation system into a factory
in the field.[42]

Factories in the Field: Rice Processing and Slave Labor

On the eve of the American Revolution exports of rice from South
Carolina reached over sixty million pounds annually.[43] This repre-

sented a staggering growth of the rice economy since 1700, when less than half a million pounds had been exported.[44] The shift in rice cultivation from inland swamps to fertile floodplains had dramatically increased yields. Growing the crop with irrigation reduced the amount of weeding needed, which greatly improved labor productivity. From the first to the second half of the eighteenth century the per capita output of milled rice produced by slaves climbed from 2,250 pounds to an average that reached between 3,000 and 3,600 pounds.[45] But improved productivity scarcely ameliorated the work burdens facing slaves, for following the harvest, rice had to be milled. The exertions required by the rice harvest were negligible compared with the Herculean toil that awaited slaves milling the crop for export. For most of the eighteenth century this crucial step in preparing rice for export markets depended upon processing the crop by hand, with a mortar and pestle. The harvest of millions of pounds of rice on Carolina and Georgia rice plantations brought no respite for slaves. Instead, it intensified their work as they struggled to hand-mill the crop for European markets in time to resume the next cycle of cultivation.

The processing of rice by hand created numerous problems for slave labor and markets in the Carolina rice economy until the 1780s, when technological improvements succeeded in mechanizing milling. An examination of the milling process prior to its mechanization reveals the effects of enslavement and mass production of rice on an African knowledge system, male and female identities, and slave culture. Active involvement in developing rice culture on Carolina plantations, on the one hand, provided slaves the means to negotiate the conditions of their labor. But the very success of rice transfer to the low-country region resulted in one of the most profitable economies of the Americas, thereby consolidating planter power. With economic success, planters exerted greater control over slave lives. They made new claims on the bodies of enslaved persons, demands that tested human endurance. The expansion of the rice culture came at great cost to black lives.

For most of the colonial period Carolina planters relied upon slaves' processing the rice by hand with a mortar and pestle to provide vast quantities of this export crop. The method used in Africa to prepare rice for daily subsistence became transformed under slavery into a grueling labor regime in which millions of pounds of rice were processed in just a few months of the year.[46] The story of this plantation crop and its milling, deeply rooted in West African culture and history, reveals the changing relationship of time, labor, and market that character- ized the commodification of rice during the eighteenth century. The pounding of rice resonated through African communities as the heart- beat of daily life, the echo of cultural identity. Under slavery it was compressed into a seasonal activity, where each stroke of the pestle made inhuman demands on labor.

As already noted, the consumption of rice, unlike cereals known to Europeans, depends upon removing without damage the grain from the hull that encases it.[47] Unlike wheat, rye, oats, and other European cereals, where the goal of processing is to produce a flour, the milling of rice aims for the opposite effect—to keep the grain whole without breakage. Until the advent of mechanized milling near the end of the eighteenth century, the only method known to planters was the African way, with the mortar and pestle. For most of the colonial period rice culture in South Carolina and Georgia relied on this system that was little changed from its origins in the West African rice region.

The mortar was made by taking a tree trunk (usually cypress or pine), and using fire to burn a cavity or receptacle for placing the un- milled grain. With the mortar hollowed out to waist height, unpro- cessed rice was then milled with a wooden pestle (about one to one and a half meters long) that weighed between seven and ten pounds.[48] Pro- cessing requires standing over the mortar, taking the pestle in hand and repeatedly lifting it up and down to remove the hulls that enclose the grain. This is a skilled operation that actually involves several steps. In recalling the process of making a mortar and pestle, an Alabama woman earlier this century drew attention to the steps involved in rice milling at a time when black families in the South continued to grow rice for subsistence on smallholdings:

> We had this great big thing that Daddy would put gallons of em
> [rice] at a time in that thing and beat it. A rice beater [mortar] we
> always called it. He cut an oak tree down and got a big stump off of
> it and sit that stump up. Tryin to make a hole in the middle of that
> stump. After he couldn't chisel as much as he could to make it even
> then he set a fire in there and burned it as far as he wanted to. He
> chiseled out almost as deep as he wanted and then he burned it.
> After burnin he sand it out and make it smooth, good and smooth.

Then he made what we call a maul [pestle]. It was a round piece of wood with a stick on it. He would take that around and put the rice in there in the stump . . . and then we would take that maul and beat it up and down on the top of the rice . . . Every once in a while we'd put our hands through it to see if all the husks, all the rice had gotten outa the husks . . . So a big windy day then we'd take that rice and spread a sheet out and then take it in a bucket and hold it up high. Let the rice fall down on the sheet and the husks would blow off. The wind would blow. We did that mo' one time to get all the husks and the rice was just as pretty and white as the rice you buy at the sto'.[49]

Rice processing involves three main operations: threshing, milling, and winnowing. Threshing involves separating the grains from the stalk (culm) after a short period of drying. This can be done by using a hand implement (flailing stick), animals for trampling the grain, or machines. Milling removes the indigestible hulls from the grain and, if a white color is desired, then the inner skin or bran. The undesired hulls and chaff are separated from the grain by winnowing.

The processing of rice by hand with a mortar and pestle is known as pounding, which is really a misnomer, since the desire to obtain whole, in preference to broken, grains requires a skilled tapping and rolling motion, where loosening the pestle grip at the right moment prior to striking the rice minimizes grain breakage. This is a delicate operation that demands care and skill, especially when the objective is to produce white rice. Pounding by hand unfolds in two distinct stages. The first step takes off the grain's hull; the second step removes the bran and nutrient-bearing germ from the softer endosperm, which polishes or whitens the rice. Following each pounding, rice is winnowed to remove unwanted materials.

Despite numerous patents for mechanical devices to improve rice milling, little headway was made in mechanization prior to the American Revolution. The first step of milling proved much easier to accomplish mechanically, because the hulls or husks came off easily. The first patents to develop devices for this step date to the end of the seventeenth century, and rudimentary systems to accomplish this came into use from the 1730s. The second step, polishing, was another matter as it represented a more delicate process. It proved difficult to detach the bran (responsible for the grain's brown or red color) without breaking the grain. Successful devices for husking and polishing did not come into widespread use until the end of the eighteenth century.

The grade of rice produced by hand milling thus varied considerably with the skill level of the person carrying out the processing. An experienced person could obtain between 65 percent and 75 percent whole grains, but half the rice might end up broken with a less-skilled, careless, or fatigued operator. While observers of rice processing during the colonial period commented upon the variability in the percentage of whole to broken rice with hand milling, the uneven quality was viewed as the result of worker apathy rather than of the brutal labor demanded by processing. Visiting North America just after the Revolutionary War, the Duke de Rochefoucault-Liancourt noted that "an efficient husker [could] . . . deliver 19 parts of whole rice and 1 part of rice dust or broken rice, while an 'indifferent' workman would turn out equal parts of each kind."[50] His comments indicate vast differences in quality by individual workers, even though he disregarded the work burden involved in processing rice by hand. In fact, different rates of milled to broken rice among slaves probably had less to do with indifference than with the skill level and other plantation duties of individual slaves.

Concern over obtaining a high percentage of whole grains from processing, however, did figure prominently in planter concerns. In eighteenth-century world markets, as in those of the present day, broken rice sold at a much-reduced price. Merchant lists from the colonial period indicate that the export market favored "very clean, bright and whole grains."[51] Higher market prices depended on milling the whole grains to remove the protein-bearing bran and then polishing them to whiteness. While this process reduced the nutritional value of white rice, it had the advantage of minimizing grain spoilage on long transatlantic voyages.[52] Such market preferences required Carolina planters to separate milled rice production into three grades: whole grains, those partially broken, and small broken ones.[53] One colonial planter, Timothy Ford, clarified the different uses of each grade of milled rice that resulted from the pounding process: "For here it must be noted that what is called the clean rice is not the *merchantable* rice; for it is easy to conceive that the beating must break many of the grains in pieces; and this divides it into *rice, midlings, & small rice*. These are all separated by sieves; the first is put up in barrels for market, the second reserved for family use; and the third for the consumption of the plantation."[54] The broken rice, not as salable in international markets, was either sold at a lower price or reserved for local consumption.[55]

However, given the labor regimen facing rice plantation slaves in the eighteenth century, achieving a high percentage of whole grains with hand milling would have proved difficult. The abbreviated time period allotted for rice processing and the stress it placed on slave labor resulted in sacrificing quality for completion of the task. Slavery additionally forced men to process rice with the mortar and pestle. A skill of African women became with slavery male as well as female work due to the high demand for Carolina rice in international markets and the intensive labor required for its processing. Men's inexperience in milling rice with a mortar and pestle would have also resulted in a higher concentration of shattered grains. With slavery the division of labor characterizing African farming systems dissolved, subjecting both male and female slaves to the radically different and demanding work regime of hand milling.

During the eighteenth century the percentage of broken rice likely remained high. Mortality rates kept the slave population from reproducing itself well into the century. Reliance on continuous slave imports from Africa meant males had to learn the skill upon arrival, the outcome resulting in high levels of broken rice. Differences in skill level between males and females directly imported from Africa partially explains some of the variability in quality of the output commented upon by numerous observers. For reasons such as these, planters deliberately sought slaves with expertise in rice culture. Women's skills in rice processing must have figured among the desired qualities in the unusual planter demand for female slaves on Carolina rice plantations.[56] But slave markets could not always respond to such demands. Planters would take any able-bodied laborer, male or female, with or without previous experience growing rice, to complete their labor force.

The desire to hasten shipment of milled rice to overseas markets led, from the earliest days of the rice economy, to numerous attempts to mechanize parts of the milling process. Initial efforts focused on developing a device that would reduce the slave labor input in the first step of rice processing, hulling. The South Carolina Assembly in 1691 granted the first patent for this purpose to a Peter Jacob Guerard for a "pendulum machine" to hull rice.[57] However this device functioned, the early patent underlines the growing importance of rice in the economy.[58] Neither this nor other patent requests in the decades to come indicated any knowledge of the principles of mechanical Asian milling machines in use at that time.

By the 1730s hand mills, consisting of two wooden blocks that revolved upon each other, came increasingly into use to remove the outer husk.[59] Rice planter R. F. W. Allston described hand milling the rough rice as a process in which the grains were passed between wooden blocks, twenty inches in diameter and six inches thick, and worked by hand. The surface of the blocks was frequently incised with channels grooved to radiate in an oblique direction from the center to the circumference, a design that would minimize grain breakage.[60] Despite such devices throughout the colonial period the process of milling rice remained "imperfect—very tedious, very destructive to the laborer . . . The planter regarded a good crop as an equivocal blessing, for if the product was great, so in proportion was the labor of preparing it for market."[61]

The search for more efficient energy sources for milling was slow, but in the early eighteenth century improvements in mechanical devices were facilitating the shift to Asian rice for the export market. *Sativa* broke less readily with milling than *glaberrima*. The increasing use of hulling machines suggests the orientation of the Carolina rice economy around the Asian or *sativa* varieties. The first mechanical mills were harnessed to animals: the so-called pecker mill (named for the resemblance of the pestle when in action to the bill of a woodpecker) and the cog mill, a large horizontal cogwheel turned by oxen or horses.[62] Both these devices came into wider use in the decades prior to the American Revolution.[63] Although grain was milled partly by hand and partly by animal power from the second half of the eighteenth century, the labor burden of slaves was not really relieved. The shift to tidal cultivation had augmented by 50 percent the per capita output of rice, and the increased harvest required that much more polishing.

The 1770s proved a watershed in the development of devices for rice milling, and a flurry of experimentation produced the desired results. Efforts increasingly centered on the seemingly intractable second step of rice pounding (polishing) to remove the layer of bran, which had proved consistently difficult to achieve by mechanical devices without grain breakage. Comparing the prevalent use of wooden-block mills for removing the husks with the process involved in the second milling step, leading Carolina rice planter Henry Laurens clarified in 1772: "For cleaning Rice . . . no Grinding will answer the purpose. Rice is ground first for the *Mortar* by a *Wooden* Mill & the *softest* kind of *Pine* is chosen for that service. The husk is ground off very clean, but nothing less than the Pestle will take off the Inside Coat, & shew the neat whiteness of the Grain."[64]

Even with the use of mechanical devices for hulling, Mark Catesby, who traveled through the rice-growing region prior to 1731, underscored the difficulty of removing the germ or bran of the grain so crucial for achieving whiteness of color. His observation understates the problem of hand milling for slave laborers: "About the middle of September it [rice] is cut down and housed . . . then to get off the outer coat or husk, they use a hand mill, yet there remains an inner film, which clouds the brightness of the grain, to get off which it is beat in large wooden mortars, and pestles of the same, by Negro slaves, which is very laborious and tedious."[65]

Milling rice with a mortar and pestle was grueling, for the worker had to stand for hours at a time, repeatedly lifting a pestle that weighed as much as ten pounds to remove the hulls and bran. The task demanded strength and endurance as well as care and finesse. Photographs of milling from the early twentieth century suggest a more benign type of work. One taken on Sapelo Island, Georgia, shows two women sharing the labor of processing rice for their family needs (Figure 4.5). In slavery days they would not have shared the labor, but worked alone. They would not have finished the task within minutes. Instead, each one would have stood upright for hours at a time lifting the heavy pestle to meet a daily production quota that would have fed the families of their Sapelo descendants for weeks.

Since at least the 1750s the task of processing rice was divided into two sessions, morning and evening work, as Johan Martin Bolzius observed: "They [slaves] gather the rice, thresh it, grind it into wooden mills, and stamp [pound] it mornings and evenings."[66] The repetitive motion of lifting pestles up and down for hours at a time proved so physically taxing and arduous that the task was divided into two milling

Figure 4.5 Women milling subsistence rice, Sapelo Island, Georgia, c. 1915

sessions per day. Even so, slaves worked late into the night during the winter months, beating the rice in large mortars to free the grain.[67]

The drudgery and labor involved in pounding rice in tandem with other plantation activities meant work demands greatly intensified with the rice harvest. Many observers from the colonial period allude to the injurious effects of rice milling on slaves, for it "was a heavy task that slowed down the crop's travel to market and with its monotonous drudgery took the heart out of the plantation hands."[68] Pounding rice by hand over many hours came after the exertion demanded in harvesting the crop by hand with a sickle. Superimposed on other plantation duties, rice milling extended the hours slaves labored each day. Commentaries accompanying patent requests for mechanical pounding devices indirectly reveal the adverse effects of hand milling on slaves. One patent request in 1733 by Villepontoux for a mechanical pounding mill, for instance, mentions in a matter-of-fact manner that high slave mortality resulted from milling the crop by hand: "The Pounding of Rice by Negroes, hath been of very great Damage to the Planters of this Province, by the excessive hard Labour that is required to Pound the said Rice, which has killed a large Number of Negroes."[69]

Another inventor who wanted to memorialize his contribution to colonial rice technology added: "In the course of which, perceiving the hardships the Negroes labour'd under in Pounding and Beating Rice and Indigo, induced your Memorialist to continue and invent Machines."[70] Since slaves were already worn out from the harvest of rice, indigo, and provision crops in early fall, the added burden of pounding rice for market schedules must have greatly contributed to slave mortality in the first half of the eighteenth century. Even into the antebellum period, death rates on rice plantations remained high.[71]

Because mechanical mills for removing hulls had come into widespread use by the American Revolution, some planters were rebuked for failing to substitute improved devices for hulling. Their commentaries similarly offer insight into the onerous labor of hand milling. Henry Laurens, for instance, chastised a planter in 1773 for failing to install husking mills that would ease the labor burden of his slaves. Despite the availability of labor-saving mechanical devices, Laurens's neighbor chose not to modernize processing: "[His crop] . . . depends wholly on the Violent Labour of the poor Negroes."[72] Milling by hand, noted another planter, came at "infinite cost to human labour" but seldom garnered concern beyond its justification for patent requests.[73] Even when use of mechanical devices had become widespread, Nathaniel Heyward, "the greatest of all rice planters . . . long continued to have his crops threshed by hand, saying that if it were done by machines his darkies would have no winter work."[74] Paternalist concern over the welfare of slaves put to such brutal work, however, remained uncommon.

Although inventors justified patent requests on the basis of reducing the hardship of manual pounding on slave labor, considerations of profit guided planter interest in mechanical devices for milling. Hand pounding slowed down the delivery of rice to European destinations.

The milling of rice too often was "not completed when spring sowing began."[75] Profits from tidal rice production consequently were not being fully realized because hand milling created labor bottlenecks on plantations. This immense seasonal pressure on labor increased the proportion of broken to whole-grained rice while delaying shipping dates for overseas markets. Loss of profit, rather than planter solicitude over the injurious effects of hand milling on slave labor, provides a far more plausible explanation for the repeated efforts and financial incentives to improve rice pounding by technological innovation during the colonial period. For slaves, only the cleaning and repair of irrigation ditches was as universally detested as rice milling.[76]

The pressures brought to bear on the slaves by market forces tested their physical endurance to its limits. Death was too frequently the result, as South Carolina scientist Alexander Garden noted in 1755: "Labour and the Loss of many of their lives testified the fatigue they underwent in Satiating the Inexpressible Avarice of their Masters . . . but the worst comes last for after the Rice is threshed, they beat it all in large Wooden Mortars to clean it from the Husk . . . [planters who work their slaves so much] often pay . . . dear for their Barbarity, by the Loss of many . . . Valuable Negroes."[77]

Technical progress on the second step of milling, removal of the inner skin of the rice grain or its bran, lagged until 1787 when Jonathan Lucas, the "Eli Whitney" of rice, invented a water-driven mill for polishing. The Lucas mill successfully husked the grain with minimal breakage and polished it to the desired whiteness. His machine achieved excellent results with the Carolina gold *sativa* variety then being planted in the colony. The tidal rivers used for irrigating rice fields during the spring and summer cultivation season served in the fall and winter as the source of water power for milling. With the diffusion of water mills throughout low-country rice plantations during the remaining decade of the century, slaves were for the most part finally relieved of the burden involved in processing the entire export crop by hand.[78]

Enslavement and the Mass Production of Rice

Like all aspects of the plantation rice system, processing was "tasked," with each slave expected to deliver a fixed amount of polished rice daily until the plantation crop was completely milled. Alexander Garden in 1755 provides an early estimate of the amount of rice each slave was expected to clean: "Each Slave is tasked at Seven Mortars for One Day, and each Mortar Contains three pecks of Rice."[79] While Garden placed the task as equal for men and women, later commentators like planter R. F. W. Allston, who drew upon family records, wrote that the daily task for milling differed between females and males, with six pecks required for men and four for women: "The method was, that each male laborer had three pecks of rough rice in a mortar, and each female two pecks, to pound before day or sun-rise; and the same at night, after finishing the ordinary task in the field."[80]

While rice culture and mortar-and-pestle processing have long faded from the low-country landscape, a comparative perspective from West Africa illuminates our understanding of the brutal work regime they imposed on slaves. Throughout the West African rice region, women continue milling the cereal by hand with the mortar and pestle. Data on hand milling a kilogram (2.2 pounds) of rice in The Gambia, an important rice-growing country in the region, make it possible to extrapolate the amount of time involved in processing the daily "task" on Carolina rice plantations.[81] The time required for an individual Gambian woman to hand-pound a kilogram of paddy *(sativa)* rice averages between 10 and 19 minutes. The variation in rate reflects differences in level of strength and skill among females as well as a woman's motivation to produce a product with a high percentage of whole grains.

Turning attention to the rice-processing task mentioned by Garden and Allston reveals a discrepancy in their accounts. On Carolina plantations a bushel of unmilled rice typically weighed about 45 pounds and resulted in a bushel of milled rice averaging 30 pounds, a paddy-to-milled conversion rate consistent with contemporary hand-pounding methods in The Gambia. But the Carolina references are expressed in pecks, which weighed about 11 pounds. If Garden's figures of 21 pecks of unhulled rice were correct, the daily processing task would demand hand milling over 230 pounds of rice daily. This could not have been completed in one day, even in two extended pounding periods. However, if Garden erred and meant 3 pecks as the task, even if it took seven mortars to accommodate that quantity, then his estimate conforms better with that of Allston, who claimed the task as 3 pecks, or 33 pounds, for one of two processing sessions. The daily task during the postharvest period in eighteenth-century South Carolina thus would have required milling some 66 pounds of paddy rice.

However, if there was, as Allston claimed, a difference between individual men and women in the amount demanded for daily processing, the female task would have been about 44 pounds of unhulled rice.[82] This figure is supported by research on the Lowndes rice plantation in South Carolina from the first decades of the nineteenth century. Two processing periods are noted as well as a gendered difference in tasking requirements, measured in bushels (a bushel of paddy rice weighs about 45 pounds). The Lowndes data support Allston's estimates, showing that the daily task for an individual man working alone was one and one-half bushels while that for a woman was one bushel, approximately 67 and 45 pounds respectively.[83]

What did this task mean in terms of actual time that a slave spent milling rice? An extrapolation of the range in processing times presented in the Gambian data brings into sharp relief colonial commentaries on the brutality of rice processing even when the task was divided into two daily sessions. At the fastest Gambian rate for hand-processing rice, 10 minutes per kilogram, completion of the daily task would have required a slave to pound rice about 5 hours daily. If, as Allston claimed, a gendered difference existed in the requirement, the fastest rate would have demanded that women mill rice for about 3 hours 20 minutes. At the slower rate of Gambian processing, the 19-minute average per kilogram, the time for task completion by a slave would have increased daily to 9½ hours for a male and 6 hours 20 minutes for a female.[84] The time required of slaves for rice processing likely fit somewhere between these two sets of values. Thus even at the fastest rate, the physical exertion demanded by repeatedly lifting a seven- to ten-pound pestle and bringing it down upon the rice for hours at a time vividly confirms the task's grueling toil mentioned in several colonial commentaries.

By dividing processing into two daily work periods, before sunrise and after sunset, planters improved the "efficiency" of labor expended while intensifying it on a daily basis. Rice processing contributed to lengthening the number of days worked in rice cultivation during the calendar year. The addition of rice milling to a full day's plantation work starkly illustrates the dramatic rupture in labor relations slavery represented over the precapitalist agricultural system known in West Africa. A task performed daily by African women in less than an hour became transformed with commodity production into extended hours of daily toil by male and female slaves over an abbreviated period of the year.

The pounding of rice, the preparation of a food that signals daybreak and the re-creation of community life in West Africa, underwent a radical transformation on eighteenth-century rice plantations. As workers arose to the first of two pounding periods, the striking of the pestle represented a new conception of time and labor, calibrated by the dictates of planter and market. Commodity production transformed the mortar and pestle into a device that harnessed human arms to a measurement of rice required by planters for processing.

The pestle represented a powerful symbol of bondage for slaves on Carolina rice plantations as well as in other areas of plantation slavery in the Americas. In many parts of Brazil use of the pestle, the *pilão*, served as a daily reminder of the arduous labor required of slave women in food processing.[85] Only in areas of the Americas where slaves had escaped, as among rice-growing maroons of the Guianas, did the mortar and pestle reassert its African meaning. For Suriname's maroons, as in other free communities of blacks, the rhythms of food preparation still heralded the dawn of a new day. The striking of the pestle in a mortar became again the heartbeat of village life, a daily reminder of the significance of rice for daily culture. The rhythm of women's pounding resonates through the fond recollection of fieldwork among Suriname's maroon descendants by anthropologist Melville Herskovits: "With the coming day the soft footfalls died down and gave way to the sound of stamping mortars and the cries of children recalling their mothers from early tasks."[86]

During the period of slavery in the United States the market pressures to satisfy an increased international demand for rice shattered this aspect of African daily existence. Rice plantations ruptured and then transformed the traditional cultural associations of hand milling into an insatiable demand for labor that was forced to work faster to complete the processing of rice as quickly as possible.

Rice Processing and Gendered Knowledge

Historical and ethnographic accounts of agricultural systems too often leave unexamined the manner in which field grains and tubers are prepared for human consumption. This results in part from the specific technological trajectory of cereal processing for people with diets based on those grains of European and Near Eastern origin. From the Roman period wheat, oats, barley, and rye were crushed into flour by hand or with animal- or water-driven rotary millstones.[87] This form of technology development in flour milling displaced the "mill girls" and slaves who figured prominently in grain preparation during antiquity.[88] The effect of this mechanical trajectory on cereals known to Europeans was to direct attention away from the significance of gender in the processing of food and to limit consideration of women's labor to the act of cooking. In many societies of the world, this represents a small proportion of the time actually spent preparing foods for consumption.

Processing consequently does not often figure in early descriptions of food systems in non-European societies. Yet in many tropical cultivation systems, the preparation of cereals and tubers often demands more time and labor than that actually spent cooking. A few examples illustrate this point. In its place of origin maize is rendered into tortillas by a time-consuming process that involves soaking the corn kernels, heating them in an alkali solution, and rolling the mixture into dough. Root crops like bitter manioc similarly require a complicated soaking process to remove poisonous alkaloids. While the seeds of many of these cereals and root crops became part of the Columbian Exchange, the preparation methods did not always transfer. Instead, in the areas where such crops diffused, women processed the adopted cereals in the manner of foods long known to them. Maize in Africa, for instance, was pounded into grits for porridge, which is consistent with the lack of west-to-east migration of Amerindian practitioners of maize culture. Its introduction in Europe involved processing it into flour for products like polenta. The processing of rice with a mortar and pestle, however, transferred, as did West African cooking methods. Diffusion of indigenous methods of food processing depended upon the presence of female bearers of the knowledge system to teach the method. This occurred with rice culture because African women were brought to the Americas as slaves.

In the modern world of mechanized agriculture, it is often difficult to remember that until recently agriculture represented repositories of cultural knowledge built from generations of observation, trial, and error. Agriculture has long provided the tissue linking culture to environment, cultural identity to food. Most traditional societies practice agriculture with a gender division of labor, which means that the knowledge underlying many practices constitutes a crucial aspect of male and female identities. Because African rice is a crop that always involves women, female knowledge in cultivation and processing would have helped establish the cereal across the Atlantic. Although both males and females planted rice on Carolina and Georgia plantations, some of the cultivation tasks resembled patterns of work in West African rice fields. Others did not. The market demand of milling under slavery required men to perform uncustomary labor with a mortar and pestle. The result was to require an even greater work output from men, even if it resulted in a lower-quality product. The significance of gendered forms of knowledge for agricultural expertise is a point to which anthropologist Claude Meillassoux has drawn attention: "It is not that men could not perform these tasks, since there was no question of social standing for slaves, but women were better prepared because they received knowledge which passed from woman to woman."[89]

Women's indigenous knowledge, transmitted from one generation to another and from mother to daughter, forms a significant aspect of rice culture in West Africa. With enslavement this knowledge crossed the Middle Passage and reemerged in the way rice was grown and processed and in the cooking styles that mark the African diaspora in the Americas. Among all the African crops that transferred to the New World, none proved as significant as rice in affirming African cultural identity. Rice became a dietary staple wherever blacks settled in environments amid social conditions favorable for its cultivation. Slaves as well as maroons adopted the crop, and their descendants planted it in freedom throughout tropical and subtropical America.

Among descendants of maroons in Suriname, the Saramaka maintain a division of labor in rice cultivation that resembles African practices. Men prepare the rice plot by clearing and burning the forest. The plot then becomes a woman's field; females harvest, hand-mill, and cook the rice. During the period of slavery rice processing remained women's work only in these areas where slaves escaped bondage. This remains the case today among the Guiana maroons. As in Africa, men make the mortars and pestles used in processing, but only women pound rice.[90] A recent anthropological study of the Saramaka observes that the growing and processing of rice remains the most important role performed by women in daily life, just as was true for their maroon forebears.[91]

In South Carolina, however, where rice became a plantation crop, slavery dismantled this gender division of labor as both men and women were forced to work in its cultivation and milling. The rice plantation economy necessitated the resolution of several problems associated with hand processing. Slavery shifted the temporal pattern of rice milling in Africa, characterized by women pounding the cereal for a short period of time each day of the year, to one that compressed milling into just a few months. The shift demanded that slaves spend grueling hours processing rice. Then, as the rice export economy placed ever greater demands on labor, rice processing required dissolving its African basis as a female responsibility so that both men and women processed the crop.

As long as slavery depended on new waves of forced migrants, men were put to work at a female task that demanded a considerable level of skill. In assuming a task they had not formerly performed, male slaves confronted planter demands to intensify labor for market schedules. The result was a milled product with a high percentage of broken rice. However, a more effective way to improve the skill level of male processing and to de-gender the task on Carolina rice plantations was to teach the processing techniques to children, young boys in addition to girls.[92] An account by African-American blacksmith and master craftsman Philip Simmons reveals how young boys acquired processing skill on Carolina rice plantations: "At age six Philip . . . wasn't strong enough to lift the regular pestle . . . so his grandfather made a small one for him to use . . . Philip could then take part in the work, even though it certainly couldn't be regarded as a full share."[93]

A personal memoir from one plantation descendant in Georgia speaks to the skill and care involved in learning to mill rice with a mortar and pestle while indicating that the techniques were introduced to children when they were young: "The children often tried it, but never succeeded, as the motion required a knack they did not possess."[94] Breaking apart the received knowledge of women in milling, passed on from generation to generation, involved teaching boys how to mill at a young age in addition to their sisters. Figure 4.6 shows a photo of two boys and a girl pounding rice in South Carolina around 1920. Among the earliest representations of hand milling, this as well as other repre-

Figure 4.6 Children pounding rice with mortar and pestle, South Carolina, c. 1920

sentations from the same period indicate that boys and men had become quite familiar with rice processing during slavery.

For the first half of the eighteenth century efforts to improve the male skill level in processing would have proved difficult. Teaching young boys the tapping motion crucial for reduced breakage of the grain with removal of the bran depended on a population that generally survived to adulthood. But the numbers of slaves in the colony failed to reproduce, and the rice fields relied on continuous imports of Africans to sustain those dying in bondage.[95] Under such conditions of high mortality skilled female labor would have been in demand, a point that adds depth to Alexander Garden's claim at mid-century that the processing task was equally divided among men and women. But from the 1750s the reproductive rate of the colony's slave population began improving, with "slave imports no longer necessary to supply the place of Negroes worn out with hard work or lost by Mortality."[96] While a recent study by historian William Dusinberre challenges the notion that mortality rates decreased on low-country rice plantations, males did learn to process the crop at a young age.[97] Nonetheless, if the percentage of slaves surviving to adulthood changed little on rice plantations during the colonial period, the vast numbers of slaves imported to the colony from West Africa's rice region in the latter part of the eighteenth century probably alleviated the skilled labor demand on females. This may have contributed to the reduction of the processing task for women, as Allston later claimed.[98] Certainly by the American Revolution a skilled and de-gendered labor force had emerged to process the millions of pounds of rice produced annually for export markets.

PRIOR TO THE Atlantic slave trade rice, indigo, and cotton were widely planted in Africa. As these crops emerged on plantations in the Americas, historians documented the slave labor regimes underlying their production. Little scholarship to date, however, has examined the methods underlying the cultivation and processing of these crops within Africa to illuminate possible antecedents to the forms of production and patterns of labor established on eighteenth-century plantations. Such a cross-cultural focus on indigenous knowledge systems could possibly reveal other African technological contributions to the agricultural history of the Americas. These have been obscured, as Daniel Littlefield has cogently noted, by a vantage point that fails to consider American plantations in relation to African systems of production.[99]

But one sobering consideration endures with its unsettling implications. African growers and pounders of rice, enslaved in the Americas, desired to consume their dietary staple in the lands of their bondage. In South Carolina they found an environment eminently suitable for the cultivation of rice. The wetlands where they experimented with rice growing in fact showed planters the way to use an African indigenous knowledge system for their own mercantile objectives. Slaves with expertise in rice farming used that knowledge to negotiate a system of labor demands similar to that known to them with indigenous African slavery. Planters, on the other hand, saw the means to control this black expertise for their own ends. During the charter generations of slavery in South Carolina, this African and gendered knowledge system did result in a mitigated form of labor over that known in other slave societies of the Americas. But black expertise only purchased a small space for negotiation, when the rice economy was nascent. As the rice trade became increasingly globalized, the gains of black expertise vanished with the labor burden imposed by milling.

African knowledge of rice farming established, then, the basis for the

Carolina economy. But by the mid-eighteenth century rice plantations had increasingly come to resemble those of sugar, imposing brutal demands on labor. Slaves with knowledge of growing rice had to submit to the ultimate irony of seeing their traditional agriculture emerge as the first food commodity traded across oceans on a large scale by capitalists who then took complete credit for discovering such an "ingenious" crop for the Carolina and Georgia floodplains. For this reason, the words "black rice" fittingly describe their struggle to endure slavery amid the enormity of the travail they faced to survive.

5

African Rice and the Atlantic World

Brazil supplied maize, beans, cassava, cashew, papaya, and pineapples; India, rice, coconuts . . . Africa . . . provided nothing important.
—Orlando Ribeiro, *Aspectos e problemas da expansão portuguesa* (1962)

*T*HE METHODS and techniques of rice cultivation in the Carolina colony show a remarkable resemblance to West African systems that developed long before the onset of the Atlantic slave trade. If there is evidence for the presence of *glaberrima* rice on the western rim of the Atlantic basin, the case for African agency in pioneering the crop in the Americas is considerably strengthened. The significant scale of rice purchases by slave ships certainly would suggest the introduction of African rice at an early date. A determination of its presence through the historical record, however, is made difficult by several considerations.

The domestication of a separate species of rice in West Africa was not widely known until well into the twentieth century, so descriptions during the period of slavery assume all rice to be *sativa* and of Asian origin. "Seed rice" refers to rice that has not had its bran removed. For consumption, rice is milled to detach the indigestible hull and usually the bran, a process that prevents germination. The use of rice color as a guide for distinguishing *glaberrima* from *sativa* poses additional problems, as references often fail to indicate whether the description refers to rice before or after milling. The historical record again fails to clarify the form in which rice was purchased by slave ships. Was this cereal already milled, or did crews depend upon slave women to mill the rice on the journey across the Middle Passage? Only by considering each of these issues can the presence of *glaberrima* be inferred for the early colonial period.

Certain characteristics of African rice distinguish it from *sativa*.[1] One is the red color of the *glaberrima* bran, which shifts between purple and black hues in different varieties. Although some *sativa* types are also red, they occur over a limited geographical area in Asia. Only recently have these varieties been exported for foreign gourmet rice markets. It is quite unlikely that such *sativa* types were brought to eighteenth-century Carolina for the purpose of establishing a commercial plantation crop. Another candidate for historical references to red rice is so-called volunteer rice, which occasionally appears in fields and results in reduced yield and crop quality. But volunteer rice is considered a weed, and growers systematically force its eradication. Thus mention in colonial accounts of red rice being deliberately planted most likely indicates African *glaberrima*.

Several contrasts are evident between African and Asian rice. African rice is better adapted to soil nutrient deficiencies, such as acidity, salinity, excessive flooding, iron toxicity, and phosphorous deficiency. It grows quickly, which makes *glaberrima* more competitive with weeds in its early growth cycle than *sativa*. But under optimum soil and water conditions, the Asian species typically provides higher yields. The key contrast that would affect the trajectory of Carolina colonial rice development was the different milling quality of each species. One factor limiting the extension of *glaberrima* cultivation over a broader area of the world, and which in fact has led to the current dominance of *sativa* rice throughout West Africa, is the notorious difficulty of milling African rice for consumption. The grains shatter with mechanized milling. Only processing by hand with a mortar and pestle, in the way African women have long milled the crop, minimizes the breakage problem.[2] This drawback to African rice would not have affected its cultivation during the early colonial period in the Americas, when mechanical devices had not yet advanced enough to replace the mortar and pestle. But as such devices came into use in the eighteenth century, the yield and milling advantages of *sativa* over *glaberrima* rice would become evident in seed selection.

Early Introductions of Rice to South Carolina

The fact that African and Asian rice do not readily cross lends credibil-
ity to the assumption of the presence of *glaberrima* in early colonial accounts, which indicate the cultivation of both red and white rice. Efforts to identify the rice species grown in the colonial period have
advanced in South Carolina due to the interest in uncovering the parentage of "Carolina gold," the fabled *sativa* rice of the antebellum period. Prized in nineteenth-century global markets, the gold type replaced an earlier *sativa* species grown for export before the American
Revolution, "Carolina white." Despite their names, the grains of both
were white in color. In searching for the antecedents to the Carolina
varieties, historian A. S. Salley examined official records for the earliest
rice shipments to the colony. He found mention of two types of rice being grown, one red and the other white. Salley attributed their origins
to the deliberate importation of seed rice to South Carolina at the end
of the seventeenth century. One lot entered the colony via a brigantine
from Madagascar in the years between 1685 and 1690. After receiving a
peck (about five kilograms) of leftover seed rice from the ship's captain,
Dr. Henry Woodward, a prominent Charleston physician and botanist,
planted it and "from part of this he had a very good Crop, but was ig-
norant for some Years how to clean it. It was soon dispersed over the
Province; and by frequent Experiments and Observations they found
out Ways of producing and manufacturing it to so great Perfection,
that it is thought it exceeds any other in value."[3]

   The second documented introduction of seed rice occurred in 1696
by a certain Dubois, treasurer of the East India Company, who sent a
bag of seed rice to the colony from India, presumably on request.
Salley then concluded that these documented introductions of seed
were the source of the two types of rice recorded as being the earliest
cultivated in colonial Carolina, "one called Red Rice in Contradistinc-
tion to the White, from the Redness of the inner Husk or Rind [bran]
of this Sort, tho' they both clean and become white alike."[4] He believed
the introduced Madagascar seed to be the source of the cultivated
white rice and the one sent by Dubois to be the progenitor of the red
variety. Writing at a time when scholars thought all rice was *sativa*,
Salley linked the initial rice types planted in the Carolina colony to

Asia via India and Madagascar. Madagascar was unpopulated until the period A.D. 800–1100 when Indo-Malayan (Malagasy) people reached the island from Ceylon, bringing with them *sativa* rice. The white rice mentioned by Salley as being one of two initially planted in South Carolina was certainly *sativa*. The red one, however, likely was not.

Several popular accounts claimed the Madagascar seed as the parent of Carolina gold, but the latter variety is not mentioned until the period just preceding the American Revolution. The "gold" seed still exists in germplasm collections in the United States, and the "white" was recently found as a rain-fed crop in the Peruvian and Brazilian upper Amazon basin. Both Carolina types are *Oryza sativa*. Carolina gold appears related to rice varieties from Madagascar and South Asia, which gives some support to popular accounts of its Madagascar parentage.[5] But the gold variety is not reported for South Carolina until later in the eighteenth century, which suggests that it resulted from a cross between the Carolina white grown over much of the preceding period and another variety, perhaps introduced later. During his travels to the region in the mid-eighteenth century, naturalist Mark Catesby claimed that the grain introduced from Madagascar was the origin of the rice then being cultivated in inland swamps, which may have been the earlier Carolina white.[6] Planted either with rainfall or in swamps, Carolina white probably accompanied the colony's shift to wetland rice cultivation in inland swamps that proved so crucial for the emerging rice economy. The "white" type led the early phase of tidal rice cultivation until the "gold" variety developed for floodplain cultivation by the close of the colonial period.[7]

The references noted by Salley are useful in establishing the early appearance of *sativa* seed in the Carolina economy and interest in the cereal as an export crop. But neither of these recorded instances of seed introduction nor Salley's interpretation reveals the origin of the red rice also planted in the colony from an early date. The red rice undoubtedly came from Africa and likely entered the colony on a slave ship. Salley in fact lends support for this contention. He quotes yet another surviving record from the same period that links one rice shipment to the arrival of a slave ship in South Carolina: "About this time [in the 1690s] 'a *Portuguese* vessel arrived, with slaves from the east, with a considerable quantity of rice, being the ship's provision: this rice

the *Carolinians* gladly took in exchange for a supply of their own produce.—This unexpected cargo was distributed, which gave new spirit
to the undertaking, but was not sufficient to supply the demand of all
those that would have procured it to plant.' "[8]

This example indicates another way seed rice arrived in the colony:
as leftover provisions not consumed on the voyage across the Middle
Passage. Salley overlooked this early instance of rice introduction; his
interest was to determine the origins of a crop he believed of unquestioned Asian provenance, hence his focus on the other two shipments.
Unaware of a native African species of rice, Salley could not appreciate
the significance of ships bringing slaves and rice from West Africa. The
red rice that figured among the first types cultivated in the Carolina
colony was almost certainly *glaberrima*, with seed rice the result of the
imperfect milling that often accompanies processing.

Such considerations raise an additional issue: the form in which slave
ships introduced rice to the Carolina colony. For it to serve the needs
of planting, the bran cannot be removed. How would such rice arrive as
leftover provisions from slave ships? In what form did slavers in West
Africa purchase rice?

A century after Richard Jobson reported that only women milled
rice along the Gambia River, French commandants in the 1720s made
a similar observation about female work along the Senegal River: "It
was their job to thresh the rice, the corn *(le Mahis ou gros Mil)*, and the
millet."[9] This raises the question whether Africans sold the rice milled
or unmilled to slave ships. Were the females retained as slaves in West
Africa required to mill the grain sold to slavers or were female slaves
aboard ships made to process it? This proves to be a vexing question, as
scant research has been done on this issue. A review of secondary sources
elicits just two primary references, of which only one is pertinent. The
reference mentions female slaves milling rice on ship deck, which suggests that the cereal was purchased unprocessed. The journal entry
from the slave ship *Mary*, outbound from Senegal, dated Monday, June
19, 1796, reads: "Men [crew] Emp[loye]d tending Slaves and Sundry
Necessaries Jobs about the Ship. Demolished the Steerage booby
hatch. The Women Cleaning Rice and Grinding Corn for corn cakes."[10]

How common was this practice? The huge volume traded along the
Upper Guinea Coast and the labor demands required for rice milling
favor the likelihood that the rice was purchased unmilled, with female

slaves processing it aboard ship. The purchase of rice in this form would certainly have contributed to the availability of seed rice for dispersal to slave destinations in the Americas.

When John Lawson visited the colony of South Carolina in 1709, he noted, in addition to the preferred Carolina white variety, the deliberate cultivation of a red type: "There are several sorts of Rice, some bearded, others not, besides the red and white; But the white Rice is the Best."[11] African rice probably experienced multiple introductions, given the sheer number of vessels trafficking in human cargo that required food for the Atlantic crossing. Certainly slave ships figured in the introduction of the cereal to the French colony of Louisiana. Historian Gwendolyn Midlo Hall records the arrival there of two slave ships from Senegambia in 1719, carrying several barrels of seed rice in addition to slaves familiar with rice cultivation—a conscious effort to establish the crop in the Louisiana colony.[12] There is no reason to believe that this seed originated anywhere but Africa.

The historical record, then, reveals numerous introductions of rice to colonial South Carolina from diverse sources. As slaves grew a favored dietary staple for subsistence in the early settlement period, they demonstrated the suitability of rice cultivation in the colony. The earliest rice planted was likely *glaberrima*, given the role of the cereal in provisioning slave ships that delivered to the Carolina colony its labor force. Experiments with the crop in different environmental settings showed its potential, and rice became a viable export. The higher yields of *sativa* and its ability to better withstand breakage with mechanical milling devices would result in the selection of Asian over African rice for export markets.

African rice was introduced again to South Carolina following the American Revolution, well after the export economy had fully developed around the higher-yielding Carolina *sativa* varieties. A notable, deliberate introduction was a shipment from slave merchants of *glaberrima* solicited by Thomas Jefferson in 1790. Jefferson hoped to reverse the Carolina emphasis on tidal rice to upland cultivation, because "the kind they now possess, which requiring the whole country to be laid under water during a season of the year, sweeps off numbers of the inhabitants annually with pestilential fevers."[13] He believed wet rice to be a crop of mixed value, for "[it] sows life and death with almost equal hand."[14] This was a reflection on endemic malaria and the belief in Jefferson's era that it resulted from breathing bad air, hence the disease's name. The form of malaria established in the lowlands of South Carolina and Georgia was the lethal, cerebral type, introduced from West Africa as a consequence of the Atlantic slave trade. *Falciparum* malaria led to high rates of mortality. Whites tried to escape its ravages by staying away from rice plantations during the summer, while only mild cases would develop among blacks who carried the sickle cell trait.

In order to reverse the deadly effects of malaria in the lowland tidal swamps, Jefferson believed planters should revive rain-fed cultivation on the uplands. In 1789 he initiated transatlantic correspondence in order to obtain varieties of upland rice from various parts of the world. In this manner he learned of rice found in various parts of Africa "growing on a dry soil, 'not like that of America,' which is very hearty food and supposed (by the parties) the best rice in the world." The letter writer, one Benjamin Vaughan, had his son Samuel send Jefferson samples of this "mountain rice." Another correspondent, Nathaniel Cutting, a ship captain in contact with traders along the coast of Sierra Leone, relayed to Jefferson a description of rice cultivation provided by the trader Cleveland, who operated from the offshore Banana Islands. Cleveland described to Cutting the cultivation of three rice varieties, with different maturation periods and planted in distinctly different microenvironments along a landscape gradient.[15] This was the red *glaberrima* rice of the upland-inland farming system cultivated in the southern portion of the West African rice region:

> The local "Red Rice, as this kind is sometimes call'd," was regarded "as a distinct species" not requiring "that the Fields . . . be laid under water, yet a great quantity of moisture's necessary to its producing a good crop." There was in addition ". . . a distinct species of rice . . . sometimes [sown] in [swamp] grounds."[16]

From his conversations with resident European traders, Cutting called this red species the "true upland Rice." But he was unable to procure the seed for delivery to Jefferson. Instead he ventured up the coast and found it in the rice area of Guinea Conakry. There he obtained a ten-gallon keg of *the heavy upland rice* for shipment to Thomas Jefferson.[17]

Jefferson called this rain-fed rice *Oryza mutica*. The term *mutica* derives from the Latin *muticus*, which means shortened or curtailed. It is difficult centuries later to know precisely what Jefferson meant by the use of the term. However, a distinguishing characteristic of *glaberrima* is the shortness of the plant's ligule. The ligule refers to the part of the plant's stalk where a leaf branches out. A thin appendage that appears at the base of a leaf, the *glaberrima* ligule is considerably shorter (less than 6 mm) than that of *sativa* (15–45 mm). The difference in ligule length distinguishes African from Asian rice. Such a significant species characteristic would likely have been noted by anyone experimenting with the cultivation of different rice varieties in the eighteenth century.[18] Jefferson's use of the term *mutica* therefore lends additional support to the tentative identification of Cutting's rice as *glaberrima*.

Upon receipt of the seed rice from West Africa, Jefferson experimented with its cultivation. He also sent a portion to the Charleston Agricultural Society and to an acquaintance in Georgia. The rice grew abundantly in the two to three years Jefferson planted it, but difficulties were encountered with its milling because they lacked at Monticello the "conveniences for husking it." By this period rice-milling devices were in widespread use, but they would have been of little use with African rice. The husking problem further suggests that the rice Jefferson received was *glaberrima*.[19]

Like many of his contemporaries, Jefferson was aware that rice was grown in West Africa. Despite the Linnaean classification of rice as of Asian origin he believed *mutica* to be a separate species, much harder to mill than other types, a view that anticipated scholarship establishing that fact for *glaberrima* more than a century later. Planters of his era were familiar with rice cultivation and knew not only in which parts of the world they could obtain slaves practiced in growing the cereal but also where they could find different varieties. But the scientific exchanges that resulted from the personal correspondence of Jefferson with ship captains and British officials were already placing slaves and Africa in the background of rice history. Emphasis was now on seed transfers and the agency of Europeans in agricultural development, not on the cropping and processing systems that mediated seed exchange and establishment. In fact, one of Jefferson's most famous observations, "the greatest service which can be rendered any country is, to add a useful plant to its culture," was made in partial reference to rice. These words, which emphasize the diffusion of seed rather than an indigenous knowledge system, credit a crucial role in crop history to men like himself, not those they enslaved.[20]

Jefferson's request for new varieties from Africa highlights a pernicious process common to intellectuals of his era. Scientists who studied the plants of the Columbian Exchange were unconsciously involved in the process of demoting an African knowledge system to just bits of information, to mere practice, to seed exchanges, and thus to invisibility. Active participants in the "production" of history, their version rested upon viewing Africans as incapable of achievement. Jefferson and the slave owners of the period were excising the history of rice from its linkage to Africa and in the process paving the way for a critical historical distortion of the origins of rice in the Americas.

The multiple introductions of rice into South Carolina and Georgia would lead by the time of the American Revolution to the development of the high-yielding *sativa* variety known as Carolina gold. Carolina gold was easily milled with the mechanical devices that were revolutionizing rice production at the time.[21] Although tidal rice was favored in export markets, other types continued to be cultivated in South Carolina. These included Carolina white in inland swamps as well as other varieties maintained by slaves in their provision gardens. John Drayton described some of these in 1802: "Besides the white and gold rice, already mentioned, there are some others in the State, of little note or consequence; principally cultivated by negros. They are called *Guinea rice, bearded rice, a short grained rice,* somewhat like barley, and a species of *highland rice.*"[22]

The description suggests that some of these were *glaberrima.* Drayton's account draws attention to the role of slave provision gardens for growing varieties of rice favored by slaves. Such gardens proved especially significant for the cultivation of crops that had long remained central to African cultural identity, such as okra, millet, yams, and black-eyed peas. At the time of Drayton's comments, a re-Africanization of the Carolina rice fields was taking place due to the massive influx of slaves imported after the American Revolution, which led to a reassertion of food preferences from Africa. In addition to rice, the place name Guinea was affixed to other crops such as "Guinea corn" (probably sorghum), cultivated from an early period of Carolina settlement.[23] The ascription of the name "Guinea" to several crops present in South Carolina indirectly reveals planter awareness of their origins in West Africa and association with slave foods and crop preferences.

A preliminary examination of references to rice in South America sheds additional light on *glaberrima* introduction in multiple locales throughout the Americas. In 1750 the Dutch governor of Suriname contrasted the advantages of the rice planted there with a red type he knew about in South Carolina, writing that "the rice in Essequibo has not the red husk which gives so much trouble in Carolina to get off."[24] His distinction between two types of rice—one red, the other not—and pointed mention of the difficulty involved in husking the red offer additional evidence for the cultivation of *glaberrima* in South Carolina during the first half of the eighteenth century.[25]

Historical sources from Brazil dating to the period prior to the mid-eighteenth century provide numerous references to rice, including a red type grown along the floodplains of the Amazon River and in low-lying swamps.[26] Interestingly, this species, initially believed to be of Brazilian origin, was known as *Oryza nutica*.[27] Some colonial authorities promoted the cultivation of this rice, "even though red, . . . because it had always served to sustain the poor."[28] The repeated reference to *nutica/mutica* in descriptions of an introduced rice suggests the presence of *glaberrima* in various locales of the eighteenth-century Americas.

Red rice again emerges in commentaries from the second half of the eighteenth century, when Portugal attempted to establish a rice plantation system in the eastern Amazon of Brazil. The objective was to develop Amazonian export markets to Portugal and thereby reduce dependency on Carolina rice imports. This led to the creation from the 1760s of tidal-irrigated rice plantations in the Amazonian states of Amapá, Pará, and Maranhão, modeled on the Carolina system and its high-yielding Carolina white rice seed. More than twenty-five thousand slaves were imported to the region, many from Guinea-Bissau and the coastal mangrove area, through the monopoly trading company of Gran Pará and Maranhão. The year 1767 witnessed the first exports of milled rice to Portugal, but the irrigated rice plantations failed to withstand competition from Carolina rice when its plantation system rebounded after the Revolutionary War. Lacking continued metropolitan support, the experiment in irrigated rice failed after a few decades.[29]

But the cultivation of a red rice in the area of the rice plantations aroused repeated official concern. In a 1772 decree, the Portuguese colonial administration mandated a year's jail sentence for whites who planted the red rice and two years of imprisonment for slaves and Indians who did so.[30] The reasons for this seemingly draconian measure are not explicit, but if the rice were *glaberrima*, then issues of quality control might have figured in the decision. Portugal was attempting to build a rice plantation economy that would reduce the metropole's dependence on imports from South Carolina. If mixing the easily breakable *glaberrima* with *sativa* in the milling process (which by then was mechanically performed with water wheels) would result in a higher percentage of broken rice and an admixture with some grain bearing a red color, then exports would carry a lower value. The threat of legal action by colonial officials may well have proved necessary to ensure a quality product of the preferred white rice for European markets.[31]

But more than a century would pass before scientists learned of the existence of *glaberrima* as a separate species of rice and established its African provenance. In the early twentieth century French commentaries on *glaberrima* from the inland delta of the Niger River drew attention to the red color of African rice. Among the indigenous *glaberrima* varieties identified in their botanical collections is one they designated *mutique (mutica)*, which was grown under lightly flooded conditions.[32] This *mutique* may have represented part of the ancient *glaberrima* germplasm of the Niger Delta that was eventually adapted for cultivation with rainfall and for shorter duration in the secondary center of rice domestication in the Guinea highlands. The progeny of these varieties were likely those described by Olfert Dapper in the mid-1600s, cited as growing in the Brazilian Amazon, and prized by Jefferson in the eighteenth century.

Although these descriptions of red rice from several areas of the Americas cannot provide conclusive evidence for the early presence of *glaberrima* on the American continent, the convergence of research drawn from disparate academic disciplines certainly invites speculation. But more archival, botanical, and archaeological research is needed in the Americas. One direction would involve archaeological studies in areas of former rice plantation economies. As with the work of Susan and Roderick McIntosh in the Niger Delta, such studies can confirm whether rice was grown in the early colonial period and perhaps even uncover samples of African rice.[33] Botanical collections of rice in such areas and analysis of existing germplasm specimens could lead to the discovery of other *glaberrima* varieties, an endeavor that would contribute to historical recovery of the African experience in the Americas.

African rice must have crossed the Atlantic at some point during the period of the Atlantic slave trade, since French botanists recovered varieties of *glaberrima* from the 1940s to 1950s in Cayenne and from a former sugar plantation area of El Salvador.[34] The *glaberrima* reported in Cayenne was collected from descendants of maroons whose escape over a nearly two-hundred-year period from the 1660s enabled many to flee coastal sugar plantations.[35] These upland varieties were found to be related to ones cultivated in Guinea Conakry, Liberia, and the Ivory Coast, where they are known as "gbaga, baga, or bagaye" after the Baga with whom they remain indelibly associated.[36] The Baga, like the Diola and other groups of mangrove rice farmers along the Upper Guinea Coast, were not organized into states. With the spread of the Atlantic slave trade, the decentralized societies of mangrove farmers along the coast increasingly became targets of slavers. By the mid-eighteenth century, population dislocations along the coast from Guinea Conakry to Sierra Leone came largely at the expense of the Baga.[37] Even though slavery caused the Baga to disappear from many areas of West Africa initially planted to these varieties, their role as expert rice farmers survived in the varietal name given their crop. Thus during the same era (c. 1793) in which slave captain Samuel Gamble documented for posterity his observation "The Bagos are very expert in Cultivating rice and in quite a Different manner to any of the Nations on the Windward Coast," the Baga were being scattered as a people across the Middle Passage.[38] The discovery of Baga *glaberrima* varieties in Cayenne perhaps bears silent testimony to their role as the agents responsible for the diffusion of rice through the Guianas.

Anthropologists Melville and Frances Herskovits, who worked in both West Africa and Suriname earlier this century, reported descendants of female maroons in Suriname planting a rain-fed rice that they believed was African: "The rice is planted on a hillside, for the Bush Negro [Saramaka] does not grow irrigated rice, but the dry African variety that thrives on the slopes." More recently anthropologist Sally Price mentions the continuous cultivation of old rice varieties by the Saramaka maroons of Suriname. These include a red variety they call the "true rice" *(bè alisi séei)*, which women plant and harvest in inland swamps and forest clearings.[39]

The centrality of rice for cultural identity in maroon history is also captured in legends recounted by their descendants, who claim their ancestors introduced the crop from Africa.[40] In the area of Cayenne where a French agronomist found the Baga varieties, the Djuka maroons maintain that rice originally came from Africa, brought by female slaves who smuggled in their hair grains from the slave ships that transported them to the New World.[41] If the legend is literally accurate, these must have been seed grains. And if women did perform milling aboard slave ships, seed rice could have been set aside for such a purpose. In studies of a separate maroon group, the Saramaka of Suriname, anthropologist Richard Price records a similar legend, where the presence of the crop is attributed to female ancestors' hiding rice in their hair as they fled sugar plantations to freedom.[42] The attribution of rice introduction to females is not confined solely to South America. In 1726 a Swiss correspondent wrote that "it was by a woman that Rice was transplanted into Carolina."[43] While legends cannot always be accorded literal truth, these accounts provide a counternarrative to the dominant one that attributes rice history in the Americas to European agency. The maroon legends affirm an African role in introducing and maintaining the crop and, significantly, the role of women in rice culture throughout the African diaspora.

This overview of historical references to rice cultivation indicates that African rice did become established in the Americas during the Atlantic slave trade and that *glaberrima* may have pioneered the varieties of rice established by blacks on the western rim of the Atlantic basin. Figure 5.1 indicates the confirmed presence of *glaberrima* as well as promising regions for searching archival records and seed collections for its introduction. This preliminary research shows that African crops did in fact play a crucial role in global germplasm exchanges. Plants from other parts of the world were adopted by African farming systems at an early date, while Africans experimented with adjusting their plant domesticates and agronomic knowledge to other areas of forced migration. Rice and slaves together crossed the Middle Passage of slavery, and African ingenuity led to the cereal's establishment in the Americas.

While rice came to the Americas as provisions aboard slave ships, its centrality for African cultural identity led to its establishment by slaves for their own subsistence. Slaves grew rice and other African plant domesticates in their provision gardens. They relied on informal networks of seed exchanges distinctly different from the botanical gardens, scientific societies, and merchant-planter contacts that diffused

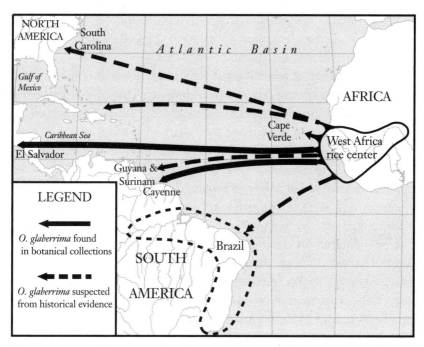

Figure 5.1 Areas of documented and suspected presence of *Oryza glaberrima* in the Americas

the crops of the Columbian Exchange among whites. For slaves, provision gardens served to maintain their dietary favorites in the Americas.

Provision Gardens and Cultural Identity

During the turmoil of the Revolutionary War, the British promise of liberty to bondsmen who joined their forces prompted slaves to flee plantations in large numbers—even though only a small percentage eventually realized their freedom. In areas where the revolutionary struggle was acute, such as South Carolina, about one-quarter of the prewar slave population fled bondage, a loss of some twenty-five thousand to thirty thousand workers, according to some estimates.[44] This loss contributed to efforts by remaining slaves to obtain larger land allotments for provision gardens, which they had repeatedly requested prior to the conflict. The turmoil of the American Revolution resulted in augmenting a slave family's provision garden in many areas so that it totaled about one acre, on average.[45] But in a manner similar to the gains of the task labor system, this was to prove short-lived. The massive import of new slaves that occurred at the end of the century resulted in the erosion of such gains.

The importance of provision gardens to slaves has long been noted. Their role in improving diet and providing an income from marketing has received particular attention.[46] But little research has focused on the role of provision gardens as the botanical gardens of the dispossessed, the marginal, those who struggled to hold on to their cultural identity under dehumanized conditions. Such a perspective illuminates the manner in which slaves maintained many African crops in the Americas and, with them, profoundly affected foodways and culinary traditions in areas of the Americas settled by blacks.

Commentaries on varieties of rice cultivated in provision gardens of South Carolina indicate the presence of several types that only slaves grew, presumably for desired taste and cooking characteristics or adaptability to diverse microenvironments. The significance of rice for provision aboard slave ships as well as its prominence as an export crop led to numerous introductions and the opportunity for slaves to maintain diverse varieties in their provision gardens. Provision gardens likely maintained the rice varieties that blacks were growing in inland swamps of South Carolina's piedmont area into the 1930s, a part of the state where its cultivation had never formed part of a plantation system.[47]

But what of the other crops introduced from Africa? What were the circumstances leading to their arrival in the Americas? How did slaves gain access to seeds and maintain favored crops in the Americas when, other than rice, there was little white interest in them? Was their arrival merely the outcome of experimental planting of exotic cultivars in botanical gardens or as items of curiosity in seed exchanges during the eighteenth century among members of agricultural and scientific societies? Joyce Chaplin's masterly study of agricultural innovation in South Carolina during this period argues that whites paid little heed to African crops grown by their slaves:

> Considering their long-standing connection with Africa established by the slave trade, it is surprising that whites in the lower South did not experiment more with African crops. Neglect of Africa paralleled their relative lack of interest in South America, probably because planters considered both places to have torrid

climates too different from their own and because they were prejudiced against regions that lacked what they would recognize as civilized cultures. They experimented with truly tropical crops from unfamiliar areas only if such plants had already proved successful in the Europeanized West Indies . . . Rather than importing African crops, planters more often discovered them in the gardens of their slaves. For these crops, blacks were the true experimenters and relied on a transatlantic network much different from that emanating from the Royal Society. Through the Atlantic slave trade, blacks had gradually transferred African plants (like sesame, guinea corn, okra) and American crops transplanted in Africa (peanuts and capsicum peppers) to lands where they were enslaved. Whites discovered uses for slaves' products only when they learned of external markets for them. This was clearly the case with peanuts. Blacks had often grown and marketed peanuts, but whites paid little heed until European chocolate manufacturers wanted the product for its bland oil.[48]

We may never know how blacks already deported to the Americas procured African dietary staples. This could have occurred by requests made of black sailors or plantation owners.[49] We know that slaves enjoyed more rights in the initial period of slavery than was the case generations later when the frontier closed and bondage consolidated.[50] But we do not know whether the complex pattern of negotiation between master and slave still possible in the charter generation of slavery extended to the procurement of African crops desired by the bondsmen. These crops were present from an early date in the Americas. While the literature on the Columbian Exchange emphasizes the significance of transatlantic commercial networks for seed transfers among Europeans, evidently slaves had their own informal networks for obtaining preferred dietary staples from Africa. Provision gardens figured crucially in the establishment of African crops in the black Atlantic world.

Many commentators on agriculture and slavery in the Americas mention the significance of provision gardens in slavery, although not all plantation regimes accorded slaves land for a garden. The right to a garden plot was frequently contested and negotiated, as was its size and the time granted to work on independent production. While some studies have pointed out the mixed benefits of slave gardens since they enabled planters to reduce food allotments and thereby disguise actual work intensification, others mention the gardens' role in providing slaves potential cash earnings from sale of produce. Whatever the significance of provision gardens for labor exploitation, slaves prized them and constantly sought ways to augment their allotment. Throughout the colonial period they repeatedly attempted to increase the size of their holding, but it was the turmoil of the American Revolution that enabled slaves to augment the average family allotment. The historical record shows that Carolina slaves planted African okra, greens, millet, sorghum, and black-eyed peas in their gardens.[51]

Provision gardens appearing in other areas of the Americas from an early date suggest that their establishment may have resulted from conventions already established in Africa. A description of Brazil under Dutch administration in 1647–48 recorded that many of the plantation slaves had "little pieces of land on which, during the limited time they have for rest (after a twelve-hour day) they sow peas, beans, millet and maize."[52] This land rights and labor system was brought to Suriname when the Dutch fled Brazil in the 1640s, and it became known as the "Pernambuco system." The priest Jean Baptiste du Tertre wrote about a similar system in the French Caribbean in 1667.[53] Another plantation area where slaves were granted provision grounds was Brazil; the right even existed in São Tomé, located off the coast of central Africa. In the Jamaican sugarcane economy, slaves attempted to grow rice as a provision crop. However, their efforts to maintain a dietary favorite were frustrated by hand milling, which burdened their exhausted bodies, as noted in this report from 1753: "This grain is sowed by some of the Negros in their gardens, and small plantations in Jamaica, and thrives very well in those that are wet, but because of the difficulty there is in separating the grain from the husk, 'tis very much neglected, seeing the use of it may be supplied by other grains, more easily cultivated and made use of with less labour."[54]

Provision gardens undoubtedly served to maintain African staples in the Americas. The widespread presence of gardens in plantation economies reveals a parallel universe of crop experimentation, seed exchanges, and dietary practices that contributed to the maintenance of African foodways among blacks forced into bondage in the Americas.[55]

THE EMPHASIS of slavery studies on plantation crops thus has not accorded sufficient attention to subsistence crops and provision grounds.

We know more about the plantation crops for export than we do, for instance, about the food crops that supplied the slave ships. Nor is there much information on how the African slave trade led to a reorganization of agricultural production within West Africa, one that may have been based disproportionately on female labor.[56] A more complete understanding of these issues should enable historians to assess anew legends that attribute rice origins to slaves.

Sorghum and African oil palm *(Elaeis guineesis)* were introduced into the Americas by slave ships, presumably because they served as food and cooking oil. Other African crops of the Columbian Exchange, such as coffee, circulated via seed transfers among members of scientific societies interested in commercial possibilities, the discovery and classification of new varieties, or in exotics for botanical gardens and collections.[57] Still intriguing is the number of European observers from the eighteenth century who attributed certain plant introductions directly to the slaves themselves, as William Grimé documents in *Ethno-botany of the Black Americans.* Figuring among such plants are okra *(Abelmoschus esculentus)*, yams *(Dioscorea cayenensis)*, pigeon peas *(Cajanus cajan)*, and cowpeas or black-eyed peas *(Vigna unguiculata).*[58] Even though Grimé incorrectly assumes rice was from Asia, his book compiles quotations from the period of the Atlantic slave trade that claim slave agency in bringing other perishable crops like okra to the Americas. The introduction of okra, a major component of gumbos—a key African diaspora dish—remains a mystery, yet the plant was established at an early date in slave gardens.[59] A historical focus on rice and other food crops of slave societies consequently will illuminate the networks used by slaves to obtain seeds of their favored dietary staples and the role of provision gardens for adaptation, experiment, and maintenance of African crops in the Americas.[60]

6

Legacies

All of this was accomplished in [the] face of seemingly insuperable
difficulties by every-day planters who had as tools only the axe, the
spade, and the hoe, in the hands of intractable negro men and
women, but lately brought from the jungles of Africa.

—David Doar, *Rice and Rice Planting in the
South Carolina Low Country* (1936)

*T*HE NINETEENTH CENTURY brought an end to slavery
throughout the Atlantic world. With the Civil War came emancipation
of slaves in the U.S. South. In 1870 passage of the Fifteenth Amend-
ment enfranchised African-American males with voting privileges. But
in the decades that followed, as Jim Crow legislation again reasserted
racial hierarchies and segregation steadily replaced slavery, descendants
of planters began their revisionist memoirs of plantation days. From
the 1920s, supporters of the "Lost Cause" generated numerous accounts that wistfully celebrated what they viewed as the benign paternalism of slavery. Descendants in South Carolina, where rice planters
figured prominently in encouraging Confederate secession from the
Union, praised planter ingenuity in developing a crop that proved so
eminently profitable. In extolling the achievements of his forebears,
one planter descendant captured the traditional white view of African
contributions to the Carolina rice economy, a perspective then becoming the orthodox interpretation of rice history:

What skill they displayed and engineering ability they showed
when they laid out these thousands of fields and tens of thousands
of banks and ditches in order to suit their purpose and attain their
ends! As one views this vast hydraulic work, he is amazed to learn
that all of this was accomplished in [the] face of seemingly insu-

perable difficulties by every-day planters who had as tools only the axe, the spade, and the hoe, in the hands of intractable negro men and women, but lately brought from the jungles of Africa.[1]

When David Doar penned these words in 1936 few whites believed that slaves had contributed anything but brawn to the rice economy of South Carolina and Georgia. One year later another planter descendant, Duncan Clinch Heyward, presented his forebears as gentleman-scholars who assiduously studied methods of Chinese rice culture to improve a system they had independently invented. His view was based on little more than paintings he had seen of Chinese cultivation systems, which he presumed must have inspired his ancestors as they did him.[2]

Scholarship on African contributions to Carolina rice history remained mired in self-serving and racist interpretations until the 1970s, when Peter Wood rigorously engaged the issue and showed that Carolina slaves played an active role in developing the rice economy. In demonstrating that many Carolina slaves possessed prior experience with the crop's cultivation in West Africa, Daniel Littlefield's book the following decade delivered yet another critical perspective on the accounts of rice history presented by planter descendants. The research of Wood and Littlefield finally corrected the demeaning distortion of the historical record that presented the role of slaves on Carolina plantations as menial. Contemporary scholarship acknowledges their contribution, even crediting slaves with adapting the crop to inland swamps.[3] But the crucial technological development in water control that led to tidewater cultivation continues to be presented in terms of planter ingenuity rather than as the product of an indigenous African knowledge system. Discussions of the principles that transformed Carolina wetlands into rice plantations remain anchored in European expertise and culture.

This book's emphasis on agrarian genealogy presents a way forward for a fuller appreciation of the contributions of both black and white Carolinians during the colonial period. Technological development is an incremental process, built upon a preexisting foundation of knowledge. On Carolina rice plantations, slaves familiar with wetland farming and the cultivation of irrigated rice provided the foundation for the water control systems that enabled the shift to tidewater cultivation.

Only after the establishment of rice culture in South Carolina did European contributions become evident. The tidewater system began as an Afro-Americanization of Carolina wetlands; European expertise then contributed additional innovations that shaped rice culture. Thus while cultivation and development of tidewater rice began as an African knowledge system, it eventually bore the hybridized imprimatur of both African and European influences.

By the American Revolution the technological and agronomic heritage of each knowledge system had combined in new ways to shape rice cultivation along the Atlantic Coast of the United States, a process geographer Paul Richards terms "agrarian creolization." By way of analogy with its linguistic namesake, Richards is referring to the convergence of different knowledge systems—such as cultivation strategies, rice varieties, and milling devices—and their recombination into new hybridized forms.[4] The outcome of this convergence in South Carolina was an agrarian landscape actively shaped by African as well as by European culture. Recognition of this fact is not intended to celebrate the roots and contributions of diverse peoples of the Americas, which are clear, but to acknowledge the depth, uncertainty, and complexity of power relations that shaped the transfer of rice culture during the charter generations of slavery.

Such issues surrounding technology transfer, indigenous knowledge, culture, and environment will certainly be clarified with additional research on Atlantic rice systems in the years to come. Recent comparative research on rice origins in other important areas of the African diaspora, such as Brazil and the Caribbean, indicates the crop's establishment with slavery more than a century earlier than in North America.[5] The value of viewing agricultural history from a comparative framework focused on the Atlantic basin is to elucidate crucial issues of technology transfer and to restore to peoples sharing the Atlantic world their appropriate historical contributions. This process of historical recovery requires us to think of the Atlantic as a medium through which power relations forced the migration of plants and peoples across geographic space. Even if Europeans forced that transition on Amerindians, Africans, and their own poor, theirs was but one cultural fund of knowledge that informed life in the Americas. Significantly, subordinated peoples used their own knowledge systems of the environments they settled to reshape the terms of their domination.

Comparative work on rice origins in the Americas reveals the crucial linkage between culture, technology, and the environment, thereby illuminating the broader African contribution within the Atlantic basin. For Africans rice culture represented an assemblage of techniques, which enabled the application of indigenous knowledge to different environmental conditions under profoundly altered social relations of production. Slaves recombined in new ways the principles that informed African rice cultivation within the diverse physical and mental landscapes that shaped their identities in the New World. In a similar fashion, Carolina planters would later segregate those rice systems into the rain-fed, inland swamp, and tidal production environment, from the least to the most productive and remunerative systems.

The enormity of the travail endured by male and female bondsmen in cultivating and milling rice, however, underscores the limited social space that existed for negotiating the terms of bondage. Slaves successfully transferred a knowledge system from Africa and actively participated in the establishment of rice as a plantation crop. Although this reduced some of the claims on their work in the rice fields, they found themselves burdened even more with milling. The very success of rice as an export crop undermined the gains achieved in field labor, undone by dependence on the mortar and pestle to mill the expanding colonial rice output.

To recognize the achievements of slaves in introducing and adapting a cereal that became the first food commodity globally traded is to highlight the contradictory qualities of indigenous knowledge. It is to place slaves' remarkable contribution against a background of brutal and unjust power relations. Diffusion of a significant African knowledge system occurred in the context of everyday efforts to grow a favored dietary staple for subsistence. Planters would realize that rice grown in wetlands produced yields that made it a viable export crop. Blacks participated in developing the rice economy through their struggle to survive the overwhelming demands on their labor.

It bears remembering that diffusion of this significant African knowledge system to the Americas emerged within the confines of transatlantic slavery. While planters used black expertise for their objectives, slaves struggled to negotiate the conditions of their labor. Thus as Africans and Europeans faced each other in new territory under dramatically altered and unequal power relations, with a cropping system known to one but not the other, knowledge of rice cultivation represented one way slaves could shift ever so slightly the terms of their bondage. The result was the establishment of a cereal that has long served to assert African cultural identity in the Americas.

Reconsidering the Columbian Exchange

Publication in 1972 of historian Alfred Crosby's monumental book *The Columbian Exchange* awakened scholars to the significance of intercontinental plant transfers for European global expansion. "The most important changes brought on by the Columbian voyages," wrote Crosby, "were biological in nature."[6] His work showed the role of epidemic diseases in reducing Native American resistance to European political-economic control and the ecological transformations that followed the voyages of Columbus. Crosby's illuminating perspective revolutionized the way scholars looked at the significance of plant and animal transfers for shaping the European-dominated world economy from the sixteenth century.

But scholars working in the tradition he established have yet to accord full significance to the role of Africans and African plants in European maritime expansion abroad. The Columbian Exchange has long emphasized crops of American, Asian, and European origin and the role of Europeans in their global dispersal.[7] This agrarian genealogy of rice history, however, reveals a different face of the Columbian Exchange by showing that rice accompanied the forced migration of Africans and was present in tropical America from the earliest settlement period. In the first centuries of slavery, more Africans crossed the Atlantic than Europeans, and the ships carrying them were frequently provisioned with African domesticates.[8] While Europeans certainly brought rice seeds from Asia to Africa as well as to the Americas, a far more significant form of transfer was unfolding with West African rice and slaves.

Understanding the black role in the Columbian Exchange has been partially obscured by the emphasis on the period after Europeans arrived in the New World, even though a subsequent volume by Alfred Crosby drew attention to the initial phase of European maritime expansion to the Atlantic islands.[9] The forms of production they pioneered and the methods Europeans used to develop plantations and to feed slaves in the Atlantic archipelago illuminates the significance of African crops. The Columbian Exchange really began more than a century earlier when the European predecessors of Christopher Columbus ventured into the Atlantic and found the Canary Islands inhabited with a people they would enslave to extinction. Over the second half of the fifteenth century the Cape Verde Islands served to enable explorations of the West African coast and to establish sugarcane plantations with the Africans they enslaved. The economies established on these islands depended upon African labor and subsistence crops indigenous to West Africa. Even though sugar cultivation would eventually pale in significance with that later developed in Brazil and the Caribbean, the Cape Verde Islands served to establish African food systems outside the continent in the initial period of European maritime expansion. The four decades prior to Columbus's departure for the Caribbean thus adumbrate the role that Africans and their food systems would play in the agricultural history of the Americas.

The Columbian Exchange at times also represented considerably more than the transfer of seeds revealed in most descriptions. While crop exchanges accompanied the movement of European ships across the world, the adoption of introduced seeds frequently depended upon an understanding of the methods of their cultivation. One limitation of the literature on agricultural diffusion and prevailing conceptions of the Columbian Exchange is that it divorces seed exchanges from their environmental setting and thus from the cultural funds of knowledge that often shape crop diffusion and adaptation. This book's emphasis on indigenous knowledge views landscapes as inscriptions of cultural practices that bear the signatures of specific ethnic traditions.[10]

The development of rice culture in the Americas required more than the movement of seeds across the Atlantic. In Virginia rice was planted and discarded as a potential export crop by whites because cultivation with rainfall was low yielding and European milling methods could not produce a whole-grained product. In the Carolina colony blacks implemented another way of growing rice, in high-yielding wetland environments, and introduced the mortar and pestle for milling. Rice cultivation in the Americas depended upon the diffusion of an entire cultural system, from production to consumption. Emphasis on the *process* of the transfer of seeds in the Columbian Exchange illuminates the relationship of techniques to distinctive cultural funds of knowledge and the dissemination of agricultural technology to the migration of specific populations.

In demanding a rethinking of the relationship of the New World to Europe, the concept of the Columbian Exchange corrected a major distortion of previous scholarship. It underscored the enormity of the role that foods domesticated by Amerindians played in facilitating the survival of Europeans and their plantation economies with overseas colonization. This fact is symbolized, for example, in the United States by the traditional corn-beans-squash-cranberry-turkey dinner that marks the Thanksgiving holiday commemorating European settlement in North America. Europeans again appear at the center of the narrative for converting the wilderness of the Americas to landscapes of export crops, using plants brought from elsewhere in the New World and Asia. However, the literature has yet to consider crops of African origin and the agency of Africans in their diffusion to the Americas. Africa remains conceptualized as a region where crops diffused to, rather than from, and where New World domesticates revolutionized the continent's agrarian systems.[11]

The slight attention accorded to African domesticates in this research reflects the minor role that scholars continue to assign food of African origin, a point addressed in *Lost Crops of Africa*, a volume by the National Research Council (NRC) of the United States: "Africa's cereals are inadvertently discriminated against through the way they are described . . . All the categories have pejorative connotations. For instance, these grains [sorghums and millets] are typically referred to as: 'coarse' (that is, not refined; fit for animal feed); . . . 'famine' food (good for eating only when starving); and . . . poor people's plants . . . scorned as fit only for consumption by the poor."[12]

To a certain extent the same argument can be made about African rice, *Oryza glaberrima*, scarcely known outside its area of origin in West Africa. Since scientific knowledge of an independent rice origin in West Africa lagged well into the twentieth century, only within recent decades has the process of historical recovery begun to illuminate the significance of slavery for the transfer and adoption of rice cultivation systems to the Americas.

A focus on the foods of African origin, such as rice, that traversed the Middle Passage demands a different emphasis than that taken in the standard narrative of the Columbian Exchange. Frequently crop adoption involved just the transfer of seeds from one area of the world to another and their addition to an existing agricultural system. But at other times the adoption of a specific plant depended upon the presence of individuals familiar with its cultivation and processing. The exchange of seeds marking the Columbian Exchange thus occurred within preexisting agricultural and food processing systems. Unless new methods of cultivation, processing, and cooking were taught, adopted plants were grown and prepared in ways already known to the people who received them. The establishment of new plants resulted from the ease with which the introduced crop fit within preexisting agricultural practices or from the transfer of specialized knowledge systems that facilitated its acceptance.

The tendency in studies of agricultural history to separate production from consumption has undervalued the importance of cereal processing and the labor and knowledge systems involved in preparing crops for consumption. Until the nineteenth century most cereals demanded considerable postharvest processing. This is traditionally women's work and represents a knowledge system perfected over time by females. The Carolina rice economy took off once the means to process rice with a mortar and pestle became common knowledge. By not according sufficient attention to the postharvest period and female knowledge systems, the Columbian Exchange literature underestimates the role of food processing for global seed transfers.

An emphasis on rice cultivation illuminates how the Columbian Exchange was sometimes made. When rice culture diffused to the Americas from the sixteenth century, an entire agricultural complex of rice seeds, farming techniques, and milling transferred. It did so because the bearers of the indigenous knowledge system were also mobile. The agricultural, botanical, and scientific exchanges that characterized European scholarship during the eighteenth century served to institutionalize these informal transfers of knowledge that routinely marked European contact with new peoples and crops.[13]

Wherever planted in the Americas, rice was associated with African labor. Yet this relationship lost focus with the passage of time. Three hundred and fifty years of the Atlantic slave trade recast social relations between European and African, erasing the complex pattern of negotiation and exchange of knowledge that typically characterized the settlement history of New World frontiers dependent upon African labor.[14] The consolidation of slavery over the next centuries resulted in the increasing portrayal of its victims as little more than animated commodities, thus dissolving any linkage between rice history, Africa, and slaves. The agricultural history of the Americas has been misunderstood and misinterpreted in ways that have significantly diminished the African origins of rice and the people who grew it, processed the grain, and prepared it as food. The view of Africans as having arrived in the Americas with nothing but their brawn has only recently begun to change. This history of rice in the Americas provides one means to reenvision the agency of slaves in the making of the Atlantic world.

Back to Africa: America, Freedom, and "Méréki"

> For the slaves had learned through the repetition of group experience that freedom was to be attained through geographical movement, and that freedom required one to risk his life against the unknown. [Geography] has performed the role of fate, but it is important to remember that it is not geography alone which determines the quality of life and culture. These depend upon the courage and personal culture of the individuals who make their homes in any given locality.
>
> —Ralph Ellison, *Going to the Territory*

In 1800 about half the population of Brazil was of African descent. In many areas of the Caribbean the percentage was even greater. Some fifty years before, African slaves formed the largest single group of non-English-speakers to arrive in the North American colonies. These men and women who, in forced bondage to others, cleared forest and swamp for agriculture, grazed cattle, and mined ores in the lands where they were enslaved, laid the foundations of the colonies of the Americas. Theirs was a painful and harrowing experience, one that denied their humanity while punishing them with brutal and abbreviated lives. As we enter a new millennium, we have yet to come to terms with the meaning of the experience of slavery and its legacy. The contribution of these involuntary migrants who helped build the foundations of the Americas is still not fully appreciated, and much more awaits our understanding.

In 1807 the British government passed legislation forbidding its subjects to trade in slaves. An outcome of steady abolitionist pressure from the end of the eighteenth century, the decision held profound implications for slavery in the Americas and Africa. Even if slavery were to continue in the New World, it would be against the law to bring in additional victims from Africa. Meanwhile, the growing number of free American blacks served the goals of abolitionists, who hoped to establish settlements in West Africa as the basis for spreading Christianity and ending African involvement in the trade.

Efforts to return blacks to West Africa began in England, shortly after a landmark legal judgment in 1772 that proclaimed no one could be a slave, regardless of origin. This decision immediately liberated some fifteen thousand blacks in England. The number of blacks who became free in British territory increased considerably as a result of the American War of Independence. At the outbreak of the conflict there were about three hundred thousand slaves in the southern colonies. Seeking to destabilize the American colonies' independence movement, the British promised freedom to slaves who supported the loyalist side in the Revolutionary War. As many as a third of them tried to flee slavery in areas of the Lower South, where the conflict was especially intense. But only about twenty thousand slaves managed to find their way aboard British ships. Some found freedom; others did not. Slaveholders loyal to the English were frequently allowed to reclaim their fugitives. Other fleeing slaves were deposited in Florida and in Canada. Some were even cynically sold anew to Caribbean plantations. About twelve hundred of the runaway slaves gained passage on loyalist ships that carried them to freedom in Nova Scotia.[15] Still others got aboard British naval vessels and landed successfully in England. With the conclusion of the Revolutionary War in 1783, the swelling population of blacks in England became a matter of increasing concern to whites. A solution was found in the "Back to Africa" movement, which sought to repatriate people of African descent to the land of their ancestors while furthering religious, abolitionist, and commercial goals. A colony of grateful blacks could serve the goals of both empire and commerce. The outcome led to the establishment of settlements along the West African coast in Sierra Leone.[16]

In 1787 English abolitionists sponsored three shiploads of poverty-stricken blacks, some 411 of them, to found the settlement in Sierra Leone.[17] Those in charge of the effort purchased a nine-mile stretch of land from the Temne along the coast of Sierra Leone to encourage voluntary repatriation to West Africa. But this attempt at settlement and other early efforts failed miserably. Death, disease, desertion, and hostilities with local peoples thwarted the repatriation objective, as did the active presence of slave traders operating on the islands of Bunce and Lomboko, just offshore from the mainland settlements. In the 1790s the British attempted to found ten missions on the mainland with freed blacks. All but one failed, and that mission was abandoned to the French.[18]

Meanwhile, sympathy in England was growing for the abolitionist cause. Resettled blacks were increasingly viewed as a potential vanguard for promoting Christianity in West Africa, which many believed would end African collusion in slavery. Even though slave owners in the southern colonies of North America had little problem reconciling Christian beliefs with full participation in human bondage, English abolitionists expected that Africans' conversion to Christianity would lead them to renounce participation in slavery. The view that spreading the word of the gospel to Africans would promote this objective led the Society for the Extinction of the Slave Trade and the Civilization of Africa to send an expedition of British missionaries to West Africa in the 1790s. They believed that "nearly the whole of this vast continent, so far as we are acquainted with it, has been from time immemorial immersed in moral darkness, adapted only to exhibit scenes of the deepest human degradation and woe."[19] Setting off along the course of the 2,500-mile Niger River on its journey through the interior of the West African rice region, the missionaries dispensed English-language Bibles. They proselytized in a language almost none could understand among populations long influenced by Islam. The ill-conceived expedition found few willing converts and considerable problems, with many of the missionaries dying from cerebral malaria.[20] The spread of Christianity to the "Dark Continent" would increasingly depend upon black repatriation.

By the beginning of the nineteenth century, abolitionist funding and support increased the number of blacks settled in Sierra Leone. Joining the black urban poor affected by the 1772 decree and the ex-slaves brought to England in 1783 was another sizable number of voluntary emigrants recruited among black settlers in Nova Scotia. These were the black American loyalists landed by the British Navy after the Revolutionary War and some two thousand Jamaican maroons, deposited in Nova Scotia by the British Navy between 1796 and 1800. Many of these blacks were born in Africa and welcomed the return home; others left because the English never made good on their promise to give them land.

These freed blacks of the African diaspora were serving another abolitionist objective: the creation of export-oriented agricultural communities in Sierra Leone. Abolitionists believed that sponsored agricultural settlements would eventually weaken the institution of American slavery, because the same commodities could be as cheaply produced on the other side of the Atlantic with free labor. If cotton, sugar, and rice could be grown profitably in Africa, there would be no need to grow them with slaves in the Americas.[21] Realization of this objective, however, would await European colonialism in the mid-1880s for its full expression.

With its declaration of abolition of the transatlantic slave trade in 1807, Britain expanded its naval presence along the Upper Guinea Coast to enforce compliance.[22] Africans captured on slave ships seized by the British Navy were landed in the Sierra Leone settlement. Caught in ports or on the high seas distant from their homes, these "recaptives" swelled the population of those being repatriated to the colony from England and Canada. Their numbers would grow even more with settlements sponsored by Christian missions from the United States.

As many as 60,000 blacks in the United States had gained their freedom from slavery by 1790; in 1830 their numbers had reached 319,000.[23] Statesmen of the early independence era like Thomas Jefferson could not bear the idea of a sovereign United States with blacks on an equal footing with whites.[24] Never comfortable with blacks, especially a growing population of freedmen, many Americans, slave owners as well as abolitionists, supported efforts to sponsor their relocation to Africa. Repatriation to Africa would remove the nation of free blacks while restricting the hopes for liberty among those still in bondage. The exposure of American freedmen to Christianity, improved agricultural techniques, and the mechanical arts would, moreover, serve as a model for "civilizing" the peoples of Africa.[25]

Such goals served as the rationale for the American Colonization Society, founded in 1816, which began sponsoring one of the first North American programs to repatriate free American blacks to West Africa. By 1820 the society had recruited eighty-six African Americans willing to emigrate, but an initial attempt to settle them on Sherbo Island off Sierra Leone in 1821 failed. The terms of the treaty ending the War of 1812 excluded American vessels from operating in English waters, even near the Sierra Leone enclave in West Africa. The search for another site resulted in the establishment of a settlement south along the coast at Cape Mesurado in Liberia. The place names given to the freedmen's new homes along the West African coast speak from the dark shadows of slavery to the yearning for freedom and liberty: Freetown in Sierra Leone, Libreville in Gabon, and Liberia.

From the 1820s freed American blacks added to the steady influx of recaptives from slave ships who joined the settlements established by missionaries from Gambia to Liberia along the African coast. The return of diaspora populations unfolded, however, amid commercial and religious objectives: the promotion of export agriculture in tandem with the promulgation of Christianity. Seeds were being introduced anew to the West African rice region. Cotton, peanuts, and cacao were planted for export along the coastal stretch long known as the Rice Coast, introduced again to the region in this new chapter of the Columbian Exchange.[26] Interest in the potential of rice had not faded with the continuing success of the slave-based Carolina rice economy. Efforts to produce crops with free labor that would weaken the plantation sector in the Americas, after all, were at the center of abolitionist concern. As early as the 1770s the export potential of rice in Senegambia was anticipated: "Rice may be produced here as much as in the Provinces of Carolina and Georgia."[27] As European and American abolitionists sponsored black repatriation to coastal Sierra Leone and Liberia decades later, another chapter in the region's rice history would thus be written.

Seeds and agricultural implements formed a crucial component of the goods accompanying black settlers to West Africa. In the agricultural world of that era, the economic basis of settlement rested on seeds for subsistence and export crop development. Rice figured among the seeds that reached the shores of Sierra Leone from North America in the early nineteenth century. When and how many times it was introduced remains unknown, but new varieties appear to have been present by the 1840s.

In 1839 a Portuguese ship containing a cargo of slaves purchased by a Spaniard operating from the island of Lomboko, south of Freetown, eluded the British Navy and departed Sierra Leone with its illegal captives bound for the slave markets of Cuba. The survivors of an arduous trip that claimed many lives were divided up and sold upon arrival in Havana. Fifty-three of them, purchased by two Spaniards, boarded another ship for the sugar plantations of Matanzas to the east. On the third night out, the slaves successfully staged an uprising. Hoping to command the remaining crew to return them to West Africa, they instead found themselves reaching land at the eastern tip of Long Island. Entangled in an international legal dispute over their ownership, these slaves were detained in a prison in New Haven, Connecticut, while the courts considered their claim for freedom.[28] They became known after the ship of their insurrection, the *Amistad*. A protracted legal battle ensued, with John Quincy Adams arguing their landmark case before the U.S. Supreme Court. Justice was done when the decision came to grant the *Amistad* refugees their freedom.

The leader of the *Amistad* uprising, Cinque, like many of his fellow rebels, was born in Sierra Leone. He spoke one of the region's principal languages, Mende, which is affiliated with the Mande linguistic family; its speakers in ancient times had spearheaded the domestication and diffusion of rice in West Africa. During the course of the trial, when lawyers for the defense finally found a Mende-speaking interpreter for the Amistads, each was interviewed. Biographical sketches were prepared and images made of each Amistad's profile. Excerpts from their interrogations attest to the significance of rice cultivation in their lives before capture.

Cinque, along with another ten rebels, had planted rice in Sierra Leone. At least three of the Amistads were kidnapped and enslaved as they traveled to their rice fields; others were seized as they journeyed to market to buy rice and clothes. Several more were set to work in rice fields in the interlude between capture and shipment across the Middle Passage. Even the Mende interpreter for the Amistads, James Covey, grew rice in Sierra Leone as a child prior to his enslavement and subsequent freedom, when he became a sailor aboard British ships.[29] Excerpts from interrogations with the Amistads reveal details about individuals and the significance of rice in their lives:

There are high mountains in his country, rice is cultivated, people have guns; has seen elephants.

He was a blacksmith in his native village, and made hoes, axes, and
   knives; he also planted rice.
He is married, but no children; he is a planter of rice . . .
He was caught on the road when going to Taurang, in the Bandi
   country, to buy clothes; he is a planter of rice.
He was taken in the night, and was taken a six days' journey, and
   sold to Garlobá, who had four wives. He staid with this man two
   years, and was employed in cultivating rice. His master's wives
   and children were employed in the same manner, and no distinc-
   tion made in regard to labor.
He is a planter of rice, and never owned or sold slaves.
He was caught in the bush by 4 men as he was going to plant rice;
   his left hand was tied to his neck; was ten days in going to
   Lomboko.
He is a planter of rice . . . High mountains in his country, but small
   streams.
He was taken while going to a town to buy rice.
His parents are dead, and he lived with his brother, a planter of rice.
He lived in a mountainous country; his town was formerly fenced
   around, but now broken down. He was seized by four men when
   in a rice field, and was two weeks in traveling to Lomboko.
He was seized by two men as he was going to plant rice.[30]

During the eighteen months of the court case, the Amistad blacks
learned some English and received religious instruction from members
of the growing abolitionist movement. Among those concerned with
their welfare was philanthropist Lewis Tappan, a founder of the New
York Anti-Slavery Society, who formed a commission to help them. After the trial Tappan's committee took charge of efforts to return the
Amistads to Sierra Leone, where they had originally been enslaved and
where many of them had been born.

   In 1841 a fully provisioned ship set sail eastward across the Atlantic
with the thirty-five surviving Amistads, the direction they had futilely
sought two years earlier. They left forever behind "Merica," the name
they gave to the land that finally released them from bondage. Accompanying them were free blacks recruited in the United States, mostly
ministers and teachers of African-American, African-Anglo, and African–West Indian heritage. The objective of the journey was to found

an American missionary settlement in Sierra Leone with the freed Amistads. The settlement became known as the Mendi Mission, after the Mende language many of them spoke.[31]

Although the mission's charter was eventually transferred from the American Missionary Association to the United Brethren in Christ (a church of American Protestants of German descent), its emphasis, like that of its predecessors, continued to focus on industry, thrift, and "civilizing" the Africans. The specific cargo carried with the Amistads is not mentioned in accounts drawn from secondary sources. However, agricultural implements and seeds were vital for establishing any Christian outpost in early nineteenth-century West Africa.

Seeds consequently figured crucially in the cargo of ships returning people of African descent from the Americas to West Africa. Whether the result of the Amistad voyage or of others sponsored by abolitionist and colonization groups, the Carolina gold variety of rice still being planted by slaves in South Carolina figured among the seeds introduced to West Africa during this period of black repatriation. In retreading the Middle Passage of their ancestors, freed blacks were returning to the land of their forebears with a crop that for hundreds of years had symbolized African identity in the Americas. We learn of this introduction of Carolina rice to the coastal region of Sierra Leone and Liberia via black settlers during Africa's colonial period decades later, when French botanists discovered another link in Atlantic rice history.

Colonial rule led the French to establish a sizable empire in the western Sahel that included the northern half of the West African rice region. Interest in getting Africans to produce agricultural commodities cheaply for France led to the subsequent emphasis on cotton and peanuts for export. The widespread cultivation of rice on wetlands, ecologically complementary to a system of cash-crop cultivation with rainfall, awakened French botanists' interest in rice. Eventually curiosity about the origins of rice varieties being grown in the inland delta of the Niger River in the French colony of Mali in the early twentieth century led to the first scientific discovery of African *glaberrima*. Other research involved experimentation with the diverse varieties found in the region. Among those reported by French botanists was one that local people variously referred to as "Méréki" and "Mériké." This rice variety thrived when grown under submersion in the deep-flooded conditions of the Niger River floodplain.[32] Initially thinking it a desirable "indigenous" variety, French botanists began breeding experiments with "Méréki" during the 1920s.[33]

But research on this variety planted in the heartland of African rice domestication showed it was in fact not *glaberrima* rice but *sativa*. Curiosity about its odd name caused French irrigation engineer and rice specialist Pierre Viguier to ask other officials about Méréki. He learned that the variety was already present in the region by the onset of colonial rule, with the first French botanical expedition reporting its existence in 1899. Viguier learned that this long-grained rice and other "new" seeds (eggplants and a variety of hot peppers) were said to have entered Mali from Sierra Leone via Guinea. Viguier corroborated the story through an English colonial official, M. A. Allridge, who had reported in 1917 that indeed a "beautiful variety of white rice was introduced formerly and cultivated with success in Sierra Leone by American missionaries."[34] Known as Méréki, this varietal name proved in fact a corruption of the name America or American, in the same manner that the Amistads shortened the name of the country that granted them their freedom. The toponym Méréki referred then to the seed's arrival from the United States. Subsequent research by French botanists showed the grain's remarkable similarity to, and likely provenance from, the Carolina gold rice seed, the variety prized on antebellum tidal plantations in South Carolina and Georgia.[35]

Though fragmentary, this evidence suggests the possibility that Carolina gold arrived in Africa around the time that the Amistads returned to Sierra Leone. Whether this was the same voyage that carried Carolina gold or Méréki to Africa remains unknown. One fact, however, is certain: the variety was first grown in Sierra Leone, where the Americans had established the Mendi Mission to settle the Amistads. The subsequent diffusion of Méréki from Sierra Leone established the variety over a broad part of the West African rice region into Guinea, the interior of Mali along the Niger River, and onward to the Ivory Coast, where it was reportedly still being grown in 1996.[36]

The circle of rice history in the Atlantic basin thus closes with the introduction of the Carolina rice of U.S. slavery to Sierra Leone and the West African rice region via freedmen and Christian missionaries. Through another African diaspora, this one based on freedom and voluntary return to the continent by some of its descendants, Carolina rice reached into the heart of Africa all the way to the floodplains of the

Niger River in Mali, where farmers domesticated *glaberrima* rice more than two millennia ago. A cereal and a knowledge system that left West Africa on ships with slaves and became established in the Americas under bondage, returned once more to African shores in freedom through the agency of black missionaries, freed slaves, and recaptives. Known as Méréki, the rice drew its name from America, the continent of human bondage. But this time the history of those who brought it would not be forgotten.

Notes

Introduction

1. The English word "maroon," like the French *marron*, derives from the Spanish *cimarrón*. The term's usage in the Americas initially referred to domestic cattle that had taken to the hills in Hispaniola, then to Amerindians who fled enslavement by the Spanish. By the end of the 1530s, the word was beginning to refer primarily to African and African-American runaways, with the term connoting the ferocity, wildness, and unbroken character of those fleeing slavery. Richard Price, ed., *Maroon Societies: Rebel Slave Communities in the Americas* (Baltimore: Johns Hopkins University Press, 1979), pp. 1–2.

2. The publication of *Black Jacobins* by C. L. R. James in 1938 proved monumental in shaping the contours of this debate. James was the first scholar to give agency to slaves as the center of analysis in his research on the Haitian Revolution, thereby stimulating much subsequent research on the African diaspora. See James, *Black Jacobins* (1938; New York: Vintage Books, 1989).

3. For the debate on African cultural survivals, see, for instance, Melville Herskovits, *The Myth of the Negro Past* (1941; Boston: Beacon Press, 1958); Sidney Mintz and Richard Price, *The Birth of African-American Culture: An Anthropological Perspective* (1976; Boston: Beacon Press, 1992).

4. Studies employing the structural approach emphasized by Mintz and Price and bearing on South Carolina include Charles Joyner, *Down by the Riverside* (Urbana: University of Illinois Press, 1984); Margaret W. Creel, *A Peculiar People: Slave Religion and Community Culture among the Gullahs* (New York: New York University Press, 1988); John Vlach, *The Afro-American Tradition in Decorative Arts* (Athens: University of Georgia Press, 1990). More recent approaches to the study of African cultures in the Americas focus on cultural exchanges and the role of free black Atlantic journeyers in creating diaspora cultures across territorial boundaries. See, for instance, Paul Gilroy, *The Black Atlantic: Modernity and Double Consciousness*

(Cambridge, Mass.: Harvard University Press, 1993). The view of cultural memory or "tradition" as a function of power, negotiation, and re-creation, and its significance for African cultural history and agency, are cogently addressed in Michel-Rolph Trouillot, *Silencing the Past: Power and the Production of History* (Boston: Beacon Press, 1995); and J. Lorand Matory, "The English Professors of Brazil: On the Diasporic Roots of the Yorùbá Nation," *Comparative Studies in Society and History*, 41, no. 1 (1999): 72–103.

5. Peter Wood, *Black Majority* (New York: Knopf, 1974). The first to question the representation of slaves in Carolina rice fields as unskilled laborers was historian Converse Clowse, who revealed the importance of African skills in colonial ranching and agriculture. See his *Economic Beginnings in Colonial South Carolina, 1670–1730* (Columbia: University of South Carolina Press, 1971).

6. Daniel C. Littlefield, *Rice and Slaves* (Baton Rouge: Louisiana State University Press, 1981).

7. See Alfred W. Crosby, *The Columbian Exchange: Biological and Cultural Consequences of 1492* (Westport, Conn.: Greenwood Press, 1972); and Eric Wolf, *Europe and the People without History* (Berkeley: University of California Press, 1982).

8. Roland Portères, "Primary Cradles of Agriculture in the African Continent," in J. D. Fage and R. A. Oliver, eds., *Papers in African Prehistory* (Cambridge: Cambridge University Press, 1970), pp. 43–58; Tadeusz Lewicki, *West African Food in the Middle Ages* (Cambridge: Cambridge University Press, 1974); Jack Harlan, J. De Wet, and A. Stemler, *Origins of African Plant Domestication* (The Hague: Mouton, 1976).

9. Francesca Bray, *The Rice Economies* (Oxford: Blackwell Press, 1986); Michael Adas, *Machines as the Measure of Men* (Ithaca, N.Y.: Cornell University Press, 1989); and J. Blaut, "On the Significance of 1492," *Political Geography*, 11 (1992): 355–385.

10. Carville Earle, *Geographical Inquiry and American Historical Problems* (Stanford: Stanford University Press, 1992), p. 9.

11. See, for instance, Jack Kloppenburg, *First the Seed* (New York: Cambridge University Press, 1990); and Stephen Brush and Doreen Stabinsky, eds., *Valuing Local Knowledge: Indigenous People and Intellectual Property Rights* (Washington, D.C.: Island Press, 1996).

1. Encounters

1. T. B. Duncan, *Atlantic Islands: Madeira, the Azores, and the Cape Verdes in Seventeenth Century Commerce and Navigation* (Chicago: University of Chicago Press, 1972); Eric Wolf, *Europe and the People without History* (Berkeley: University of California Press, 1982); Alfred W. Crosby, *Ecological Imperialism: The Biological Expansion of Europe, 900–1900* (New York: Cambridge University Press, 1986), pp. 70–85.

2. Quote from the Venetian pilot Alvise da Cadamosto, c. 1468, in George Brooks, *Landlords and Strangers: Ecology, Society, and Trade in Western Africa, 1000–1630* (Boulder: Westview Press, 1993), p. 126.

3. Walter Rodney, *A History of the Upper Guinea Coast, 1545 to 1800* (New York: Monthly Review Press, 1970).

4. The introduction of American cereals, like maize, to West Africa in the

early sixteenth century extended cereal production to the African tropics. Marvin Miracle, *Maize in Tropical Africa* (Madison: University of Wisconsin Press, 1966).

5. Ibid.; W. O. Jones, *Manioc in Africa* (Stanford: Stanford University Press, 1959).

6. Daphne Roe, *A Plague of Corn: A Social History of Pellagra* (Ithaca, N.Y.: Cornell University Press, 1973); Redcliffe Salaman, *The History and Social Influence of the Potato* (Cambridge: Cambridge University Press, 1949); Miracle, *Maize in Tropical Africa*.

7. Michael Adas, *Machines as the Measure of Men* (Ithaca, N.Y.: Cornell University Press, 1989).

8. Orlando Ribeiro, *Aspectos e problemas da expansão portuguésa*, Estudos de Ciencias Políticas e Sociais (Lisbon: Junta de Investigações do Ultramar, 1962), p. 27.

9. Portuguese agency in introducing rice culture from Asia to Africa represents a long-standing bias in historiography that was only questioned by French botanists in the twentieth century. On the argument for Portuguese introduction, see ibid., pp. 49, 88, 116.

10. Societies of the coastal mangrove rice area of the West African coast are termed acephalous for their relative absence of social stratification. On the eve of the Atlantic slave trade these included the Baga, Diola, Balanta, Bullom/Sherbo, and Temne. See Rodney, *Upper Guinea Coast*, chaps. 1–2; António Carreira, *Os Portuguêses nos rios de Guiné, 1500–1900* (Lisbon: privately published, 1984); Brooks, *Landlords and Strangers*, chaps. 2–5; and Olga Linares, *Power, Prayer, and Production* (New York: Cambridge University Press, 1992).

11. August Chevalier, "Sur le riz africains du groupe Oryza glaberrima," *Revue de botanique appliquée et d'agriculture tropicale*, 17 (1937): 413–418, esp. p. 418.

12. Senegambia refers to the countries of Senegal and The Gambia, which share a similar ethnic and cultural history. Anglophone Gambia is surrounded by francophone Senegal as a result of European geopolitical struggles for territory that date to the military garrisons established during the Atlantic slave trade. Such enclaves eventually served as the basis for European territorial claims to colonies in Africa at the end of the nineteenth century. The Gambia represents little more than a river basin enclosed on all sides by Senegal. The modern West African country is referred to as The Gambia; prior to 1965 the British referred to their colony as the Gambia, without capitalizing the article. This distinction between the pre- and postindependence periods is followed in the text.

13. Gomes Eanes de Azurara, *The Chronicle of the Discovery and Conquest of Guinea*, 2 vols. (London: Hakluyt, 1899), 2:263–264.

14. G. Crone, *The Voyages of Cadamosto* (London: Hakluyt, 1937), p. 70.

15. Paul Pélissier, *Les paysans du Sénégal* (St. Yrieix, France: Imprimerie Fabrègue, 1966), pp. 711–712; Duarte Pacheco Pereira, *Esmeraldo de Situ Orbis*, trans. G. H. T. Kimble (London: Hakluyt, 1937), pp. 91–99.

16. Valentim Fernandes, *Description de la Côte Occidentale d'Afrique*, trans. and notes by T. Monod, A. Teixeira da Mota, and R. Mauny (Bissau, Guinea-Bissau: Centro de Estudos de Guiné Portuguêsa, 1951), pp. 40, 49.

17. Brooks, *Landlords and Strangers*, pp. 126–141.

18. English chronicler John Sparke mentioned in ibid., pp. 295–296.

19. Rodney, *Upper Guinea Coast*, p. 21; Carreira, *Os Portuguêses nos Rios de*

Guiné, pp. 27–28; Brooks, *Landlords and Strangers,* pp. 276–296; Boubacar Barry, *Senegambia and the Atlantic Slave Trade* (Cambridge: Cambridge University Press, 1998), pp. 79, 107–108, 117–118.

20. On female traders, see A. Donelha, *An Account of Sierra Leone and the Rivers of Guinea and Cape Verde* (Lisbon: Junta de Investigacões Cientificados, 1977), p. 149. See also A. Texeira da Mota, *Some Aspects of Portuguese Colonisation and Sea Trade in West Africa in the 15th and 16th Centuries* (Bloomington: Indiana University, 1978), p. 15; and Carreira, *Os Portuguêses nos Rios de Guiné,* pp. 27–28. Other mentions of Portuguese rice purchases include La Fosse (c. 1479), Fernandes (c. 1506–1510), Almada (c. 1594), and Donelha (c. 1625), summarized in Brooks, *Landlords and Strangers,* pp. 260, 276–296, 315–318.

21. Brooks, *Landlords and Strangers,* p. 175.

22. Ribeiro, *Aspectos e problemas,* pp. 143–147; Duncan, *Atlantic Islands,* p. 168; J. W. Blake, *West Africa: Quest for God and Gold, 1545–1578* (London: Curzon Press, 1977), pp. 91–92; and Brooks, *Landlords and Strangers,* pp. 130–147, 279; Carreira, *Os Portuguêses nos Rios de Guiné,* pp. 47–62. On rice cultivation in inland swamps of Santiago, Cape Verde, see Ribeiro, *Aspectos e problemas,* p. 143. Da Mota, *Portuguese Colonisation and Sea Trade,* mentions the importance of slave labor in both farming and cattle raising on the Cape Verde Islands.

23. Brooks, *Landlords and Strangers,* p. 149.

24. On the Atlantic islands for provisions, see Ira Berlin, *Many Thousands Gone: The First Two Centuries of Slavery in North America* (Cambridge, Mass.: Harvard University Press, 1998), p. 68.

25. John Atkins, *Voyage to Guinea, Brasil, and the West Indies,* UCLA microfilm (London, 1735); Frances Moore, *Travels into the Inland Parts of Africa* (London: Edward Cave, 1738), pp. 165–182; Michael Adanson, *A Voyage to Senegal, the Isle of Goree and the River Gambia* (London: Nourse, 1759), p. 105; Theodore Canot, *Adventures of an African Slaver* (New York: Albert & Charles Boni, 1928); K. G. Davies, *The Royal African Company* (New York: Atheneum, 1970); Rodney, *Upper Guinea Coast,* p. 21; Blake, *Quest for God and Gold,* pp. 91–92; Philip Curtin, *Economic Change in Pre-Colonial Africa* (Madison: University of Wisconsin, 1975), pp. 100–111; and Brooks, *Landlords and Strangers,* p. 260.

26. Fernandes, *Description de la Côte Occidentale,* p. 47.

27. Throughout the Sahel, crops are planted with the retreat of fresh water on river floodplains or in inland swamps where the water table recedes with the advance of the dry season. These systems are especially important for food production in the climatically risky Sahelian region where rainfall seldom exceeds 1000 mm and averages 600–800 mm over a single rainy season of about three to four months. Fernandes's account of two harvests refers to planting rice and cereals with a short growing season during the wet season and on the floodplain with the recession of water during the dry season. The flood-recession or décrue crop includes millet, sorghum, rice, and vegetables.

28. Richard Jobson, *The Golden Trade* [1623] (Devonshire: Speight and Walpole, 1904), p. 59.

29. Gomes's observation appears in Th. Monod, R. Mauny, and G. Duval, *De la première découverte de la Guinée: Récit par Diogo Gomes (fin XV siècle)* (Bissau, Guinea-Bissau: Centro de Estudos da Guiné Portuguêsa, 1959), pp. 42, 66. On the arid conditions over the period c. A.D. 1100 to c. 1500 in West Africa, see Brooks, *Landlords and Strangers,* p. 7.

30. Quoted from Rodney, *Upper Guinea Coast*, pp. 20–21.

31. Pélissier, *Paysans du Sénégal*, p. 714. Author's translation.

32. Rodney, *Upper Guinea Coast*, p. 21; and ibid.

33. Etienne-Félix Berlioux, *André Brüe ou l'origine de la Colonie française du Sénégal* (Paris: Librairie de Guillaumin, 1874), p. 165.

34. Daniel C. Littlefield, *Rice and Slaves* (Baton Rouge: Louisiana State University, 1981), pp. 93–95.

35. Yasmine Marzouk-Schmitz, "Instruments aratoires, systèmes de cultures, et différenciation intra-ethnique," *Cahiers ORSTOM*, sér. Sci. Hum., 20, nos. 3–4 (1984): 399–425, esp. p. 404.

36. Paul Richards, *Coping with Hunger* (London: Allen and Unwin, 1986); Richards, "Culture and Community Values in the Selection and Maintenance of African Rice," in Stephen Brush and Doreen Stabinsky, eds., *Valuing Local Knowledge: Indigenous People and Intellectual Property Rights* (Washington, D.C.: Island Press, 1996), pp. 209–229.

37. Dutch translation and excerpt drawn from Olfert Dapper's manuscript "New Description of Africa," in Richards, "Culture and Community Values," pp. 213–214. On Dapper, see also Adam Jones, *From Slaves to Palm Kernels* (Wiesbaden: Franz Steiner, 1983); Jones, "Decompiling Dapper: A Preliminary Search for Evidence," *History in Africa*, 17 (1990): 171–209; and G. Thilmans, "Le Sénégal dans l'oeuvre d'Offried Dapper," *Bulletin de l'IFAN*, ser. B., 33 (1971): 508–563. Actually, Dapper may have reversed the order of the sequence in his description as the harvest of rain-fed rice usually precedes that of the other forms.

38. See Richards, "Culture and Community Values," for Dapper's insight as still apt for describing contemporary rice systems. Richards's observation follows decades of fieldwork and historical research in Sierra Leone.

39. Moore, *Travels into the Inland Parts*, p. 31.

40. Adanson, *Voyage to Senegal*, p. 166.

41. René Caillié, *Travels through Central Africa to Timbuctoo and across the Great Desert, to Morocco, Performed in the Years 1824–1828* (London: Colburn and Bentley, 1830), p. 162.

42. S. M. X. Golberry, *Travels in Africa, performed during the years 1785, 1786 and 1787, in the Western Countries of this Continent*, 2 vols., trans. William Mudford (London: R. Bent and J. Mudie, 1803), 2:351–352, cited in Jennie Dey, "Women and Rice in The Gambia: The Impact of Irrigated Rice Development Projects on the Farming System" (Ph.D. dissertation, University of Reading, 1980), p. 33.

43. One thousand millimeters of rainfall, or forty inches, delimits the northernmost-range of the tsetse fly vector that carries trypanosomes lethal to domesticated herbivores. This usually confines indigenous longhorn varieties of cattle kept by nomads of Niger (as well as the introduced zebu breeds, sheep, goats, horses, donkeys, and camels) to the area north of Guinea-Bissau. The smaller indigenous shorthorn breed of cattle, known as ndama, is trypanosome-resistant and can be raised throughout West Africa. See Curtin, *Economic Change*, pp. 218–219; and Brooks, *Landlords and Strangers*, p. 12.

44. Moore, *Travels into the Inland Parts*, p. 37.

45. Thomas Winterbottom, *An Account of the Native Africans in the Neighbourhood of Sierra Leone* (London: C. Whittingham, 1803), p. 49.

46. Caillié, *Travels through Central Africa to Timbuctoo*, p. 210.

47. Pierre Viguier, *La riziculture indigène au Soudan français* (Paris: Larose,

1939). These are likely *glaberrima* floating varieties, which can reach six meters in length; see D. Catling, *Rice in Deep Water* (London: International Rice Research Institute/Macmillan, 1992), p. 364.

48. Christian Roche, *Histoire de la Casamance* (Dakar, Senegal: Karthala, 1985), pp. 43–44, 56.

49. Richards, "Culture and Community Values," p. 213.

50. Ibid., p. 217.

51. Quoted in Brooks, *Landlords and Strangers,* p. 318.

52. Moore, *Travels into the Inland Parts,* pp. vi, 127.

53. Ibid., p. 139.

54. Golberry, *Travels in Africa,* 2:351–352.

55. Dapper in Thilmans, "Le Sénégal," p. 535; and Labat quoted in Gwendolyn Midlo Hall, *Africans in Colonial Louisiana* (Baton Rouge: Louisiana State University Press, 1992), p. 39.

56. Jobson, *The Golden Trade,* p. 68.

57. Rhodes House mss., Afr.s 945, Oxford University, n.d., located in correspondence from the 1770s.

2. Rice Origins and Indigenous Knowledge

1. See, for instance, Denise Paulme, *Les gens du riz* (Paris: Librairie Plon, 1954), p. 129; Francis Snyder, *Capitalism and Legal Change* (New York: Academic Press, 1981); Henri Raulin, "Techniques agraires et instruments aratoires au Sud du Sahara," *Cahiers ORSTOM,* sér. Sci. Hum., 20, nos. 3–4 (1984): 339–358; and Olga Linares, *Power, Prayer, and Production* (Cambridge: Cambridge University Press, 1992).

2. David P. Gamble, *The Wolof of Senegambia, Together with Notes on the Lebu and the Serer,* Ethnographic Survey of Africa, 14 (London: International African Institute, 1957).

3. Francesca Bray, *The Rice Economies* (Oxford: Basil Blackwell, 1986), pp. 8–9; R. Barker and R. Herdt, with B. Rose, *The Rice Economy of Asia* (Washington, D.C.: Resources for the Future, 1985), p. 14.

4. Barker, Herdt, and Rose, *Rice Economy,* p. 14.

5. See, for instance, Orlando Ribeiro, *Aspectos e problemas da expansão portuguésa,* Estudos de Ciencias Políticas e Sociais (Lisbon: Junta de Investigações do Ultramar, 1962), p. 49; and Paul Pélissier, *Les paysans du Sénégal* (St. Yrieix, France: Imprimerie Fabrègue, 1966), pp. 710–734.

6. A. G. Hopkins, *An Economic History of West Africa* (New York: Columbia University Press, 1973).

7. The encouragement of swamp rice for food production characterized both British and French colonialism in West Africa. Judith Carney, "The Social History of Gambian Rice Production: An Analysis of Food Security Strategies" (Ph.D. dissertation, Department of Geography, University of California, Berkeley, 1986); L. Becker and R. Diallo, "The Cultural Diffusion of Rice Cropping in Côte d'Ivoire," *Geographical Review,* 86, no. 4 (1996): 505–528, esp. p. 513.

8. A. Chevalier, "Sur le riz africains du groupe Oryza glaberrima," *Revue de botanique appliquée et d'agriculture tropicale,* 17 (1937): 418. More than thirty varieties were identified at the turn of the century, some adjusted to planting in rivers (floating rice), others grown along floodplains or with rainfall.

9. R. J. Rochevicz, "Documents sur le Genre Oryza," *Revue de botanique appliquée et d'agriculture tropicale*, 135 (1932): 950.

10. Chevalier, "Sur le riz"; R. Portères, "Historique sur les premiers échantillons d'Oryza glaberrima St. recueillis en Afrique," *Journal d'agriculture tropicale et de botanique appliquée*, 11, nos. 10–11 (1955): 535–537.

11. A. Chevalier, "Époques auxquelles des plantes cultivés et des mauvaises herbes pantropiques se sont répandues dans les pays chauds de l'ensemble du globe," *Revue de botanique appliquée et d'agriculture tropicale* (1925): 443; Chevalier, "Sur le riz," p. 413; J. Cayouette and S. Darbyshire, "Taxa Described by Steudel from the Labrador Plants Collected by the Moravian Missionary Albrecht and Distributed by Hohenacker," *Taxon*, 43, no. 2 (1994): 169–171.

12. A. Chevalier and O. Roehrich, "Sur l'origine botanique des riz cultivés," *Comptes rendus de l'Academie de Sciences*, 159 (1914): 560–562; Rochevicz, "Documents sur le Genre Oryza," pp. 949–961; A. Chevalier, "L'importance de la riziculture dans le domaine colonial français et l'orientation à donner aux récherches rizicoles," *Laboratoire d'agronomie coloniale* (Paris) (1936); Chevalier, "Sur le riz," p. 418; Chevalier, "La culture de riz dans la Vallée du Niger," *Revue de botanique appliquée et d'agriculture tropicale*, 190 (1937): 44–50; Chevalier, "Le Sahara, centre d'origine de plantes cultivés," *Mémoires de la Société de Biogéographie*, 6 (1938): 307–322; P. Viguier, "La riziculture indigène au Soudan français. Première Partie," *Annales agricoles d'Afrique Occidentale française et etrangère*, 1 (1937): 287–326; A. Haudricourt and L. Hédin, *L'homme et les plantes cultivés* (Paris: Editions de la Maison des Sciences de l'Homme, 1943).

13. Chevalier, "Sur le riz"; Chevalier, "La culture de riz"; Viguier, "La riziculture indigène"; Pélissier, *Les paysans*; R. Portères, "African Cereals: Eleusine, Fonio, Black Fonio, Teff, Brachiaria, Paspalum, Pennisetum, and African Rice," in Jack Harlan, J. De Wet, and A. Stemler, eds., *Origins of African Plant Domestication* (The Hague: Mouton, 1976).

14. A. de Candolle, *Origin of Cultivated Plants* (1886; New York: Hafner, 1964).

15. V. G. Childe, *Man Makes Himself* (New York: Mentor, 1951); R. Mauny, "Notes historiques autour des principales plantes cultivés d'Afrique occidentale," *Bulletin de l'IFAN*, 4, no. 2 (1953).

16. N. I. Vavilov, *The Origin, Variation, Immunity, and Breeding of Cultivated Plants: Selected Writings* (New York: Ronald Press, 1951). Had Vavilov survived Stalin's purge, he might have explored further the centers of crop domestication in Africa; he had planned additional research on the continent.

17. Rochevicz, "Documents sur le Genre Oryza," pp. 949–961; Mauny, "Notes historiques," p. 718; R. Charbolin, "Rice in West Africa," in C. L. A. Leakey and J. B. Wills, eds., *Food Crops of the Lowland Tropics* (Oxford: Oxford University Press, 1977), pp. 7–25; A. Carpenter, "The History of Rice in Africa," in I. Buddenhagen and J. Persley, eds., *Rice in Africa* (London: Academic Press, 1978), pp. 3–10.

18. For the earliest confirmed reference to domestication in Muslim texts, see M. Tymowski, "Les domaines des princes de Songhay (Soudan occidental): Comparaison avec la grande propriété foncière au début de l'époque féodal," *Annales*, 15 (1971): 1637–43.

19. Tadeusz Lewicki, *West African Food in the Middle Ages* (Cambridge: Cambridge University Press, 1974), p. 22.

20. Chevalier, "Sur le riz africains du groupe Oryza glaberrima," pp. 413–418.

21. See E. W. Bovill, *The Golden Trade of the Moors* (London: Oxford University Press, 1958), pp. 128–132; Walter Rodney, *A History of the Upper Guinea Coast* (New York: Monthly Review Press, 1970), p. 21; J. W. Blake, *West Africa: Quest for God and Gold, 1545–1578* (London: Curzon Press, 1977), pp. 91–92; George Brooks, *Landlords and Strangers: Ecology, Society, and Trade in Western Africa, 1000–1630* (Boulder: Westview Press, 1993), p. 260.

22. A. Chevalier, "Les céréales des regions subsahariennes et des oasis," *Revue de botanique appliquée et d'agriculture tropicale* (1932): 755.

23. Lewicki, *West African Food*, pp. 34–35.

24. The suffixes of -lo, -ro, and -o in these languages of the Niger-Congo group mean food and nourishment, while the prefix ma- is applied to foods or liquids with the meaning of "full." Mandinka is part of the Mande linguistic group; Wolof forms part of the West Atlantic language family. R. Portères, "Primary Cradles of Agriculture in the African Continent," in J. D. Fage and R. A. Oliver, eds., *Papers in African Prehistory* (Cambridge: Cambridge University Press, 1970), pp. 47–48. *Maaro* is the term for rice in the Inland Niger Delta.

25. See Ribeiro, *Aspectos e problemas*; Pélissier, *Les paysans*.

26. Portères, "Primary Cradles," p. 49. Asian rice remained of limited geographic extent until the nineteenth century, however, when American missionaries introduced new varieties in the Sierra Leone and Liberia region settled by African captives freed from slave ships. Paul Richards, "Culture and Community Values in the Selection and Maintenance of African Rice," in Stephen Brush and Doreen Stabinsky, eds., *Valuing Local Knowledge: Indigenous People and Intellectual Property Rights* (Washington, D.C.: Island Press, 1996), pp. 211–212.

27. Portères, "Primary Cradles," p. 48.

28. Chevalier, "L'importance de la riziculture," pp. 27–28.

29. Ibid., p. 41.

30. See, for instance, Ribeiro, *Aspectos e problemas*.

31. This diffusionist model of rice origins from the middle Niger River is associated with the research of Roland Portères; however, Jack Harlan suggests the possibility of multiple sites of rice development throughout West Africa in association with the gathering of its wild ancestor, *Oryza barthii*. See R. Portères, "Vieilles agricultures de l'Afrique intertropicale: Centres d'origine et de diversification variétal primaires et berceaux d'agricultures antérieurs au XVIe siècle," *L'agronomie tropicale*, 5, nos. 9–10 (1950): 489–507; Portères, "African Cereals: Eleusine, Fonio, Black Fonio, Teff, Brachiaria, Paspalum, Pennisetum, and African Rice," in J. Harlan, J. De Wet, A. Stemler, eds., *Origins of African Plant Domestication* (The Hague: Mouton, 1976); and Jack Harlan, "Wild-Grass Seed Harvesting in the Sahara and Sub-Sahara of Africa," in D. R. Harris and G. C. Hillman, eds., *Foraging and Farming: The Evolution of Plant Exploitation* (London: Unwin Hyman, 1989), pp. 79–98.

32. Portères, "Primary Cradles."

33. Portères, ibid., based his estimates for *glaberrima* domestication on the presence of megalithic stone sites in the savanna from Mali to Senegal. These large erect stones with associated burials are thought to mark ancient watercourses and thus rice cultivation sites in the West African rice region. In Portères's time these stone sites were dated between 1500 B.C. and 800 B.C., but subsequent research has provided later dates from A.D. 750. See Graham Connah, *African Civilizations* (New York: Cambridge University Press, 1987), pp. 113, 178.

34. R. J. McIntosh and S. K. McIntosh, "The Inland Niger Delta before the Empire of Mali: Evidence from Jenne-jeno," *Journal of African History*, 22 (1981): 1–22; S. K. McIntosh and R. J. McIntosh, "The Early City in West Africa: Towards an Understanding," *African Archaeological Review*, 2 (1984): 73–98; S. K. McIntosh and R. J. McIntosh, "Cities without Citadels: Understanding Urban Origins along the Middle Niger," in T. Shaw, P. Sinclair, B. Andah, and A. Okpoko, eds., *The Archaeology of Africa: Food, Metals, and Towns* (New York: Routledge, 1993), pp. 622–641.

35. African iron smelting dates to the middle of the first millennium B.C., with the earliest documented sites in the rice area appearing in southwestern Mauritania and Niger. D. Phillipson, *African Archaeology* (Cambridge: Cambridge University Press, 1993), p. 174. On its relationship to metal tools, see R. J. McIntosh and S. K. McIntosh, "The Inland Niger Delta"; S. K. McIntosh and R. J. McIntosh, "The Early City in West Africa."

36. Brooks, *Landlords and Strangers*, pp. 82, 100–114, 276–277, 289–303; Pélissier, *Les paysans*, pp. 623–708; Denise Paulme, "Des rizicultures africaines: les Baga (Guinée française)," *Les cahiers d'outre-mer*, 39 (1957): 257–278.

37. Phillipson, *African Archaeology*, p. 144.

38. Pearl millet *(Pennisetum glaucum)* and *fonio (Digitaria exilis)* were already domesticated in the region. Jack Harlan, "The Tropical African Cereals," in Harris and Hillman, eds., *Foraging and Farming*, pp. 335–343. Mande or Manding is a linguistic group that is a subset of the larger Niger-Congo language family. The Mande language group has inhabited the western Sudan since at least 5000 B.C. Its core is sometimes referred to as Mandekan. The Mande language group is further divided into a western and eastern branch associated with its diffusion over a broad region of West Africa. There are more than forty Mande languages; among the better known are Soninké, Mende, Mandinka, Bambara, Malinke, Dyula, Vai, Susu, and Dan. See also Roderick J. McIntosh, *The Peoples of the Middle Niger* (Malden, Mass.: Blackwell, 1998), p. 33.

39. As they became Islamicized in later centuries, the Nono became known as the Marka. See R. J. McIntosh, *Peoples of the Middle Niger*, pp. 116, 142–143; J. Gallais, *Le Delta intérieur du Niger* (Dakar, Senegal: IFAN, 1967); S. K. McIntosh and R. J. McIntosh, *Prehistoric Investigations in the Region of Jenne, Mali*, part 2: *The Regional Survey and Conclusions* (Cambridge: Cambridge University Press, 1980); R. J. McIntosh and S. K. McIntosh, "The Inland Niger Delta"; G. Szumowski, "Fouilles au norde du Macina et dans la région de Ségou," *Bulletin de l'IFAN*, sér. B, nos. 1–2 (1957): 224–258; R. Haaland, "Man's Role in the Changing Habitat of Mema under the Old Kingdom of Ghana," ILCA Working Document no. 2, International Livestock Centre for Africa, Addis Ababa, 1979.

40. The Ghana Empire lay far to the north of the country known as Ghana today. See Basil Davidson, *A History of West Africa* (New York: Doubleday, 1965), pp. 40–51; Donald Wright, *The World and a Very Small Place in Africa* (Armonk, N.Y.: M. E. Sharpe, 1997), pp. 26–37.

41. Blacksmiths may have spearheaded this diffusion as they moved south and west along trade routes in search of wood for iron smelting. Brooks, *Landlords and Strangers*, p. 51, establishes their migration to Senegambia over the A.D. 700–1100 period. See also Larry Becker and Roger Diallo, *Characterization and Classification of Rice AgroEcosystems in Côte d'Ivoire* (Bouaké, Ivory Coast: WARDA, 1992); Roland

Portères, "Les noms des riz en Guinée," *Journal d'agriculture tropicale et de botanique appliquée*, 13, no. 9 (1966): 1–346, esp. p. 10.

42. The development of iron-making skills centuries earlier had led to a remarkable diversification of hand tools in West African rice culture. F. Sigaut, "Essai d'identification des instruments à bras de travail de sol," *Cah. ORSTOM*, sér. Sci. Hum., 20, nos. 3–4 (1984): 360–362.

43. Chevalier, "Sur le riz," pp. 413–418.

44. See R. J. McIntosh and S. K. McIntosh, "The Inland Niger Delta," pp. 2–8.

45. National Resource Council, *Lost Crops*, p. 23.

46. Richards, "Culture and Community Values," pp. 209–229, esp. p. 212. Richards claims that while east of the Bandama River in central Ivory Coast rice cultivation does occur, it is always a modern introduction based on Asian rice.

47. R. Franke and B. Chasin, *Seeds of Famine* (Trenton, N.J.: Allanheld, 1980); D. Catling, *Rice in Deep Water* (London: IRRI/Macmillan, 1992), pp. 359–361.

48. Franke and Chasin, *Seeds of Famine*, pp. 21–25. The Sahel, which means "shore" in Arabic, refers to the arid climatic belt that extends some 200–300 miles from the southern border of the Sahara. In typical years, merely 300–600 mm (12–23 inches) of rain falls. The Sahel includes the countries of Senegal, Mali, Niger, and Chad but involves a larger number of countries affected by periodic drought, especially those directly to the south in the semiarid savanna or Sudanic zone that experience 650–900 mm (26–34 inches) of rainfall. This zone includes The Gambia, Casamance province of southern Senegal, and the northern parts of Guinea, Burkina Faso, and Nigeria.

49. For example, the Sahara Desert moved 140 kilometers south during the 1980–1984 period, bringing drought to Sahelian countries. But in 1984–85 the Sahara advanced north 100 kilometers. When the Sahel expands into the savanna Sudanic climatic zone, drought results. See review in R. Monastersky, "Satellites Expose Myth of Marching Sahara," *Science News*, 140 (1991): 38.

50. Catling, *Rice in Deep Water*, p. 359; W. M. Adams, *Wasting the Rain: Rivers, People, and Planning in Africa* (Minneapolis: University of Minnesota Press, 1993).

51. Philip Curtin, *Economic Change in Pre-Colonial Africa* (Madison: University of Wisconsin, 1975), pp. 218–219; Brooks, *Landlords and Strangers*, p. 12.

52. On the antiquity of land use in the region, see Connah, *African Civilizations*, p. 101; Phillipson, *African Archaeology*, pp. 119–142; and R. J. McIntosh, *Peoples of Middle Niger*, pp. 1–33. Contemporary estimates for the number of animals in the area include 1.5 million cattle and an additional 2.5 million sheep and goats. Matthew Turner, "Overstocking the Range: A Critical Analysis of the Environmental Science of Sahelian Pastoralism," *Economic Geography*, 69, no. 4 (1993): 402–421, esp. pp. 410–411. Some cattle are additionally kept inside the enclosure of houses, which helps reduce human exposure to *falciparum* malaria, the most deadly, and endemic, form to which the sickle cell trait developed in exposed human populations. Its advantage was to reduce morbidity for those with the trait but not the disease. Rates of exposure to this most virulent form of malaria are lowered because the animals offer an alternative host to mosquitoes in search of a blood meal. Dr. Thomas Teuscher, West African Rice Development Association (WARDA), pers. comm., August 24, 1999.

53. P. Viguier, *La riziculture indigène au Soudan français* (Paris: Larose, 1939),

p. 86; J. Dresch, "La riziculture en Afrique occidentale," *Bulletin de la Société de Géographie*, 312 (1949): 299–300; H. M. Raulin, "Techniques agraires," pp. 339–358, esp. p. 346; A. Lericollais and J. Schmitz, "La calebasse et la houe," *Cah. ORSTOM*, ser. Sci. Hum., 20, nos. 3–4 (1984): 427–452, esp. p. 438.

54. For an apt discussion of this point, see Michel-Rolph Trouillot, *Silencing the Past: Power and the Production of History* (Boston: Beacon Press, 1995).

55. Viguier, *La riziculture indigène*, p. 2.

56. These were the schemes funded by the Office du Niger in Mali, the Office du Sahel in Senegal, and the Commonwealth Development Corporation in Gambia. See Viguier, *La riziculture indigène;* K. S. Baldwin, *The Niger Agricultural Project* (Oxford: Basil Blackwell, 1957); M. Cowen, "Early Years of the Colonial Development Corporation: British State Enterprise Overseas during Late Colonialism," *African Affairs*, 83, no. 330 (1984): 63–75; Richards, *Indigenous Agricultural Revolution*, p. 75; Richards, "Culture and Community Values," p. 211.

57. On floating rices, see Chevalier, "Sur le riz africains du groupe Oryza glaberrima," p. 418; and Viguier, *La riziculture indigène*, p. 60.

58. G. Currens, "Women, Men, and Rice: Agricultural Innovation in Northwestern Liberia," *Human Organization*, 35, no. 4 (1976): 355–365; Richards, *Indigenous Agricultural Revolution*, p. 100.

59. Chevalier, "Sur le riz africains," p. 413.

60. This observation was suggested by Dr. Matthew Turner, Department of Geography, University of Wisconsin, pers. comm., January 17, 2000.

61. Paul Richards, *Coping with Hunger* (London: Allen and Unwin, 1986), p. 134. Even the names women give to some varieties may reveal a gender bias, as happened during a period of community discord in the Gambia in the 1950s when colonial development projects improved access to tidal swamps and introduced higher-yielding seeds on rice fields traditionally planted by women. However, females lost control over the benefits of these improved plots to male heads of household and relocated their individual plots elsewhere, naming from then on the variety they had long planted in the tidal swamp "No Man's Business." Carney fieldwork, 1987.

62. Sterility characterizes the first generation of crosses between *glaberrima* and *sativa* varieties. Charbolin, "Rice in West Africa," p. 12, and West Africa Rice Development Association (WARDA), *Annual Report* (Bouaké, Ivory Coast: WARDA, 1995), p. 27.

63. National Research Council (NRC), *Lost Crops of Africa* (Washington, D.C.: National Academy Press, 1996), pp. 26–29.

64. See Viguier, "La riziculture indigène," 1:291.

65. Slave captain Samuel Gamble (c. 1793) described the gender division of labor in Baga rice cultivation in Guinea Conakry. Quoted in Daniel Littlefield, *Rice and Slaves* (Baton Rouge: Louisiana State University, 1981), pp. 93–95. See also Pélissier, *Les paysans*, pp. 744–756; and Linares, *Power, Prayer, and Production*, p. 20.

66. On rain-fed farming and its significance in an upland to lowland planting system in Sierra Leone, see Richards, *Coping with Hunger;* and on Liberia, Magdalene David, "The Impact of Rural Transformation on the Productive Role of Liberian Women: The Case of Rice Production," *Liberia-Forum*, 3/4 (1987): 27–37. This area of the Guinea highlands has served as an important corridor of human

migration not only during the Atlantic slave trade but for hundreds of years before and after.

67. This rice system presents greater variability in labor patterns than the others so exceptions do occur, as in wetlands being cultivated by males of immigrant ethnic groups and with men sometimes weeding upland fields. Richards, *Coping with Hunger*, p. 178; David, "The Impact of Rural Transformation," pp. 27–37; Becker and Diallo, "Characterization and Classification," p. 205.

68. Sigaut, "Essai d'identification," p. 362.

69. Viguier, *La riziculture indigène*, p. 6; Pélissier, *Les paysans*, p. 572; Raulin, "Techniques agraires," pp. 345–350; Sigaut, "Essai d'identification," pp. 359–374, esp. p. 368; Lericollais and Schmitz, "La calebasse et la houe," p. 443.

70. Sigaut, "Essai d'identification," pp. 360–367, draws attention to the importance and unusual diversity of hoes in African farming systems, unparalleled in Eurasian systems where the hoe plays a minor role in cultivation. Dependence upon the hoe in African agriculture is not indicative of technological stagnation; rather, the hoe developed with the objective of minimally disturbing landscapes subject to erosion, often in areas unfavorable to draft animal traction. Hoes played a minor or accessory role in the evolution of Eurasian farming systems based on draft animal traction, an observation that suggests the need to explore farming implements cross-culturally in order to elucidate crop history.

71. This is the "pick axe," with a two-inch blade, mentioned by Golberry at the end of the eighteenth century.

72. Yasmine Marzouk-Schmitz, "Instruments aratoires, systèmes de cultures et différentiation intra-ethnique," *Cahiers du ORSTOM*, sér. Sci. Hum., 20, nos. 3–4 (1984): 399–425, esp. p. 402; Dresch, "La riziculture en Afrique occidentale," pp. 307–309.

73. This is the "iron curved scratching tool" first mentioned by Olfert Dapper circa 1640. See Richards, "Culture and Community Values," p. 213.

74. Richards, *Indigenous Agricultural Revolution*; Richards, "Culture and Community Values"; Becker and Diallo, "Characterization and Classification," p. 505.

75. Several researchers have commented upon the diverse availability of seed varieties adapted to short- and long-duration planting regimes, salinity, and drought tolerance. See Pélissier, *Les paysans*; Christian Roche, *Histoire de la Casamance* (Dakar, Senegal: Karthala, 1985), pp. 43–44; Richards, *Indigenous Agricultural Revolution*; Richards, *Coping with Hunger*; Becker and Diallo, "Cultural Diffusion."

76. W. Andriesse and L. O. Fresco, "A Characterization of Rice-Growing Environments in West Africa," *Agriculture, Ecosystems, and Environment*, 33 (1991): 377–395. See also Richards, *Coping with Hunger*, p. 73, for mention of at least eleven types of small-scale irrigation practices, native to West Africa, which depend upon locally specific differences in topography, soil, and flooding; Adams, *Wasting the Rain*, pp. 70–71; I. W. Buddenhagen and G. J. Persley, eds., *Rice in Africa* (London: Academic Press, 1978); and Catling, *Rice in Deep Water*, p. 372.

77. D. H. Grist, *Rice*, 4th ed. (London: Longmans, Green and Co., 1968); Bray, *Rice Economies*. An excellent description of upland and inland rice farming systems is provided in Richards, *Coping with Hunger*.

78. Lericollais and Schmitz, "La calebasse et la houe," pp. 427–452, esp. p. 438. The technique of directly sowing germinated grains continues in parts of

Ivory Coast today. Dr. Thomas Teuscher, West African Rice Development Association, pers. comm., August 24, 1999.

79. Food and Agricultural Organization (FAO), *Rice Mission Report to The Gambia* (Rome: FAO, 1983).

80. Dresch, "La riziculture en Afrique occidentale," p. 307.

81. See description of these soils in Pélissier, *Les paysans*, p. 714; Roche, *Histoire de la Casamance*, p. 76; and Richards, *Coping with Hunger*, p. 38.

82. Mangrove soils, unlike those of freshwater floodplains in West Africa and South Carolina, are chemically very complex and the deep black clays are rich in organic matter. Concentrations of sulfites are built up under anaerobic conditions. When exposed to air during a prolonged period of drought, these sulfites are oxidized to sulfates with the soil pH falling to a highly acid range, around pH 2–3. See F. R. Moorman and N. Van Breeman, *Rice: Soil, Water, and Land* (Los Baños, Philippines: International Rice Research Institute, 1978).

83. See Richards, *Indigenous Agricultural Revolution*, pp. 26–27.

84. See Olga Linares, "From Tidal Swamp to Inland Valley: On the Social Organization of Wet Rice Cultivation among the Diola of Senegal," *Africa*, 5 (1981): 557–594; Linares, *Power, Prayer, and Production*; Snyder, *Capitalism and Legal Change*; Paulme, *Les gens du riz*; and the special issue of *Cahiers ORSTOM*, série Sciences Humaines, 20, no. 1, 1984.

85. Quoted in Littlefield, *Rice and Slaves*, pp. 93–95.

86. See, for instance, Wittfogel's notion of Oriental despotism, long used to characterize stratified and centralized Asian rice societies, which is summarized in Daniel Worster, *Rivers of Empire* (New York: Oxford University Press, 1985), pp. 22–60. On West African mangrove producers, see Pélissier, *Les paysans*; and Linares, *Power, Prayer, and Production*.

87. Rodney, *Upper Guinea Coast*.

88. Pélissier, *Les paysans*; Linares, "From Tidal Swamp"; Linares, *Power, Prayer and Production*.

89. Raulin, "Techniques agraires," suggests that this indispensable technique of the mangrove system may have originated with flood recession farming.

90. The West African rice region remains an important locus internationally for research and development; the West African Rice Development Association (WARDA) is located in Bouaké, the Ivory Coast.

3. Out of Africa

1. The need to focus more research on the reorganization of African food systems during the Atlantic slave trade is underscored by George Brooks, *Landlords and Strangers: Ecology, Society, and Trade in Western Africa, 1000–1630* (Boulder: Westview, 1993), pp. 177–178.

2. John Thornton, *Africa and Africans in the Making of the Atlantic World, 1400–1680* (New York: Cambridge University Press, 1992), p. 93.

3. Richard Jobson, *The Golden Trade* [1623] (Devonshire: Speight and Walpole, 1904), p. 90.

4. Walter Rodney, *A History of the Upper Guinea Coast, 1545 to 1800* (New York: Monthly Review Press, 1970), pp. 253–270; Paul Lovejoy, *Transformations in Slavery* (Cambridge: Cambridge University Press, 1983), pp. 108–134; Boubacar

Barry, *Senegambia and the Atlantic Slave Trade* (Cambridge: Cambridge University Press, 1998), pp. 107–108.

5. On cereal production by African captives, see Francis Moore, *Travels into the Inland Parts of Africa* (London: Edward Cave, 1738), p. 43; G. Mollien, *Travels in Africa* (London: Sir Richard Phillips & Co., 1820), p. 110; Walter Rodney, "African Slavery and Other Forms of Social Oppression on the Upper Guinea Coast in the Context of the Atlantic Slave Trade," in J. E. Inikori, ed., *Forced Migration* (London: African Publishing Company, 1982), pp. 6–70; C. Robertson and M. Klein, "Women's Importance in African Slave Systems," in Robertson and Klein, eds., *Women and Slavery in Africa* (Madison: University of Wisconsin, 1983), pp. 3–28.

6. Mungo Park, *Travels into the Interior of Africa* [1799] (London: Eland, 1954), p. 9.

7. By 1600 the function of indigenous slaves in West African societies was shifting from the earlier emphasis on reproduction and domestic retainers to agriculture. See Lovejoy, *Transformations*, p. 31; Rodney, "African Slavery," pp. 6–70.

8. "Fula slaves ruling the Wolofs" is little more than an observation of Wolof dependence on slave labor and an exaggeration of slave rights. Cadamosto quoted in Lovejoy, *Transformations*, p. 27; Fernandes and De Almada cited in Rodney, *Upper Guinea Coast*, p. 236. The term "slaves" designated war captives and those pawned in famine; it was often a temporary social position from which one might obtain freedom. See Thornton, *Africa and Africans*, pp. 80–91.

9. "Rich men of São Tomé had large groups of slaves ranging from 150 to 300 who had the 'obligation to work for their master every day of the week except Sunday, when they worked to support themselves.' " Quoted in Thornton, *Africa and Africans*, pp. 170–171.

10. Oral histories collected during the twentieth century in Senegambia and Guinea Conakry show the continuity of such labor patterns after the abolition of the Atlantic slave trade. A residue of the labor system survives in Senegambia today as "strange farming" *(navétanne)*, where seasonal migrants provide agricultural labor for usually three to four half days per week in exchange for lodging, food, and access to farmland. See Ken Swindell, "Serawoolies, Tillibunkas, and Strange Farmers: The Development of Migrant Groundnut Farming along the Gambia River, 1848–95," *Journal of African History*, 21 (1980): 93–104; and P. David, *Les navétannes: histoire des migrants saisonniers de l'arachide en Sénégambie des origines a nos jours* (Dakar, Senegal: Nouvelles Editions Africaine, 1980).

11. Quoted in W. Derman, *Serfs, Peasants, and Socialists* (Berkeley: University of California, 1973), p. 36. Although Caillié's observation is from the 1820s, it details the labor rights of those in agricultural servitude, who are mentioned more generally a century earlier by Equiano and Prince Rahman Ibrahima. See D. Grant, *The Fortunate Slave* (New York: Oxford University Press, 1968); P. Edwards, *Equiano's Travels* (London: Heinemann, 1968); and T. Alford, *Prince among Slaves* (New York: Oxford University Press, 1977). Another commentary on the task system by Hugh Clappeton (1824), British envoy to the Sokoto Caliphate in northern Nigeria, fixes slave responsibility in agriculture between the hours of sunrise and 2 P.M. Quoted in Lovejoy, *Transformations*, pp. 206–207. On the partial autonomy from labor claims in African slave villages, see Mollien, *Travels in Africa*; Rodney, *Upper Guinea Coast*.

12. Inikori, ed., *Forced Migration*, pp. 6–70; Lovejoy, *Transformations*; Alford, *Prince*, p. 7.

13. See the accounts in Grant, *Fortunate Slave*; Edwards, *Equiano's Travels*, p. 10; and Mary Cable, *Black Odyssey* (New York: Penguin, 1971).

14. See Robertson and Klein, "Women's Importance in African Slave Systems"; Claude Meillassoux, "Female Slavery," in Robertson and Klein, eds., *Women and Slavery in Africa*, pp. 49–66; and Meillassoux, *The Anthropology of Slavery: The Womb of Iron and Gold* (Chicago: University of Chicago, 1991).

15. Philip Curtin, *Economic Change in Pre-Colonial Africa* (Madison: University of Wisconsin Press, 1975), p. 170; Peter Weil, "Agrarian Production, Intensification, and Underdevelopment: Mandinka Women of the Gambia in Time Perspective," paper delivered at a Title XII Conference, Women in Development, University of Delaware, Newark, May 7, 1981; Barry, *Senegambia*, pp. 107–108.

16. Abolition affected just a portion of Africa, mainly the area of the Upper Guinea Coast within reach of British naval ships operating out of the settlement that English abolitionists had established in Sierra Leone in 1787. The area patrolled for enforcing abolition from 1808 included the coastal waters and territory sandwiched between the Gambia River and Liberia. But enforcement was uneven, and slave traders operated clandestinely. Of those who participated in the famed slave uprising aboard the *Amistad* off the Cuban coast that brought the mutineers to New England in 1839 and the case before the U.S. Supreme Court, many originated in Sierra Leone, enslaved by traders who eluded the British Navy. Over the entire period of presumed abolition, slaving continued, especially to the south along the African coast in areas controlled by the Portuguese.

17. John W. Barber, *A History of the Amistad Captives* (New Haven: E. L. and J. W. Barber, 1840), pp. 3–32.

18. Elizabeth Donnan, *Documents Illustrative of the History of the Slave Trade to America*, 4 vols. (Washington, D.C.: Carnegie Institution, 1930–1935), 1:393–394, 440; 2:192, 247–269, 279–288, 303–304; 3:61, 158, 293, 373–378; 4:530. See also Bernard Martin and Mark Spurrell, *The Journal of a Slave Trader (John Newton), 1750–1754* (London: Epworth Press, 1962), pp. 20, 27–49, 78–79; Rodney, *Upper Guinea Coast*, p. 78; K. G. Davies, *The Royal African Company* (New York: Atheneum, 1970), pp. 228, 279; Peter Wood, *Black Majority* (New York: Knopf, 1974), p. 59; J. Walvin, *Black Ivory* (Washington, D.C.: Howard University Press, 1992), pp. 50–51; Barry, *Senegambia*, pp. 117–118. On Bristol slavers purchasing rice along the Guinea coast, see A. G. Hopkins, *An Economic History of West Africa* (New York: Columbia University Press, 1973), p. 89.

19. Marvin Miracle, *Maize in Tropical Africa* (Madison: University of Wisconsin Press, 1966), p. 91; Phyllis Martin, *The External Trade of the Loango Coast, 1576–1870* (Oxford: Clarendon Press, 1972), p. 13. Some places along the coast in fact were known for their surplus production of maize, yams, beans, and pepper, which were specifically intended to feed slaves during the Middle Passage. See Albert van Dantzig, "Effects of the Atlantic Slave Trade on Some West African Societies," in J. E. Inikori, ed., *Forced Migration* (London: African Publishing Company, 1982), p. 198.

20. De Sandoval mentioned in Thornton, *Africa and Africans*, pp. 154–160. Portuguese vessels carried nearly all the slaves that made the trip to the Cape Verde Islands and America prior to the 1620s. These vessels routinely stopped in Spanish

Jamaica and Portuguese Maranhão for rest and victuals. On the Atlantic islands and provisioning, see Ira Berlin, *Many Thousands Gone: The First Two Centuries of Slavery in North America* (Cambridge, Mass.: Harvard University Press, 1998), p. 68.

21. The average mortality rate derives from the last century of transatlantic slavery; losses were even higher in previous centuries. Elizabeth Donnan, *Documents Illustrative*; Philip D. Curtin, *The Atlantic Slave Trade* (Madison: University of Wisconsin Press, 1969).

22. Miracle, *Maize*, pp. 87–93. Slave ships frequently had to wait until their holds were filled with captives and food before embarking across the Atlantic and, once across, often stopped in other ports before arriving in North America.

23. Barry, *Senegambia*, pp. 117–118.

24. Miracle, *Maize*.

25. W. O. Jones, *Manioc in Africa* (Stanford: Stanford University Press, 1959), p. 62.

26. Roland Portères, "Primary Cradles of Agriculture in the African Continent," in J. D. Fage and R. A. Oliver, eds., *Papers in African Prehistory* (Cambridge: Cambridge University Press, 1970), pp. 43–58, p. 49; A. Chevalier and O. Roehrich, "Sur l'origine botanique des riz cultivés," *Comptes rendus de l'Academie de Sciences*, 159 (1914): 560–562.

27. Donald R. Wright, *The World and a Very Small Place in Africa* (Armonk, N.Y.: M. E. Sharpe, 1997), p. 82.

28. Curtin, *Atlantic Slave Trade*, p. 96; Philip Curtin, *The Rise and Fall of the Plantation Complex* (Cambridge: Cambridge University Press, 1990), p. 21.

29. See Timothy Weiskel, "Toward an Archaeology of Colonialism: Elements in the Ecological Transformation of the Ivory Coast," in Donald Worster, ed., *The Ends of the Earth* (New York: Cambridge University Press, 1988), pp. 141–171, esp. pp. 161–164, for discussion of the role of islands off the coast of Africa for indigenous African agricultural experimentation with new food and cash crops.

30. Orlando Ribeiro, *Aspectos e problemas da expansão portuguésa*, Estudos de Ciencias Políticas e Sociais (Lisbon: Junta de Investigações do Ultramar, 1962); T. B. Duncan, *Atlantic Islands: Madeira, the Azores, and the Cape Verdes in Seventeenth Century Commerce and Navigation* (Chicago: University of Chicago Press, 1972); Brooks, *Landlords and Strangers*.

31. Brooks, *Landlords and Strangers*, pp. 174, 292–296.

32. Ribeiro, *Aspectos e problemas*, p. 147.

33. None of the references to rice cultivation in Santiago claim that it is of African origin. Ibid., pp. 143–145; Duncan, *Atlantic Islands*, p. 168; J. W. Blake, *West Africa: Quest for God and Gold, 1545–1578* (London: Curzon Press, 1977), pp. 91–92; Brooks, *Landlords and Strangers*, pp. 139–147.

34. Ribeiro, *Aspectos e problemas*, p. 141.

35. Blake, *West Africa*, pp. 91–92, 103.

36. Ribeiro, *Aspectos e problemas*, pp. 146–147; Brooks, *Landlords and Strangers*, p. 149; Stuart B. Schwartz, *Sugar Plantations in the Formation of Brazilian Society: Bahia, 1550–1835* (New York: Cambridge University Press, 1998), p. 84. Seed rice has not been milled so that its husk and endosperm remain intact for germination.

37. F. C. Hoehne, *Botánica e agricultura no Brasil no século XVI.* (São Paulo: Companhia Editora Nacional, 1937), pp. 33–39.

38. Alfred W. Crosby, *The Columbian Exchange: Biological and Cultural Consequences of 1492* (Westport, Conn.: Greenwood Press, 1972), p. 70. Yams were also being planted in Peru, p. 107.

39. For Mexico the record dates from 1549. See Curtin, *Atlantic Slave Trade,* pp. 98–99.

40. Ibid., p. 108.

41. Ribeiro, *Aspectos e problemas,* pp. 143–144; Duncan, *Atlantic Islands,* p. 167; Curtin, *Rise and Fall,* p. 26.

42. See Ribeiro, *Aspectos e problemas,* pp. 152–156; A. Teixeira da Mota, *Some Aspects of Portuguese Colonisation and Sea Trade in West Africa in the 15th and 16th Centuries* (Bloomington: University of Indiana Press, 1978), p. 16.

43. Jean Suret-Canale, *Essays on African History* (Trenton, N.J.: Africa World Press, 1988), p. 67.

44. Initially serving as the financiers of the sugar economy, the Dutch occupied Pernambuco from 1629 until 1654. The numbers of African slaves grew from about 20,000 in 1600 to between 35,000 and 50,000 by the middle of the century. See Pedro Paulo de Abreu Funari, "A arqueologia de Palmares," in João José Reis and Flávio dos Santos Gomes, eds., *Liberdade por um fio* (São Paulo: Companhia das Letras, 1996), pp. 26–51, esp. p. 29.

45. Thornton, *Africa and Africans,* p. 174. When Pernambuco was reclaimed by the Portuguese after 1644, many of these Jewish settlers then moved to Suriname. See Jacob R. Marcus and Stanley Chyet, *Historical Essay on the Colony of Surinam, 1788* (Cincinnati: American Jewish Archives, 1974), pp. 20, 23–24. On New Christians (Jewish converts to Christianity) and Jewish emigration to Cape Verde and West Africa in the early period of Portuguese maritime expansion, see Brooks, *Landlords and Strangers,* pp. 159–160, 178–179, 185–187.

46. Wilhelm Piso, *História natural e médica da India ocidental* (Rio de Janeiro: Instituto Nacional do Livro, 1957), p. 50.

47. John Hemming, *Red Gold* (Cambridge, Mass.: Harvard University Press, 1978), pp. 288–289.

48. Excerpt from Stuart B. Schwartz, "Resistance and Accommodation in Eighteenth-Century Brazil: The Slaves' View of Slavery," *Hispanic American Historical Review,* 57 (1977): 69–81, appears as "The Slaves' View of Slavery: A Plantation Rebellion near Ilheus, Bahia, and the Rebels' Written Demands for a Settlement," in Robert Edgar Conrad, *Children of God's Fire: A Documentary History of Black Slavery in Brazil* (University Park: Pennsylvania State University Press, 1984), p. 400. Matthias Röhrig Assunção, "Quilombos Maranhenses," in João José Reis and Flávio dos Santos Gomes, eds., *Liberdade por um fio: História dos quilombos no Brasil* (São Paulo: Companhia das Letras, 1996), pp. 433–466, esp. p. 437.

49. Richard Price, "Subsistence on the Plantation Periphery: Crops, Cooking, and Labour among Eighteenth-Century Suriname Maroons," *Slavery and Abolition,* 12, no. 1 (1991): 107–127; Richard Price and Sally Price, *Stedman's Surinam* (Baltimore: Johns Hopkins University Press, 1992).

50. R. Price and S. Price, *Stedman's Surinam,* pp. 208–219.

51. On Jamaica and slaves growing rice in their provision gardens, see W. E. Grimé, *Ethno-botany of the Black Americans* (Algonac, Mich.: Reference Publications, 1979), p. 154; on Nicaragua, see Karl Henry Offen, "The Miskitu Kingdom Landscape and the Emergence of a Miskitu Ethnic Identity, Northeastern Nicaragua

and Honduras, 1600–1800" (Ph.D. dissertation, Department of Geography, University of Texas at Austin, 1999); for Colombia, Robert West, *The Pacific Lowlands of Colombia* (Baton Rouge: Louisiana State University Press, 1957). Cuba, Panama, northwest coastal Ecuador, and the Gulf Coast of Mexico are also areas of concentrated black settlement and rice-based cuisines.

52. Albert Virgil House, *Planter Management and Capitalism in Ante-Bellum Georgia* (New York: Columbia University Press, 1954); James Clifton, "Golden Grains of White: Rice Planting on the Lower Cape Fear," *North Carolina Historical Review*, 50 (1973): 365–393; Clifton, "The Rice Industry in Colonial America," *Agricultural History*, 55 (1981): 266–283.

53. Figures on slaves involved in rice cultivation vary, because numbers of the coastal slave population also include those growing cotton and in domestic service. The estimates provided in the text are drawn chiefly from Peter Coclanis, *The Shadow of a Dream* (New York: Oxford University Press, 1989), p. 142; P. Coclanis and J. Komlos, "Time in the Paddies: A Comparison of Rice Production in the Southeastern United States and Lower Burma in the Nineteenth Century," *Social Science History*, 11, no. 3 (1987): 345–346; Mart A. Stewart, *What Nature Suffers to Groe* (Athens: University of Georgia Press, 1996), pp. 253–255; D. E. Swan, *The Structure and Profitability of the Antebellum Rice Industry* (New York: Arno Press, 1975), pp. 14–19; Charles A. Gresham and Donal D. Hook, "Rice Fields of South Carolina: A Resource Inventory and Management Policy Evaluation," *Coastal Zone Management Journal*, 9 (1982): 183–203.

54. Coclanis, *Shadow of a Dream*, p. 70, places the average low-country holding in the nineteenth century as 871 acres.

55. On colonial production figures, see Coclanis, *Shadow of a Dream*, pp. 255n122. Figures for the pre–Civil War period are from the U.S. Census Office, *Agriculture of the U.S., 1860, 8th Census* (Washington, D.C.: U.S. Census Office, 1864); Swan, *Structure and Profitability*, p. 14. Swan estimates the annual export for the late antebellum period as 168 million pounds of clean rice. Mechanized milling reduces rough, or paddy, rice to about three-fourths of its original amount. The actual amount of rice grown in South Carolina and Georgia exceeded recorded exports because a portion was retained for consumption, which represented about 10 percent of the Carolina harvest. See Converse Clowse, *Economic Beginnings in Colonial South Carolina, 1670–1730* (Columbia: University of South Carolina Press, 1971), p. 168.

56. Memoirs by planter descendants include R. Q. Mallard, *Plantation Life before Emancipation* (Richmond: Whitte and Shepperson, 1892); U. B. Phillips, *American Negro Slavery* (New York: D. Appleton and Co., 1918); A. S. Salley, "Introduction of Rice into South Carolina," *Bulletin of the Historical Commission of South Carolina*, 6 (1919); Ralph Betts Flanders, *Plantation Slavery in Georgia* (Chapel Hill: University of North Carolina Press, 1933); Caroline Couper Lovell, *The Golden Isles of Georgia* (Boston: Little, Brown, 1932); David Doar, *Rice and Rice Planting in the South Carolina Low Country* (1936; Charleston: Charleston Museum, 1970); Herbert Ravenel Sass and D. E. Huger Smith, *A Carolina Rice Plantation of the Fifties* (New York: Morrow, 1936); and Duncan Heyward, *Seed from Madagascar* (Chapel Hill: University of North Carolina, 1937). See the detailed case studies of William Dusinberre, *Them Dark Days* (Oxford: Oxford University Press, 1996) to dispel any doubt about the horrific conditions of slavery on antebellum rice plantations of South Carolina and Georgia.

57. Wood, *Black Majority*, pp. 57–64.

58. Daniel C. Littlefield, *Rice and Slaves* (Baton Rouge: Louisiana State University Press, 1981). Betty Wood, *Slavery in Colonial Georgia* (Athens: University of Georgia Press, 1984), p. 103, also indicates a similar trend for Georgia, noting that three-fourths of the slaves shipped there during the critical period of tidewater rice expansion (1766–1771) originated from West Africa's Rice Coast.

59. See Clowse, *Economic Beginnings*, pp. 121–126, on the "imaginative planter" view of whites as ingeniously discovering cultivation of a crop previously unknown to them.

60. Philip D. Morgan, "Work and Culture: The Task System and the World of Low Country Blacks, 1700 to 1880," *William and Mary Quarterly*, 3rd ser., 39 (1972): 563–599, esp. pp. 565–566.

61. Clowse, *Economic Beginnings*, pp. 108–109; J. Leitch Wright, Jr., *The Only Land They Knew* (New York: Free Press, 1981), pp. 148–149, 159. On African-Indian relationships in the Americas, see Jack Forbes, *Africans and Native Americans* (Chicago: University of Chicago Press, 1993), p. 87.

62. Wood, *Black Majority*, pp. 103, 302–304.

63. Ibid., pp. 301–304, app. C, pp. 333–341; Margaret W. Creel, *A Peculiar People: Slave Religion and Community Culture among the Gullahs* (New York: New York University, 1988), pp. 29–44.

64. Berlin, *Many Thousands Gone*.

65. Wood, *Black Majority*, pp. 25–26, 36, 143–145; M. Eugene Sirmans, *Colonial South Carolina: A Political History, 1662–1763* (Chapel Hill: University of North Carolina Press, 1966), p. 24.

66. Wood, *Black Majority*, p. 62.

67. Clifton, "Golden Grains of White," p. 370.

68. Wood, *Black Majority*, pp. 57–58.

69. I. W. Burkhill, *A Dictionary of the Economic Plants of the Malay Peninsula*, 2 vols. (London: Crown Agents for the Colonies, 1935), 2:1601.

70. The quotation of Randolph, May 27, 1700 (British Public Record Office, Proprieties, Board of Trade records, xxvi, pp. 286–287), appears in A. S. Salley, "Introduction of Rice into South Carolina," p. 7.

71. The quotation from April 27, 1690: "Our rice is better esteem'd of in Jamaica than that from Europe sold ther for a ryall a pound its price here new husk't is 17/ [shillings] a hundred weight." Cited in Mabel L. Webber, "Letters from John Stewart to William Dunlop," *South Carolina Historical and Genealogical Magazine*, 32 (1931): 22; Clifton, "Rice Industry," p. 269.

72. Wood, *Black Majority*, p. 55.

73. Ibid., pp. 57–58.

74. Doar, *Rice and Rice Planting*; Charles Kovacik and John Winberry, *South Carolina: The Making of a Landscape* (Boulder: Westview Press, 1987); Judith A. Carney and Richard Porcher, "Geographies of the Past: Rice, Slaves, and Technological Transfer in South Carolina," *Southeastern Geographer*, 33, no. 2 (1993): 127–147.

75. John Otto, *The Southern Frontiers, 1607–1860* (New York: Greenwood Press, 1989).

76. On colonial livestock raising, see Thomas Nairne, "A Letter from South Carolina," in Jack P. Greene, ed., *Selling a New World: Two Colonial South Carolina Promotional Pamphlets* [1710] (Columbia: University of South Carolina Press,

1989), pp. 33–73, esp. p. 42; Salley, "Introduction of Rice," p. 172; Wood, *Black Majority*, pp. 30–32, 105–114.

77. On Coelho, see Thornton, *Africa and Africans*, p. 135. For a discussion of African herding and its relationship to New World cattle ranching, see Peter Wood, " 'It Was a Negro Taught them': A New Look at African Labor in Early South Carolina," *Journal of Asian and African Studies*, 9 (1974): 160–179, esp. pp. 168–173; Melville Herskovits, "The Culture Areas of Africa," *Africa*, 3 (1930): 67–73, esp. pp. 67, 70–72.

78. On slaves expanding the Carolina frontier for their owners, see Wood, "It Was a Negro," pp. 168–169; Wood, *Black Majority*, pp. 30–32. For another view on the origins of Western cattle ranching in the United States, see Terry G. Jordan, *Trails to Texas: Southern Roots of Western Cattle Ranching* (Lincoln: University of Nebraska, 1981), pp. 14, 29, 33.

79. On numbers of imported slaves, see Clowse, *Economic Beginnings*, p. 252; Wood, *Black Majority*, pp. 143–145; Coclanis, *Shadow of a Dream*, p. 64.

80. Heyward, *Seed from Madagascar*; Sam B. Hilliard, "Antebellum Tidewater Rice Culture in South Carolina and Georgia," in James Gibson, ed., *European Settlement and Development in North America: Essays on Geographical Change in Honour and Memory of Andrew Hill Clark* (Toronto: University of Toronto Press, 1978); Richard Porcher, "Rice Culture in South Carolina: A Brief History, the Role of the Huguenots, and Preservation of Its Legacy," *Transactions of the Huguenot Society of South Carolina*, 92 (1987): 11–22; David Whitten, "American Rice Cultivation, 1680–1980: A Tercentenary Critique," *Southern Studies*, 21, no. 1 (1982): 215–226.

81. Clifton, "The Rice Industry," p. 275.

82. Norman Hawley, "The Old Plantations in and around the Santee Experimental Forest," *Agricultural History* 23 (1949): 86–91.

83. John B. Irving, *A Day on the Cooper River* (Charleston: R. K. Bryan Co., 1969), p. 154. The remains of similar systems can be seen behind Murphy Island in the Santee Delta, where an extensive salt marsh is located near a freshwater stream, and at Drayton Hall on the Ashley River.

84. Edmund Ravenel, "The Limestone Springs of St. John's, Berkeley," *Proceedings of the Elliott Society of Science and Art of Charleston, South Carolina*, Feb. 1 (1859): 28–32, esp. p. 29.

85. Heyward, *Seed from Madagascar*; Hilliard, "Antebellum Tidewater," p. 99, points out the continued growing of rice with reservoirs in inland swamps during the eighteenth century amid the shift of cultivation to tidal floodplains.

86. Porcher, "Rice Culture."

87. Advertisement for land sale, dated January 19, 1738, *South Carolina Gazette*, Charleston, 1738; Clifton, "The Rice Industry," pp. 275–276, observes notices of tidal swamps for sale first appearing during the 1730s in the *South Carolina Gazette*—1731 for the Cape Fear River area in North Carolina, and 1737 for the Black River in South Carolina.

88. Douglas C. Wilms, "Development of Rice Culture in 18th Century Georgia," *Southeastern Geographer*, 12 (1972); Julia Floyd Smith, *Slavery and Rice Culture in Low Country Georgia, 1750–1860* (Knoxville: University of Tennessee Press, 1985).

89. Wilms, "Development of Rice Culture," p. 49.

90. Clifton, "The Rice Industry," p. 276.

91. D. Richardson, "The British Slave Trade to Colonial South Carolina," *Slavery and Abolition*, 12 (1991): 125–172, esp. pp. 127–128.

92. Ibid., pp. 135–136. On slave imports, see also Creel, *Peculiar People*, pp. 29–44.

93. Beauchamp Platagenet, quoted in Littlefield, *Rice and Slaves*, p. 100.

94. Ibid., p. 8; Creel, *Peculiar People*, pp. 35–36.

95. Moore, *Travels into the Inland Parts of Africa*, pp. 70–71, 244.

96. Henry Laurens to Smith and Clifton on July 17, 1755, quoted in Littlefield, *Rice and Slaves*, p. 9; Creel, *Peculiar People*, p. 35.

97. Sources for newspaper advertisements appear in Clifton, "The Rice Industry," p. 273; and Wood, "It was a Negro," pp. 170–171.

98. Christopher Fyfe, *A History of Sierra Leone* (Oxford: Oxford University Press, 1962), pp. 4–7; Littlefield, *Rice and Slaves*, pp. 21, 35–40, 54–76, 140; see also Edward Ball, *Slaves in the Family* (New York: Farrar, Straus and Giroux, 1998), pp. 192–193, 238.

99. Quotation from an unnamed rice planter in Doar, *Rice and Rice Planting*, p. 8.

100. Noted by John Gerar William de Brahm, "De Brahm's Report," in Louis de Vorsey, Jr., ed., *Report on the General Survey in the Southern District of North America* (Columbia: University of South Carolina Press, 1971), pp. 61–131, esp. p. 92. De Brahm was a royal surveyor in the southern colonies from 1751 to 1771. See also R. F. W. Allston, "Essay on Sea Coast Crops," *De Bow's Review*, 16 (1854): 589–615; Clifton, "The Rice Industry," pp. 275–276; Whitten, "American Rice," pp. 9–15.

101. Hilliard, "Antebellum Tidewater," p. 100.

102. Joyce Chaplin, *An Anxious Pursuit: Agricultural Innovation and Modernity in the Lower South, 1730–1815* (Chapel Hill: University of North Carolina Press, 1993).

103. John Drayton, *A View of South Carolina* [1802] (Columbia: University of South Carolina Press, 1972), p. 36; Chaplin, *An Anxious Pursuit*, p. 231.

104. Hilliard, "Antebellum Tidewater."

105. Leland Ferguson, *Uncommon Ground: Archaeology and Early African America, 1650–1800* (Washington, D.C.: Smithsonian, 1992), pp. xxiv, xxv, 147.

106. See James Scott Strickland, " 'No More Mud Work': The Struggle for the Control of Labor and Production in Low Country South Carolina, 1863–1880," in Walter J. Fraser and Winfred B. Moore, eds., *The Southern Enigma* (Westport, Conn.: Greenwood Press, 1983), pp. 43–62; Berlin, *Many Thousands Gone*, p. 167. Only the labor involved in rice milling was as detested by slaves as mud work.

107. Amelia Wallace Vernon documents the survival of rice cultivation among African Americans in Mars Bluff, South Carolina, located in the piedmont area of the state, distant from the coastal rice region. Amelia Wallace Vernon, *African Americans at Mars Bluff, South Carolina* (Baton Rouge: Louisiana State University Press, 1993). On white efforts to restrict black land access following emancipation, see S. Hahn, "Hunting, Fishing, and Foraging: Common Rights and Class Relations in the Post-Bellum South," *Radical History Review*, 26 (1982): 37–64.

108. Lewis Gray, *History of Agriculture in the Southern United States to 1860*, 2 vols. (Gloucester, Mass.: Peter Smith, 1958), 1:281.

109. Richard Porcher, "A Field Guide to the Bluff Plantation," O'Brien Foundation, New Orleans, 1985, pp. 26–27.

110. House, *Planter Management*, p. 25.

111. Doar, *Rice and Rice Planting*, p. 12.

112. A similar trunk was located at Tea Farm Plantation in Ravenel, South Carolina. On the archaeological discovery, see George Neil, "Archaeologists Uncover 'Rice Trunk,'" *Friends of Drayton Hall Interiors*, 15, no. 2 (1996): 4–5. For dates of the early Carolina rice plantations, see M. Lane, *Architecture of the Old South* (Savannah: Beehive Press, 1984).

113. Sass and Smith, *A Carolina Rice Plantation of the Fifties*, p. 23. For memoirs of planter descendants, see Flanders, *Plantation Slavery in Georgia*; Lovell, *The Golden Isles of Georgia*; Doar, *Rice and Rice Planting*; and Heyward, *Seed from Madagascar*.

114. Strickland, "No More Mud Work," pp. 43–62.

115. J. Carney and M. Watts, "Manufacturing Dissent: Work, Gender, and the Politics of Meaning in a Peasant Society," *Africa*, 60 (1990): 207–241.

116. Gray quoted in Morgan, "Work and Culture," p. 564.

117. Ibid.; Gray, *History of Agriculture*, 2:550–551.

118. See Morgan, "Work and Culture," and Philip D. Morgan, *Slave Counterpoint: Black Culture in the Eighteenth-Century Chesapeake and Lowcountry* (Chapel Hill: University of North Carolina Press, 1998), for an excellent overview of the task labor system and its significance.

119. Morgan, *Slave Counterpoint*, p. 181; Leslie Schwalm, *A Hard Fight for We: Women's Transition from Slavery to Freedom in South Carolina* (Urbana: University of Illinois Press, 1997), p. 14.

120. Morgan, "Work and Culture," p. 566.

121. Bolzius quoted in Morgan, "Work and Culture," p. 565. The entire document by Bolzius appears in K. G. Loewald, B. Starika, and P. Taylor, "Johan Bolzius Answers a Questionnaire on Carolina and Georgia," *William and Mary Quarterly*, 3rd ser., 14 (1957): 218–261.

122. Leigh Ann Pruneau, "All the Time Is Work Time: Gender and the Task System on Antebellum Low Country Rice Plantations" (Ph.D. dissertation, Department of History, University of Arizona, 1997), p. 9.

123. Morgan, "Work and Culture," pp. 568–569.

124. Morgan, "Work and Culture."

125. Clarence Ver Steeg, *Origins of a Southern Mosaic* (Athens: University of Georgia, 1984), pp. 105–106.

126. Ira Berlin attributes the emergence of the task system to slave isolation from the Anglo-American world, an isolation that enabled the retention of an African cultural heritage under similar environmental conditions. While the view suggests an African origin for the task system, it did not develop on many other slave plantation systems that were characterized by absentee owners. See Berlin, *Many Thousands Gone*. For yet another view, see Morgan, "Work and Culture," pp. 567–569.

127. Pruneau, "All the Time."

128. Berlin, *Many Thousands Gone*, pp. 308–309. The Atlantic slave trade continued, of course, despite being declared illegal.

129. Ibid., p. 314.

130. Littlefield, *Rice and Slaves*, pp. 99–100.

131. Lawson (1714, 77–78) and Hewatt (1779, 1:159) quoted in Littlefield, *Rice and Slaves*, p. 101.

132. Quoted in ibid., pp. 101–102; Wood, *Black Majority*, pp. 56–58.

133. Catesby quoted in Littlefield, *Rice and Slaves*, p. 102.

134. C. S. Orwin, *A History of English Farming* (London: Thos. Nelson and Sons, 1949), pp. 41–45, discusses this form of cultivation through drainage, mentioned in Littlefield, *Rice and Slaves*, p. 104. On Dutch land reclamation, see W. H. TeBrake, *Medieval Frontier Culture and Ecology in Rijnland* (College Station: Texas A&M Press, 1985).

135. Littlefield, *Rice and Slaves*, p. 104.

136. References to rice cultivation in Spain date from the tenth century, because of Muslim introduction. See Andrew M. Watson, *Agricultural Innovation in the Early Islamic World* (New York: Cambridge University Press, 1983), p. 17; Raymond E. Crist, "Rice Culture in Spain," *Scientific Monthly*, 84, no. 1 (1957): 66–74; Thomas F. Glick, *Irrigation and Society in Medieval Valencia* (Cambridge, Mass.: Harvard University Press, 1970). For Italy, see Giovani Biroli, *Del riso: trattato economico-rustico* (Milan: Tipografia di Giovanni Silvestri, 1807); Giambattista Spolverini, *La coltivazione del riso* (Milan: Tipografia dé Classici Italiano, 1813); Giovanni Guida, *Manuale di risocoltura* (Novara: Tipografia Nazionale di P. Busconi, 1838); Oreste Bordiga and Leopoldo Silvestrini, *Del riso e della sua coltivazione* (Novara: Tipografia della Rivista di Contabilità, 1880); Luigi Messedaglia, "Per la storia delle coltura nostre piante alimentari: il riso," *Rivista di storia delle scienze mediche e naturali*, 20 (1938): 1–15; H. A. Tempany, "The Italian Rice Industry," *Malaysian Agricultural Journal* (1932): 274–292; Michele Lecce, "Un'azienda risiera veronese nel XVII e XVIII secolo," *Economia e storia*, 1 (1959): 64–80; P. Bullio, "Problemi e geografia della risicoltura in Piemonte nei secoli XVII e XVIII," *Annali della Fondazione Luigi Einaudi*, 3 (1969): 37–112; Littlefield, *Rice and Slaves*, p. 105.

137. See Watson, *Agricultural Innovation*, pp. 104–111. On irrigation in the classical world, see Glick, *Irrigation and Society*, p. 189. On the United States, see P. Daniel, *Breaking the Land: The Transformation of Cotton, Tobacco, and Rice Cultures since 1880* (Urbana: University of Illinois Press, 1985); Henry C. Dethloff, *A History of the American Rice Industry, 1685–1985* (College Station: Texas A&M Press, 1988); L. Post, "The Rice Country of Southwestern Louisiana," *Geographical Review*, 30, no. 4 (1940): 574–590.

138. Quoted in Karen Hess, *The Carolina Rice Kitchen: The African Connection* (Columbia: University of South Carolina Press, 1992), p. 19. As ambassador to France, Jefferson had made a trip to Italy in 1786 to find a rain-fed rice variety for the United States, because he viewed wet rice as "a plant which sows life and death with almost equal hand." E. M. Betts, *Thomas Jefferson's Garden Book, 1766–1824* (Philadelphia: American Philosophical Society, 1944), p. 120.

139. Gardner Stickney, "Indian Use of Wild Rice," *American Anthropologist*, 9, no. 4 (1896): 115–122; Littlefield, *Rice and Slaves*, pp. 105–106.

140. Although rice seed from Madagascar might have diffused to Carolina, little evidence supports Heyward's memoir, which suggests an Asian influence on the rice cultivation system. The historical record does not reveal similarities in rice growing between Madagascar and South Carolina and therefore gives no indica-

tion of any influence of Asian growing techniques on colonial Carolina cultivation. See Littlefield, *Rice and Slaves*, p. 107.

141. Wood, "It was a Negro," p. 161.

142. Ibid., p. 162.

4. This Was "Woman's Wuck"

1. Thomas Nairne, mentioned in Peter Wood, *Black Majority* (New York: Knopf, 1974), pp. 106–107; see also Daniel C. Littlefield, *Rice and Slaves* (Baton Rouge: Louisiana State University Press, 1981), pp. 56–57.

2. Long-handled hoes are also depicted on the dustjacket and page ii of Ira Berlin's *Many Thousands Gone: The First Two Centuries of Slavery in North America* (Cambridge, Mass.: Harvard University Press, 1998). Lewis Gray, *History of Agriculture in the Southern United States to 1860*, 2 vols. (Gloucester, Mass.: Peter Smith, 1958), 1:194–195.

3. Leslie Schwalm, *A Hard Fight for We: Women's Transition from Slavery to Freedom in South Carolina* (Urbana: University of Illinois Press, 1997), p. 21.

4. Gray, *History of Agriculture*, 1:195.

5. R. Berleant-Schiller and R. and L. Pulsipher, "Subsistence Cultivation in the Caribbean," *New West Indian Guide*, 60, nos. 1–2 (1986): 1–40.

6. These points are repeatedly mentioned by two contributors to a special issue of *Cahiers ORSTOM*, série Sciences Humains, 20, nos. 3–4 (1984): H. M. Raulin, "Techniques agraires et instruments aratoires au sud de Sahara," pp. 339–358, esp. p. 350; and F. Sigaut, "Essai d'identification des instruments à bras de travail de sol," pp. 360–367. Sigaut, pp. 360–362, compares traditional African with European farming systems.

7. Ibid., and A. Lericollais and J. Schmitz, "La calebasse et la houe," *Cah. ORSTOM*, sér. Sci. Hum., 20, nos. 3–4 (1984): 438.

8. Alice Huger Smith created this drawing for the memoir by Elizabeth Allston Pringle, *A Woman Rice Planter* (1914; Cambridge, Mass.: Harvard University Press, 1961).

9. A. Lericollais and J. Schmitz, "La calebasse et la houe," *Cah. ORSTOM*, sér. Sci. Hum., 20, nos. 3–4 (1984): 438.

10. Theodore Ravenel, "The Last Days of Rice Planting," in David Doar, *Rice and Rice Planting in the South Carolina Low Country* (1936; Charleston: Charleston Museum, 1970), pp. 43–50, esp. pp. 49–50. Another description and illustration of women performing this technique appears in Pringle, *Woman Rice Planter*, pp. 11–12: "Young men brought the clay water . . . while young girls, with bare feet and skirts well tied up, danced and shuffled the rice about with their feet until the whole mass was thoroughly clayed."

11. Gray, *History of Agriculture*, 2:728.

12. See Doar, *Rice and Rice Planting*; R. F. W. Allston, "Essay on Sea Coast Crops," *De Bow's Review*, 16 (1854): 589–615, and Allston, "Memoir of the Introduction and Planting of Rice in South Carolina," *De Bow's Review*, 1 (1846): 320–357; Duncan Heyward, *Seed from Madagascar* (Chapel Hill: University of North Carolina Press, 1937), pp. 9–10. In West Africa, direct seeding of rice in floodplains depends on the availability of seed varieties timed to tidal amplitude.

13. On the African basis of the mortar and pestle, see Peter Wood, " 'It was a

Negro Taught them': A New Look at African Labor in Early South Carolina," *Journal of Asian and African Studies*, 9 (1974): 160–179; Judith A. Carney, "Rice Milling, Gender, and Slave Labour in Colonial South Carolina," *Past and Present*, 153 (1996): 108–134. On rice processing in India, see K. T. Achaya, *Indian Food: A Historical Companion* (New York: Oxford University Press, 1994). The fulcrum is about a foot in length and fixed underneath a beam of wood, located more than halfway along the pestle. A large stone may be tied to the beam above the pestle to give extra weight to its pounding. The fulcrum mortar and pestle is depicted in D. H. Grist, *Rice*, 4th ed. (London: Longmans, Green and Co., 1968), illus. following p. 216. Comments on Punta Gorda, Belize, are drawn from the author's fieldwork in the area.

14. Dale Rosengarten, "Social Origins of the African-American Lowcountry Basket" (Ph.D. dissertation, Harvard University, 1997), esp. pp. 273–311. These fanner baskets were woven from bullrush and sweet grass. On the Gullah tradition of fanner baskets, see Joseph Opala, *The Gullah* (Freetown, Sierra Leone: United States Information Service, 1987).

15. Karen Hess, *The Carolina Rice Kitchen: The African Connection* (Columbia: University of South Carolina Press, 1992), esp. pp. 2–26; Ntozake Shange, *If I Can Cook/You Know God Can* (Boston: Beacon Press, 1998), pp. 33, 48–49.

16. Jacob Motte Alston, cited in Charles Joyner, *Down by the Riverside* (Urbana: University of Illinois, 1984), p. 96. See also the description provided by Allston, "Memoir of the Introduction," p. 327.

17. Sally Price, *Co-wives and Calabashes* (Ann Arbor: University of Michigan Press, 1993), p. 32. On the Cuban term, see Jeffrey Alford and Naomi Duguid, *Seductions of Rice* (New York: Artisan, 1998), p. 29. Shange, *If I Can Cook*, p. 49, claims the dried crust results as an outcome of cooking rice to favor grain separation: "In order to avoid making . . . [rice] like a thick soup where the rice becomes one mass instead of standing, each grain on its own—it is necessary to let the rice at the bottom of the pot get a crustlike bottom, assuring that all the moisture has evaporated."

18. West Africans sometimes use palm oil to flavor rice dishes.

19. Karen Hess, pers. comm., March 29, 1996. Many rice dishes associated with African settlement in the Americas bear distinctive African signatures in preparation. These dishes combine the cooking of rice with beans, such as the Cuban "Moros y Cristianos" (Moors and Christians), prepared with black beans; Hoppin' John in South Carolina and Louisiana (black-eyed peas or cowpeas); and a similar dish in the Caribbean based on pigeon peas and rice. Other African food traditions in the Americas are the Louisiana jambalaya, based on rice, sauces, and seasonings, and gumbo, with the addition of okra. An additional African foodway is the preparation of stews from well-cooked greens, fatback pork, and hot pepper seasonings. The use of oilseeds represents yet another characteristic African cooking method, with many indigenous and introduced plants valued for their seeds and oil. Kathleen A. d'Azevedo, "Kwi Cooking: Influences of the West African Cooking Tradition" (M.A. thesis, California State University at San Francisco, 1974), p. 38.

20. Parboiling also developed in India.

21. For instance, elderly informants who lived in Oklahoma, descendants of Black Seminoles who settled there after their removal from Florida in the early

1840s, remember the method. Linda Salmon, pers. comm., March 20, 2000. Kate Sheehan, in Janice Jorgensen, ed., *Encyclopedia of Consumer Brands*, vol. 1 (Washington, D.C.: St. James Press, 1994), pp. 608–609.

22. On disease risks in rice cultivation see especially Wood, *Black Majority;* Peter Coclanis, *The Shadow of a Dream* (New York: Oxford University Press, 1989). High mortality rates characterized rice production all the way to the Civil War. See William Dusinberre, *Them Dark Days* (Oxford: Oxford University Press, 1996).

23. Heyward, *Seed from Madagascar,* p. 55.

24. Berlin, *Many Thousands Gone*, p. 167.

25. Excellent descriptions of the rice calendar occur in J. H. Easterby, "The South Carolina Factor as Revealed in the Papers of Robert F. W. Allston," *Journal of Southern History*, 7, no. 2 (1941): 160–172; Doar, *Rice and Rice Planting;* Albert Virgil House, *Planter Management and Capitalism in Ante-Bellum Georgia* (New York: Columbia University Press, 1954); Gray, *History of Agriculture*, vol. 2; Joyner, *Down by the Riverside;* Mart A. Stewart, *What Nature Suffers to Groe* (Athens: University of Georgia Press, 1996); Schwalm, *Hard Fight;* Daina Ramey, " 'She Do a Heap of Work': An Analysis of Female Slave Labor on Glynn County Rice and Cotton Plantations," *Georgia Historical Quarterly*, 82 (1998): 707–734.

26. Schwalm, *Hard Fight;* Leigh Ann Pruneau, "All the Time Is Work Time: Gender and the Task System on Antebellum Low Country Rice Plantations" (Ph.D. dissertation, University of Arizona, 1997); Ramey, "Heap of Work."

27. Berlin, *Many Thousands Gone*, p. 168; Pruneau, "All the Time," p. 15.

28. Bolzius quoted in Klaus G. Loewald, Beverly Starika, and Paul Taylor, "Johan Bolzius Answers a Questionnaire on Carolina and Georgia," *William and Mary Quarterly*, 3rd ser., 14 (1957): 257.

29. Heyward, *Seed from Madagascar,* p. 31; Allston, "Sea Coast Crops," p. 609. See Joyner, *Down by the Riverside*, p. 48, for a drawing by one planter descendant of women sowing rice in the African manner of covering the seed by foot.

30. T. Addison Richards, "The Rice Lands of the South," *Harper's New Monthly Magazine*, 19 (November 1859): 726.

31. See also Heyward, *Seed from Madagascar,* pp. 28, 31; Schwalm, *Hard Fight,* pp. 23,37; Frances Kemble, *Journal of a Residence on a Georgia Plantation in 1838–1839* [1863] (Athens: University of Georgia Press, 1984), p. 156; and Ramey, "Heap of Work." Elizabeth Pringle, one of the last Carolina planters, wrote in 1913 that among male laborers: "The hoe they consider purely a feminine implement." *Woman Rice Planter,* p. 79.

32. Schwalm, *Hard Fight*, p. 9.

33. Doar, *Rice and Rice Planting*, pp. 13–15; Joyner, *Down by the Riverside*, pp. 46–47.

34. Joyner, *Down by the Riverside*, p. 46. Indigo, planted on the higher lands behind the riverine rice fields, got under way in the 1740s but declined as a cash crop after the American Revolution. Charles Kovacik and John Winberry, *South Carolina: The Making of a Landscape* (Boulder: Westview Press, 1987), pp. 74–75; and Joyce Chaplin, *An Anxious Pursuit: Agricultural Innovation and Modernity in the Lower South, 1730–1815* (Chapel Hill: University of North Carolina Press, 1993), pp. 191–208. Indigo cultivation and dyeing diffused to West Africa from the Nile Valley circa A.D. 700–1100. See George Brooks, *Landlords and Strangers: Ecology, Society, and Trade in Western Africa, 1000–1630* (Boulder: Westview Press, 1993),

p. 56. On female slaves and indigo dyeing in West Africa, see Claire Robertson and Martin Klein, "Women's Importance in African Slave Systems," in Robertson and Klein, eds., *Women and Slavery in Africa* (Madison: University of Wisconsin Press, 1983), pp. 3–28, esp. pp. 15–16.

35. Pelatiah Webster, "Journal of a Visit to Charleston, 1765," in H. Roy Merrens, ed., *The Colonial South Carolina Scene: Contemporary Views, 1697–1774* (Columbia: University of South Carolina Press, 1977), p. 221.

36. Henry C. Dethloff, *A History of the American Rice Industry, 1685–1985* (College Station: Texas A&M Press, 1988), p. 23.

37. Converse Clowse, *Economic Beginnings in Colonial South Carolina, 1670–1730* (Columbia: University of South Carolina Press, 1971), p. 244; James Clifton, "The Rice Industry in Colonial America," *Agricultural History,* 55 (1981): 266–283, esp. pp. 280–281.

38. M. Eugene Sirmans, *Colonial South Carolina: A Political History, 1662–1763* (Chapel Hill: University of North Carolina Press, 1966), pp. 107–108; Clowse, *Economic Beginnings,* pp. 128–129; Clifton, "The Rice Industry," pp. 280–281. Demand for rice expanded during the eighteenth century throughout Europe since it was used for brewing beer and to make paper.

39. Richard Splatt, Charles Towne, to William Crisp, London, January 17, 1726, quoted in Dethloff, *American Rice Industry,* p. 11.

40. Heyward, *Seed from Madagascar,* p. 21; Leila Sellers, *Charleston Business on the Eve of the American Revolution* (Chapel Hill: University of North Carolina Press, 1934), pp. 151, 154–156; Clowse, *Economic Beginnings,* pp. 128–129.

41. Peter Wood, pers. comm., August 31, 1999, provides this observation.

42. Michael Mullin, *American Negro Slavery: A Documentary History* (Columbia: University of South Carolina Press, 1976). See related discussion by Clifton, "Rice Industry," p. 279, for the relevance of this view of South Carolina rice plantations during the colonial era.

43. Dethloff, *American Rice Industry,* p. 10.

44. Ibid.

45. Estimates appear in Coclanis, *Shadow,* p. 97.

46. Melville Herskovits, *The Myth of the Negro Past* (1941; Boston: Beacon Press, 1958); Wood, *Black Majority* and "It was a Negro"; Littlefield, *Rice and Slaves,* p. 105.

47. I. W. Burkhill, *A Dictionary of the Economic Plants of the Malay Peninsula,* 2 vols. (London: Crown Agents for the Colonies, 1935), 2:1601.

48. One rice pestle in the South Carolina State Museum, dating from the nineteenth century, weighs 8.5 pounds (Fritz Hamer, pers. comm.); those used in The Gambia typically weigh 7–10 pounds.

49. In many accounts of rice milling, husking refers to milling off the hulls as well as the bran. Onnie Lee Logan, as told to Katherine Clark, *Motherwit: An Alabama Midwife's Story* (New York: Dutton, 1989), p. 9. Among the Saramaka of Suriname men also make mortars and pestles. Sally Price, *Co-wives and Calabashes* (Ann Arbor: University of Michigan Press, 1993), p. 11.

50. Clowse, *Economic Beginnings,* p. 129. The Duke of Rochefoucault (1800, ii:446), quoted in Gray, *History of Agriculture,* 1:278.

51. Reference is to the merchant demand list of Josiah Smith, Jr., quoted in Sellers, *Charleston Business,* p. 68.

52. When rice is polished, many of its nutrient-bearing minerals are lost and the result may lead to the nutritional disease known as beriberi. On spoilage of cereal grains, see Dethloff, *American Rice Industry*, p. 35, and Carville Earle, *Geographical Inquiry and American Historical Problems* (Stanford: Stanford University Press, 1992), p. 114.

53. On rice grades, see U. B. Phillips, *American Negro Slavery* (New York: D. Appleton and Co., 1918), p. 90; Gray, *History of Agriculture*, 1:287.

54. J. W. Barnwell, ed., "Diary of Timothy Ford, 1785–1786," *South Carolina Historical and Genealogical Magazine*, 13 (1912): 183–184.

55. Quoted from James Freeman (1712) in R. Merrens, ed., *The Colonial South Carolina Scene* (Columbia: University of South Carolina Press, 1977), p. 46. On broken rice serving as food for slaves, see A. Pace, *Luigi Castiglioni's Viaggio: Travels in the United States of North America, 1785–87* (Syracuse: Syracuse University Press, 1983), p. 169.

56. On slave imports directly from Africa, see Berlin, *Many Thousands Gone*, pp. 313–315. On planter preferences for slaves familiar with rice growing with the shift to tidal production, see Littlefield, *Rice and Slaves;* and D. Richardson, "The British Slave Trade to Colonial South Carolina," *Slavery and Abolition*, 12 (1991): 135–172.

57. Wood, *Black Majority*, p. 58n86.

58. Clifton, "Rice Industry," p. 272.

59. Mark Catesby (1731–1747) in Merrens, *The Colonial South Carolina Scene*, p. 100. Bolzius (1751) mentions grinding rice in wooden mills.

60. Allston, "Memoir of the Introduction," p. 342; Gray, *History of Agriculture*, 1:282.

61. Doar, *Rice and Rice Planting*, p. 18, quoting a report by Dr. E. Elliot, *De Bow's Review*, 1851.

62. Allston, "Memoir of the Introduction," p. 342; J. Drayton, *A View of South Carolina* [1802] (Columbia: University of South Carolina Press, 1972), pp. 120–124; Sellers, *Charleston Business*, p. 150; V. S. Clark, *History of Manufactures in the U.S.*, 2 vols. (New York: Peter Smith, 1949), pp. 177–178; Gray, *History of Agriculture*, 1:280–283; Richard Porcher, "Rice Culture in South Carolina: A Brief History, the Role of the Huguenots, and Preservation of Its Legacy," *Transactions of the Huguenot Society of South Carolina*, 92 (1987): 11–22; Chaplin, *An Anxious Pursuit*, pp. 252–253.

63. George C. Rogers and David Chestnutt, eds., *The Papers of Henry Laurens* (Columbia: University of South Carolina Press, 1968–), 8:70–71.

64. Letter to Peter Le Poole from Henry Laurens (1772) in ibid., p. 409.

65. Mark Catesby, quoted in Merrens, *The Colonial South Carolina Scene*, p. 100.

66. Loewald, Starika, and Taylor, "Johan Bolzius," p. 259.

67. Berlin, *Many Thousands Gone*, p. 147.

68. Garden, quoted in Wood, *Black Majority*, p. 79.

69. *South Carolina Gazette*. Advertisement for patent to produce pounding mill by Villepontoux and Holmes, dated July 21–28, 1733.

70. Robert Deans, who had been a surveyor and builder for many years in Carolina prior to the American Revolution, in a note to the South Carolina Treasury, received November 10, 1776, in Rogers and Chestnutt, *Papers of Henry Laurens*, 8:70n5.

71. See Dusinberre, *Them Dark Days.*

72. Letter to John Lewis Gervais from Henry Laurens (March 2, 1773), in Rogers and Chestnutt, *Papers of Henry Laurens,* 8:634–635.

73. Mentioned in Sellers, *Charleston Business,* p. 27.

74. Phillips, *American Negro Slavery,* p. 249, quoted in Rosengarten, "African-American Lowcountry Basket," p. 225.

75. Sellers, *Charleston Business,* p. 28.

76. Berlin, *Many Thousands Gone,* p. 167.

77. Samuel G. Stoney, *Plantations of the South Carolina Low Country* (Charleston: Carolina Art Association, 1938), pp. 33–34.

78. Dethloff, *American Rice Industry,* p. 29; Chaplin, *An Anxious Pursuit,* p. 254. See also, Pace, *Viaggio,* p. 169. Mortar-and-pestle processing continued, however, with rice retained for plantation consumption. It also continued in areas where the main plantation crop was cotton but slaves planted rice as a provision crop. See Amelia Wallace Vernon, *African Americans at Mars Bluff, South Carolina* (Baton Rouge: Louisiana State University Press, 1993).

79. Correspondence between Alexander Garden, M.D., and the Royal Society of Arts, quoted in Wood, *Black Majority,* p. 79.

80. Allston, "Memoir of the Introduction," p. 342; Drayton, *View,* p. 151.

81. Carney fieldwork data, The Gambia, 1993.

82. Estimates of the weight of a peck of rice and other figures are drawn from Allston, "Memoir of the Introduction," p. 342; Phillips, *American Negro Slavery,* p. 252; Doar, *Rice and Rice Planting,* p. 18.

83. Pruneau, "All the Time," pp. 68, 97, 155. Unlike many other plantation duties, the task of rice processing seems not to have increased over time.

84. Estimates result from converting the shortest and longest processing times for hand milling a kilogram of rice in The Gambia; then conversion of kilograms to pounds at the 10- and 19-minute rate for the respective male and female task; and dividing those figures by 60 minutes to determine hours spent rice milling.

85. M. Karasch, "Slave Women on the Brazilian Frontier in the Nineteenth Century," in David B. Gaspar and Darleen C. Hine, eds., *More than Chattel* (Bloomington: University of Indiana Press, 1996), p. 86.

86. Melville Herskovits and Frances Herskovits, *Rebel Destiny: Among the Bush Negroes of Dutch Guiana* (New York: McGraw-Hill, 1934), p. 185. These authors provide additional detail on women's work in rice processing in describing the rhythm of one Saramaka woman, with child still asleep on her back, "stamping rice, hulls flying about her. Her mortar, which was made of a hollowed-out log, like a drum, was large and reached almost to her hips. On the ground was a large tray which she used for winnowing the rice. With slow, regular beats she lifted and dropped the pestle, and as her body swung with its slow motion the head of the sleeping child on her back rolled this way and that" (p. 3).

87. L. A. Moritz, *Grain Mills and Flour in Classical Antiquity* (Oxford: Oxford University Press, 1958), pp. 62, 74, 105, 115–116, 133–136. On the British use of hand-operated iron mills on slave ships for crushing coarse grains like maize for provisions, see Elizabeth Donnan, *Documents Illustrative of the History of the Slave Trade to America,* 4 vols. (Washington, D.C.: Carnegie Institution, 1930–1935), vol. 1 (1441–1700), p. 406.

88. Moritz, *Grain Mills,* pp. 29, 34, 74, 97, 133. The pattern of using female slaves for domestic work and food preparation was even evident in old Irish law

texts, which indicate that females performed the task of grinding cereal with a rotary quern in the early Christian period. F. Kelly, *Early Irish Farming* (Dublin: Dublin Institute for Advanced Studies, 1997), p. 439.

89. Claude Meillassoux, "Female Slavery," in C. Robertson and M. Klein, eds., *Women and Slavery in Africa* (Madison: University of Wisconsin Press, 1983), p. 56. On the gender division of labor, see M. Klein, "Women and Slavery in the Western Sudan," in Robertson and Klein, eds., *Women and Slavery*, pp. 85–86. On women and indigenous African slavery, see also Claude Meillassoux, *The Anthropology of Slavery: The Womb of Iron and Gold* (Chicago: University of Chicago Press, 1991).

90. M. Herskovits and F. Herskovits, *Rebel Destiny*, pp. 90–99.

91. S. Price, *Co-wives and Calabashes*, pp. 14–18, 25, 30–31. For detailed discussions on Saramaka history, see Richard Price, *The Guiana Maroons: A Historical and Bibliographical Introduction* (Baltimore: Johns Hopkins University, 1983).

92. The fragmentary evidence from South Carolina suggests that boys became involved at an early age in rice milling and that this was an outcome of plantation slavery. However, rice processing also became de-gendered among descendants of maroon communities in Suriname. While women and girls dominate mortar-and-pestle processing among contemporary Saramaka and Djuka communities, Djuka boys were occasionally observed hand-pounding rice this century in the interwar period. See M. C. Kahn, *Djuka: The Bush Negroes of Dutch Guiana* (New York: Viking, 1931), p. 86. Maroon communities were formed principally by male runaways, and necessity required that men pound cereals for consumption. See R. Price, *The Guiana Maroons*, p. 293; and S. Price, *Co-wives and Calabashes*, pp. 14–15, 18, 30–31.

93. John Vlach, *The Afro-American Tradition in Decorative Arts* (Athens: University of Georgia Press, 1992), pp. 3–5.

94. Quote from Caroline Couper Lovell, *The Golden Isles of Georgia* (Boston: Little, Brown, 1932), p. 187. The earliest representations of hand milling date to the 1920s and 1930s, when men and boys appear in photographs on former plantations, processing rice with a mortar and pestle.

95. Donnan, *Documents Illustrative*, 4:313, mentioned in Peter Wood, "More Like a Negro Country: Demographic Patterns in Colonial South Carolina, 1700–1740," in Stanley Engerman and Eugene Genovese, eds., *Race and Slavery in the Western Hemisphere: Quantitative Studies* (Princeton: Princeton University Press, 1975), pp. 131–171, esp. p. 154.

96. Report by South Carolina governor James Glen in 1754, quoted in Wood, "More Like a Negro Country," p. 132, from original citation in Donnan, *Documents Illustrative*, 4:313. But whether conditions improved on rice plantations in Carolina is contentious. Dusinberre, *Them Dark Days*, observes that work and living conditions jeopardized slave survival on rice plantations throughout the antebellum period.

97. Dusinberre, *Them Dark Days*.

98. Allston, "Introduction and Planting," p. 342.

99. Littlefield, *Rice and Slaves*, pp. 4–6.

5. African Rice and the Atlantic World

1. This discussion draws upon National Research Council, *Lost Crops of Africa* (Washington, D.C.: National Academy Press, 1996), pp. 29, 36; R. Charbolin,

"Rice in West Africa," in C. L. A. Leakey and J. B. Wills, eds., *Food Crops of the Lowland Tropics* (Oxford: Oxford University Press, 1977), pp. 7–25, esp. p. 12; and West Africa Rice Development Association (WARDA), *Annual Report* (Bouaké, Ivory Coast: WARDA, 1995), p. 27.

2. A. Chevalier, "Sur le riz africains du groupe Oryza glaberrima," *Revue de botanique appliquée et d'agriculture tropicale*, 17 (1937): 418. Chevalier, for example, distinguished *sativa* from *glaberrima* milling in West Africa by the fact that the latter can only be milled by hand with a mortar and pestle.

3. A. S. Salley, "Introduction of Rice into South Carolina," *Bulletin of the Historical Commission of South Carolina*, 6 (1919): 10–13. The difficulty in cleaning the rice suggests the mortar-and-pestle method of removing the hulls was still not widely known.

4. Ibid., p. 11.

5. On the introduction of the gold variety in the period around the American Revolution, see John Drayton, *A View of South Carolina* [1802] (Columbia: University of South Carolina Press, 1972), p. 125. Researchers at the International Center for Tropical Agriculture in Cali, Colombia, found the rice varieties. Dr. Thomas Hargrove, pers. comm., December 7, 1995. On the linkage of Carolina gold to Madagascar rice, see August Chevalier, "L'importance de la riziculture dans le domaine colonial français et l'orientation à donner aux récherches rizicoles," *Laboratoire d'agronomie coloniale* (1936): 41.

6. Mark Catesby, *The Natural History of Carolina, Florida, and the Bahama Islands*, 2 vols. (1743; London: B. White, 1771), 1:xviii.

7. See Duncan Heyward, *Seed from Madagascar* (Chapel Hill: University of North Carolina Press, 1937). On the Carolina white variety, see also R. F. W. Allston, "Memoir of the Introduction and Planting of Rice in South Carolina," *De Bow's Review*, 1 (1846): 606–607. Indirect support for Carolina rice development comes from South America, where the Carolina white, not gold, variety was imported for plantation rice development in the eastern Amazon in 1772. See Manoel Barata, *Formação histórico do Pará* (Belém, Brazil: Universidade Federal do Pará, 1973); C. R. Boxer, *The Dutch Seaborne Empire, 1600–1800* (London: Penguin, 1965), p. 193. Derk HilleRisLamber, a rice agronomist in Suriname, has found mention of a dryland white variety imported from Carolina in Dutch reports written before 1801, pers. comm., September 15, 1998. These observations are substantiated independently by R. F. W. Allston, "Essay on Sea Coast Crops," *De Bow's Review*, 16 (1854): 607, who noted the cultivation of Carolina white in Guiana.

8. P. Collinson, "Of the Introduction of Rice and Tar in Our Colonies," *Gentleman's Magazine*, 36, June 1766, pp. 278–280, cited in Salley, "Introduction of Rice," pp. 14–16.

9. Labat quoted in Gwendolyn Midlo Hall, *Africans in Colonial Louisiana* (Baton Rouge: Louisiana State University, 1992), p. 39.

10. Elizabeth Donnan, *Documents Illustrative of the History of the Slave Trade to America*, 4 vols. (Washington, D.C.: Carnegie Institution, 1930–1935), vol. 3 (1932), pp. 121, 376.

11. John Lawson, *A Voyage to Carolina* [1709], ed. Hugh Talmadge Lefler (Chapel Hill: University of North Carolina Press, 1967), pp. 81–82. On early rice seed introductions, also see Catesby, *The Natural History*; Drayton, *View of South Carolina*, p. 125; Allston, "Essay on Sea Coast," pp. 606–607; Allston, "Memoir of the Introduction," p. 324; Salley, "Introduction of Rice," pp. 10–11; Lewis Gray,

History of Agriculture in the Southern United States to 1860, 2 vols. (Gloucester, Mass.: Peter Smith, 1958), 1:277–284; and Daniel C. Littlefield, *Rice and Slaves* (Baton Rouge: Louisiana State University Press, 1981), p. 102.

12. Peter Wood, " 'It Was a Negro Taught them': A New Look at African Labor in Early South Carolina," *Journal of Asian and African Studies*, 9 (1974): 162–163, 170; Hall, *Colonial Louisiana*, p. 10.

13. Quoted in Karen Hess, *The Carolina Rice Kitchen: The African Connection* (Columbia: University of South Carolina Press, 1992), p. 19.

14. E. M. Betts, *Thomas Jefferson's Garden Book, 1766–1824* (Philadelphia: American Philosophical Society, 1944), p. 120.

15. On the correspondence between the sea captain, Nathaniel Cutting, and Jefferson, see Paul Richards, "Culture and Community Values in the Selection and Maintenance of African Rice," in Stephen Brush and Doreen Stabinsky, eds., *Valuing Local Knowledge: Indigenous People and Intellectual Property Rights* (Washington, D.C.: Island Press, 1996), pp. 216–220.

16. Ibid., p. 217.

17. Quote in ibid., p. 218; Betts, *Jefferson's Garden*, p. 380.

18. On *mutica* as another name for mountain or upland rice, see Richards, "Culture and Community," p. 218. On the characteristics of African and Asian rice, see R. Rose Innes, *A Manual of Ghana Grasses* (Surrey: Ministry of Overseas Development, 1977), pp. 193–194. African rice is also noted for its small and pear-shaped grains, bran of a red color, tough seed coat, smooth and hairless hulls, and a rounded, rather than pointed, ligule.

19. Betts, *Jefferson's Garden*, p. 381. Quote from December 1, 1808. At the time of Jefferson's experiments with *glaberrima*, most commercial rice was cleaned by machines, the mortar-and-pestle processing no longer characteristic of rice milling. In that case, perhaps Sally Hemmings, or her African grandmother, should have advised Jefferson to parboil the rice, thereby facilitating removal of the hulls through an entirely different process known to Africans. Paul Richards, pers. comm., January 31, 2000.

20. Betts, *Jefferson's Garden*, p. vii. Remarkably, Jefferson regarded the olive tree and the introduction of rain-fed rice cultivation as equal in historical importance to the Declaration of Independence and the guarantee of religious freedom.

21. Drayton, *View of South Carolina*, p. 125; Henry C. Dethloff, *A History of the American Rice Industry, 1685–1985* (College Station: Texas A&M Press, 1988).

22. Drayton, *View of South Carolina*, p. 125.

23. Ibid.; Allston, "Memoir of the Introduction." See Wood, "It Was a Negro," p. 163, on Guinea corn, and Catesby, *Natural History*, for other African introductions bearing a "Guinea" moniker.

24. In this quotation, husking refers to removing the bran as well as the hulls, since the product desired in European markets was white rice—which *glaberrima* can also become with much effort in hand milling. Mentioned in Hiko-Ichi Oka, "Report of Trip for Investigations of Rice in Latin American Countries," National Institute of Genetics, Mishima, Japan, 1961, p. 21.

25. On the propensity of the red hulls to adhere to grains of *glaberrima*, see NRC, *Lost Crops of Africa*, pp. 21, 29; Richards, "Culture and Community Values," p. 210.

26. See R. Gayozo, *Compéndio histórico-político dos princípios da lavoura do*

Maranhão (Paris: Fougeron, 1818); César Augusto Marques, *Dicionário histórico e geográfico da província do Maranhão* [1870] (Rio de Janeiro: Cia. Editôra Fon-Fone Seleta, 1970); T. Chermont, "Memória sobre a introducção de arroz branco no estado do Gram-Pará," *Revista Trimensal do Instituto Histórico Geográphico e Ethnográphico do Brasil,* 48 (1885): 770–784; Dauril Alden, "Manoel Luis Vieira: An Entrepreneur in Rio de Janeiro during Brazil's Eighteenth Century Agricultural Renaissance," *Hispanic American Historical Review* 39 (1959): 521–537; Manuel Nunes Dias, *Fomento e mercantilismo: a Companhia Geral do Grão Pará e Maranhão (1755–1778),* 2 vols. (Belém, Brazil: Universidade Federal do Pará, 1970); J. de Viveiros, *História do comércio do Maranhão, 1612–1895,* 3 vols. (São Luis, Brazil: Edição Facsimilar, 1895); Barata, *Formação histórico;* John Hemming, *Amazon Frontier* (London: Macmillan, 1987); Rosa Acevedo, *A escrita do história paraense* (Belém, Brazil: Universidade Federal do Pará, 1997), pp. 53–91.

27. Although rice was not domesticated in Brazil, a wild *Oryza* species did occur there, *O. glumaepatula.* G. C. X. Oliveira, "Padroes de variação fenotípica e ecologia de Oryzae (Poaceae) Selvagens da Amazônia" (M.A. thesis, University of São Paulo, Brazil, 1993). The reference to *O. mutica* appears in Alexandre Rodrigues Ferreira, writing in 1884, in "Viagem filosófica ao Rio Negro," *Revista do Instituto Histórico e Geográfico Brasileiro,* 48 (1983): 132, and in Acevedo, *Escríta do história,* p. 54.

28. Ferreira, "Viagem filosófica ao Rio Negro," quoted in Acevedo, *Escríta do história,* p. 54.

29. Gayozo, *Compéndio histórico,* p. 192; Barata, *Formação histórico;* Acevedo, *Escrita do história.* The Brazilian rice plantation system was made possible through slave imports by two monopoly trading companies, the Companhia de Grão Pará e Maranhão and another one for Pernambuco in the country's northeast sugar plantation region. The Maranhão company obtained most of its slaves from the Upper Guinea coastal ports of Cacheu and Bissau, located in the heart of West Africa's rice region in contemporary Guinea-Bissau, while the Pernambuco company concentrated on importing slaves from Luanda, Angola. Herbert S. Klein, "The Portuguese Slave Trade from Angola in the Eighteenth Century," in J. E. Inikori, ed., *Forced Migration: The Impact of the Export Slave Trade on African Societies* (London: African Publishing Company, 1982), pp. 221–241.

30. Marques, *Dicionário,* pp. 435–436; Barata, *Formação histórico;* Acevedo, *Escrita do história.*

31. Acevedo, *Escrita do história.*

32. See, for instance, A. Chevalier and O. Roehrich, "Sur l'origine botanique des riz cultivés," *Comptes rendus de l'Academie de Sciences,* 159 (1914): 560–562; Chevalier, "Sur le riz"; A. Camus and P. Viguier, "Riz flottants du Soudan," *Revue de botanique appliquée et d'agriculture tropicale,* 17 (1937): 201–203. Four varieties of *mutique* of five-month duration are identified by P. Viguier, *La riziculture indigène au Soudan français* (Paris: Larose, 1939).

33. No archaeological research to date has sought to locate African rice in the Americas, yet rice samples should be well preserved in the perpetually wet soils of rice regions (historical archaeologist Leland Ferguson, pers. comm.). Phytolith analysis, which examines the silica signature that distinguishes all grasses, could be used to distinguish Asian from African rice (anthropologist Deborah Pearsall, pers. comm.). Brazil, Cuba, and Suriname are representative of tropical American areas

with an early history of rice cultivation where the crop remains important. In these areas, germplasm collections from farmer fields may contain *glaberrima* varieties.

34. A. Vaillant, "Milieu cultural et classification des varietés de riz des Guyanes français et hollandaise," *Revue internationale de botanique appliquée et d'agriculture tropicale*, 33 (1948): 520–529; R. Portères, "Présence ancienne d'une varieté cultivée d'*Oryza glaberrima* en Guyane française," *Journal d'agriculture tropicale et de botanique appliquée*, 11, no. 12 (1955): 680; R. Portères, "Historique sur les premiers échantillons d'*Oryza glaberrima* St. recueillis en Afrique," *Journal d'agriculture tropicale et de botanique appliquée*, 11, nos. 10–11 (1955): 535–537; R. Portères, "Un problème ethnobotanique: relations entre le riz flottant du Rio Nunez et l'origine médinigérienne des Baga de la Guinée française," *Journal d'agriculture tropicale et de botanique appliquée*, 11, nos. 10–11 (1955): 538–542; R. Portères, "Riz subspontanés et riz sauvages en El Salvador (Amérique Centrale)," *Journal d'agriculture tropicale et de botanique appliquée*, 7, nos. 9–10 (1960): 441–446; R. Portères, "Les noms de riz en Guinée," *Journal d'agriculture tropicale et de botanique appliquée*, 13, no. 9 (1966): 1–346; R. Portères, "African Cereals: Eleusine, Fonio, Black Fonio, Teff, Brachiaria, Paspalum, Pennisetum, and African Rice," in J. Harlan, J. De Wet, and A. Stemler, eds., *Origins of African Plant Domestication* (The Hague: Mouton, 1976), p. 441; Richards, "Culture and Community Values," p. 218.

35. R. Price, *First-Time: The Historical Vision of an Afro-American People* (Baltimore: Johns Hopkins University Press, 1983); R. Price, *The Guiana Maroons: A Historical and Bibliographical Introduction* (Baltimore: Johns Hopkins University Press, 1983).

36. Portères, "Problème ethno-botanique."

37. Walter Rodney, *A History of the Upper Guinea Coast, 1545 to 1800* (New York: Monthly Review Press, 1970), p. 112. On stateless societies and the Atlantic slave trade, see Walter Hawthorne, "The Production of Slaves Where There Was No State: The Guinea-Bissau Region, 1450–1815," *Slavery and Abolition*, 20, no. 2 (1999): 97–124.

38. Quoted in Littlefield, *Rice and Slaves*, pp. 93–95.

39. Melville Herskovits and Frances Herskovits, *Rebel Destiny: Among the Bush Negroes of Dutch Guiana* (1934; New York: McGraw-Hill, 1971), p. 100; Sally Price, *Co-wives and Calabashes* (Ann Arbor: University of Michigan Press, 1993), pp. 25, 32.

40. Jean Hurault, *La vie materielle des noirs refugies Boni et des indiens Wayana du Haut-Maroni* (Paris: ORSTOM, 1965); Richard Price, *First-Time*.

41. Vaillant, "Milieu cultural," p. 522. The French were not the only scientists interested in maroon rice varieties. As early as 1907, the Dutch head of agricultural research in Suriname, Dr. Van Hall, sent the maroon variety "Bruin Missie" to U.S. plant breeders. It became the parent stock of several U.S. rice varieties, including one popular marketed variety, "Gulfrose." Derk HilleRisLamber, rice agronomist, Suriname, pers. comm., December 20, 1998.

42. Price, *First-Time*, pp. 129–133. R. Price, ed., *Maroon Societies: Rebel Slave Communities in the Americas* (Baltimore: Johns Hopkins University Press, 1979), p. 298, records another maroon legend which again indicates the importance of rice technology to females: "Here is the story of our ancestors and of their difficulties while they were at war with the bakra ["whites"] . . . some of the women,

frightened by the noise of battle, would run and take a rice mortar, heft it onto their shoulders, and flee with it into the forest."

43. Peter Wood, *Black Majority* (New York: Knopf, 1974), p. 36, fn 2.

44. British ships carried some to freedom in Nova Scotia; others escaped to the North, but most were reenslaved as the losing forces abandoned them. See Ira Berlin, *Many Thousands Gone: The First Two Centuries of Slavery in North America* (Cambridge, Mass.: Harvard University Press, 1998), p. 304; Charles Kovacik and John Winberry, *South Carolina: The Making of a Landscape* (Boulder: Westview Press, 1987), p. 85. The impact of slave flight from Carolina rice plantations may have involved greater numbers, with some twelve thousand fleeing slavery, even though most were captured and reenslaved in Florida or the Caribbean. Edward Ball, *Slaves in the Family* (New York: Farrar, Straus and Giroux, 1998), p. 230.

45. Berlin, *Many Thousands Gone*, p. 302. This was the result of slaves fleeing to freedom and some being manumitted by the English or transported to Nova Scotia.

46. See, for instance, Ira Berlin and Philip Morgan, eds., *Cultivation and Culture* (Charlottesville: University Press of Virginia, 1993); and David B. Gaspar and Darlene C. Hine, eds., *More than Chattel: Black Women and Slavery in the Americas* (Bloomington: University of Indiana Press, 1996).

47. Amelia Wallace Vernon, *African Americans at Mars Bluff, South Carolina* (Baton Rouge: Louisiana State University Press, 1993).

48. Joyce Chaplin, *An Anxious Pursuit: Agricultural Innovation and Modernity in the Lower South, 1730–1815* (Chapel Hill: University of North Carolina Press, 1993), p. 156. Her quote draws upon a question raised by Wood, *Black Majority*, pp. 119–122. Sesame (or benne, as it is called in Africa and by the Gullah) came to South Carolina via Africa but is an Asian domesticate that had diffused to Africa long before the Atlantic slave trade. See Richard S. MacNeish, *The Origins of Agriculture and Settled Life* (Norman: University of Oklahoma Press, 1992), pp. 299–318. Peanuts, while domesticated in South America, were also brought to the U.S. South via West Africa. See W. E. Grimé, *Ethno-botany of the Black Americans* (Algonac, Mich.: Reference Publications, 1979), pp. 19–20, 73.

49. On the importance and role of black sailors on transatlantic ships during the eighteenth century, see James Walvin, *Black Ivory* (Washington, D.C.: Howard University Press, 1994); W. Jeffrey Bolster, *Black Jacks: African American Seamen in the Age of Sail* (Cambridge, Mass.: Harvard University Press, 1997).

50. Berlin, *Many Thousands Gone*.

51. See Wood, *Black Majority*, pp. 167–191; Charles Joyner, *Down by the Riverside* (Urbana: University of Illinois Press, 1984), pp. 2, 196–224; Littlefield, *Rice and Slaves*, p. 31.

52. Pierre Moreau, quoted in John Thornton, *Africa and Africans in the Making of the Atlantic World, 1400–1680* (New York: Cambridge University Press, 1992), p. 174.

53. Ibid.

54. Ibid., pp. 170–171; Gert Oostinde, "The Economics of Surinam Slavery," *Economics and Social History in the Netherlands*, 5 (1993): 17; Orlando Ribeiro, *Aspectos e problemas da expansão portuguésa*, Estudos de Ciencias Políticas e Sociais (Lisbon: Junta de Investigações do Ultramar, 1962), pp. 152–156. Sloane on Jamaica is quoted in Grimé, *Ethno-botany of the Black Americans*, p. 154.

55. On African plants used in Afro-Brazilian religion, see Robert Voeks, *Sacred Leaves of Candomblé* (Austin: University of Texas Press, 1997).

56. See, for example, Claude Meillassoux, "Female Slavery," in C. Robertson and M. Klein, eds., *Women and Slavery in Africa* (Madison: University of Wisconsin Press, 1983), pp. 49–66; Meillassoux, *The Anthropology of Slavery: The Womb of Iron and Gold* (Chicago: University of Chicago Press, 1991); and the volumes edited by Inikori, *Forced Migration*, and Robertson and Klein, *Women and Slavery*.

57. Grimé, *Ethno-botany of the Black Americans;* Lucille Brockway, *Science and Colonial Expansion: The Role of the British Royal Botanical Gardens* (New York: Academic Press, 1979); Chaplin, *An Anxious Pursuit.* Missionaries, especially Moravians, were also involved in plant collection. Their role in supplying plants to German botanists from remote areas in conjunction with their missionary activity has yet to receive proper emphasis, especially as they were involved in missionizing Surinamese maroons from the 1770s and indigenous communities of the Americas. On the Moravians in Suriname, see R. Price, *First-Time* and "Subsistence on the Plantation Periphery: Crops, Cooking, and Labour among Eighteenth-Century Suriname Maroons," *Slavery and Abolition*, 12, no. 1 (1991): 107–127, for their role in sending seeds to German botanists, like Steudel; see also J. Cayouette and S. Darbyshire, "Taxa Described by Steudel from the Labrador Plants Collected by the Moravian Missionary Albrecht and Distributed by Hohenacker," *Taxon*, 43, no. 2 (1994): 169–171.

58. Grimé, in *Ethno-botany of the Black Americans* (1976), investigated secondary sources for early mention in the Americas of crops grown by slaves.

59. Ibid.

60. An important beginning in this direction is the survey of Caribbean subsistence cultivation provided by R. Berleant-Schiller and L. Pulsipher, "Subsistence Cultivation in the Caribbean," *New West Indian Guide*, 60, nos. 1–2 (1986): 1–40.

6. Legacies

1. David Doar, *Rice and Rice Planting in the South Carolina Low Country* (1936; Charleston: Charleston Museum, 1970), p. 8.

2. Duncan Heyward, *Seed from Madagascar* (Chapel Hill: University of North Carolina Press, 1937).

3. See Joyce Chaplin, *An Anxious Pursuit: Agricultural Innovation and Modernity in the Lower South, 1730–1815* (Chapel Hill: University of North Carolina Press, 1993).

4. On agrarian creolization, see Paul Richards, "Culture and Community Values in the Selection and Maintenance of African Rice," in Stephen Brush and Doreen Stabinsky, eds., *Valuing Local Knowledge: Indigenous People and Intellectual Property Rights* (Washington, D.C.: Island Press, 1996), pp. 209–229. For a suggestive and appropriately titled book on this idea for colonial Virginia, see Mechal Sobel, *The World They Made Together* (Princeton: Princeton University Press, 1987).

5. Judith A. Carney, "The Role of African Rice and Slaves in the History of Rice Cultivation in the Americas," *Human Ecology*, 26, no. 4 (1998): 525–545.

6. Alfred W. Crosby, *The Columbian Exchange: Biological and Cultural Consequences of 1492* (Westport, Conn.: Greenwood Press, 1972), p. xiv.

7. Ibid.; Karl W. Butzer, "Biological Transfer, Agricultural Change, and En-

vironmental Implications of 1492," *International Germplasm Transfer: Past and Present*, Special Publication 23. (Madison: Crop Science Society of America, 1995), pp. 3–29. On other indigenous African crops, see Timothy Weiskel, "Toward an Archaeology of Colonialism: Elements in the Ecological Transformation of the Ivory Coast," in Donald Worster, ed., *The Ends of the Earth* (New York: Cambridge University Press, 1988), pp. 141–171.

8. See, for instance, Robert Edgar Conrad, *Children of God's Fire* (University Park: Pennsylvania State University Press, 1994), pp. 26, 34.

9. Alfred Crosby, *Ecological Imperialism: The Biological Expansion of Europe, 900–1900* (New York: Cambridge University Press, 1986).

10. Dennis Cosgrove, "Geography Is Everywhere: Culture and Symbolism in Human Landscapes," in D. Gregory and R. Walford, eds., *Horizons in Human Geography* (Basingstoke: Macmillan Education, 1989); Carville Earle, *Geographical Inquiry and American Historical Problems* (Stanford: Stanford University Press, 1992); Judith A. Carney, "Rice Milling, Gender, and Slave Labour in Colonial South Carolina," *Past and Present*, 153 (1996), and "The Role of African Rice."

11. On the history of the introduction and diffusion of particular crops to Africa, see W. O. Jones, *Manioc in Africa* (Stanford: Stanford University Press, 1959); Marvin Miracle, *Maize in Tropical Africa* (Madison: University of Wisconsin Press, 1966); Crosby, *The Colombian Exchange;* and Stanley B. Alpern, "The European Introduction of Crops into West Africa in Precolonial Times," *History in Africa*, 19 (1992): 13–43; Weiskel, "Archaeology of Colonialism," pp. 161–165.

12. National Research Council, *Lost Crops of Africa* (Washington, D.C.: National Academy Press, 1996), pp. 12–13.

13. Lucille Brockway, *Science and Colonial Expansion: The Role of the British Royal Botanic Gardens* (New York: Academic Press, 1979); J. Kloppenburg, *First the Seed* (New York: Cambridge University Press, 1990); Chaplin, *An Anxious Pursuit;* Carney, "Rice Milling."

14. Peter Wood, *Black Majority* (New York: Knopf, 1974); Ira Berlin, *Many Thousands Gone: The First Two Centuries of Slavery in North America* (Cambridge, Mass.: Harvard University Press, 1998).

15. On the eve of the American Revolution one out of five persons was a slave. But only a small percentage succeeded in achieving freedom. The retreating British Navy carried away about 10,000 to 12,000 slaves from Charleston and another 5,000 to 6,000 from Savannah. More than 8,000 low-country slaves were turned over to their loyalist owners and resettled in East Florida, then under English rule (1763–1784). Some escaped to Florida's Seminole Indians; others were sold to Caribbean plantations. See Jane Landers, *Black Society in Spanish Florida* (Urbana: University of Illinois Press, 1999), p. 159; Berlin, *Many Thousands Gone*, pp. 303–304; Edward Ball, *Slaves in the Family* (New York: Farrar, Straus and Giroux, 1998), pp. 214–216.

16. P. J. Staudenraus, *The African Colonization Movement, 1816–1865* (New York: Columbia University Press, 1961), pp. 8–9; Elliott P. Skinner, *African Americans and U.S. Policy toward Africa, 1850–1924* (Washington, D.C.: Howard University Press, 1992).

17. Staudenraus, *African Colonization*, places the number of repatriated blacks at 350; Basil Davidson, *A History of West Africa* (New York: Anchor, 1965), pp. 300–306, lists 411.

18. Mary Cable, *Black Odyssey* (New York: Penguin, 1977), p. 137.

19. Ibid.

20. Ibid., pp. 137–138.

21. Skinner, *African Americans*, pp. 48–49; Staudenraus, *African Colonization*, pp. 49–50.

22. Abolition only had an impact on the part of the Upper Guinea Coast under the sphere of British influence, and even there slavery continued clandestinely. To the south in areas of Portuguese control, slavery was practiced for many more decades.

23. Skinner, *African Americans*, p. 39.

24. Mavis C. Campbell, *Back to Africa: George Ross and the Maroons* (Trenton, N.J.: Africa World Press, 1993), pp. i–ii.

25. Ibid., p. 305; Skinner, *African Americans*, p. 27; Martin R. Delany and Robert Campbell, *Search for a Place: Black Separatism and Africa* [1860], ed. Howard Bell (reprint, Ann Arbor: University of Michigan Press, 1969), p. 15.

26. Roland Portères, "Primary Cradles of Agriculture in the African Continent," in J. D. Fage and R. A. Oliver, eds., *Papers in African Prehistory* (Cambridge: Cambridge University Press, 1970), pp. 43–58; Delany and Campbell, *Search for a Place*, p. 56; Richards, "Culture and Community Values," pp. 209–229, esp. pp. 211–212.

27. Rhodes House mss., Afr.s 945, Oxford University, n.d., located in correspondence from the 1770s.

28. Slaves facing transport across the Middle Passage frequently attempted revolt or committed suicide, but only rarely were they successful in taking over as they did on the *Amistad*. See Sidney Kaplan, "Black Mutiny on the Amistad," in Jules Chametzky and Sidney Kaplan, eds., *Black and White in American Culture* (Amherst: University of Massachusetts Press, 1969), pp. 291–295.

29. Covey became free when a British ship captured the outbound Portuguese slaver that was illegally carrying him and hundreds of others across the Middle Passage. The recaptives were set free in Freetown, where Covey obtained a mission education and passage, later, as a sailor on a British ship bound for New York. A desperate search by the legal defense team for someone who could understand the Amistads located Covey just in time for the trial.

30. John W. Barber, *A History of the Amistad Captives* (New Haven: E. L. and J. W. Barber, 1840), pp. 9–15.

31. Christopher Fyfe, *A History of Sierra Leone* (London: Oxford University Press, 1962), pp. 220–223, 420; Barber, *A History of the Amistad Captives*, pp. 1–32.

32. Pierre Viguier, *La riziculture indigène au Soudan français* (Paris: Larose, 1939), pp. 53, 68–69.

33. August Chevalier, "L'importance de la riziculture dans le domaine colonial français et l'orientation à donner aux récherches rizicoles," *Laboratorie d'agronomie coloniale* (1936): 41; Chevalier, "Sur le riz africains du groupe Oryza glaberrima," *Revue de botanique appliquée et d'agriculture tropicale*, 17 (1937): 418; and Roland Portères, "Les noms de riz en Guinée," *Journal d'agriculture tropicale et de botanique appliquée*, 13, no. 9 (1966): 58–59, 224–225, 310–311.

34. Viguier, *La riziculture indigène*, p. 42.

35. Ibid.

36. L. Becker and R. Diallo, "The Cultural Diffusion of Rice Cropping in Côte d'Ivoire," *Geographical Review*, 86, no. 4 (1996): 513.

References

Books

Acevedo, Rosa. 1997. *A escrita do história paraense*. Belém, Brazil: Universidade Federal do Pará.

Achaya, K. T. 1994. *Indian Food: A Historical Companion*. New York: Oxford University Press.

Adams, W. M. 1992. *Wasting the Rain: Rivers, People, and Planning in Africa*. Minneapolis: University of Minnesota.

Adanson, M. 1759. *A Voyage to Senegal, the Isle of Goree, and the River Gambia*. London: Nourse.

Adas, Michael. 1989. *Machines as the Measure of Men*. Ithaca, N.Y.: Cornell University Press.

Alford, Jeffrey, and Naomi Duguid. 1998. *Seductions of Rice*. New York: Artisan.

Atkins, John. 1735. *Voyage to Guinea, Brasil, and the West Indies*. Originally published in London. UCLA microfilm.

Azurara, Gomes Eanes de. 1899. *The Chronicle of the Discovery and Conquest of Guinea*, vol. 2. London: Hakluyt.

Baldwin, K. D. S. 1957. *The Niger Agricultural Project*. Oxford: Basil Blackwell.

Ball, Edward. 1998. *Slaves in the Family*. New York: Farrar, Straus and Giroux.

Barata, Manoel. 1973. *Formação histórico do Pará*. Belém, Brazil: Universidade Federal do Pará.

Barber, John W. 1840. *A History of the Amistad Captives*. New Haven: E. L. and J. W. Barber.

Barry, Boubacar. 1998. *Senegambia and the Atlantic Slave Trade*. Cambridge: Cambridge University Press.

Berlin, Ira. 1998. *Many Thousands Gone: The First Two Centuries of Slavery in North America*. Cambridge, Mass.: Harvard University Press.

Berlin, Ira, and Philip Morgan. 1993. "Labor and the Shaping of Slave Life in the

Americas." In Berlin and Morgan, eds., *Cultivation and Culture*. Charlottesville: University Press of Virginia, pp. 1–45.

Berlioux, Etienne-Félix. 1874. *André Brüe ou l'origine de la Colonie française du Sénégal*. Paris: Librairie de Guillaumin.

Betts, E. M. 1944. *Thomas Jefferson's Garden Book, 1766–1824*. Philadelphia: American Philosophical Society.

Biroli, Giovani. 1807. *Del riso: trattato economico-rustico*. Milan: Tipografia di Giovanni Silvestri.

Blake, J. W. 1977. *West Africa: Quest for God and Gold, 1545–1578*. London: Curzon Press.

Bolster, W. Jeffrey. 1997. *Black Jacks: African American Seamen in the Age of Sail*. Cambridge, Mass.: Harvard University Press.

Bordiga, Oreste, and Leopoldo Silvestrini. 1880. *Del riso e della sua coltivazione*. Novara: Tipografia della Rivista di Contabilità.

Bovill, E. W. 1958. *The Golden Trade of the Moors*. London: Oxford University Press.

Boxer, C. R. 1965. *The Dutch Seaborne Empire, 1600–1800*. London: Penguin.

Bray, Francesca. 1986. *The Rice Economies*. Oxford: Blackwell.

Brockway, Lucille. 1979. *Science and Colonial Expansion: The Role of the British Royal Botanic Gardens*. New York: Academic Press.

Brooks, George. 1993. *Landlords and Strangers: Ecology, Society, and Trade in Western Africa, 1000–1630*. Boulder: Westview Press.

Brush, Stephen, and Doreen Stabinsky, eds. 1996. *Valuing Local Knowledge: Indigenous People and Intellectual Property Rights*. Washington, D.C.: Island Press.

Buddenhagen, I. W., and G. J. Persley, eds. 1978. *Rice in Africa*. London: Academic Press.

Burkhill, I. W. 1935. *A Dictionary of the Economic Plants of the Malay Peninsula*. 2 vols. London: Crown Agents for the Colonies.

Butzer, Karl. 1995. "Biological Transfer, Agricultural Change, and Environmental Implications of 1492." In *International Germplasm Transfer: Past and Present*, Special Publication 23. Madison: Crop Science Society of America, pp. 3–29.

Cable, Mary. 1977. *Black Odyssey*. New York: Penguin.

Caillié, René. 1830. *Travels through Central Africa to Timbuctoo, and across the Great Desert, to Morocco, Performed in the Years 1824–1828*. London: Colburn and Bentley.

Campbell, Mavis C. 1993. *Back to Africa: George Ross and the Maroons*. Trenton, N.J.: Africa World Press.

Candolle, A. de. 1964 [1886]. *Origin of Cultivated Plants*. New York: Hafner.

Canot, Theodore. 1928. *Adventures of an African Slaver*. New York: Albert & Charles Boni.

Carpenter, A. 1978. "The History of Rice in Africa." In I. Buddenhagen and J. Persley, eds., *Rice in Africa*. London: Academic Press, pp. 3–10.

Carreira, António. 1984. *Os Portuguêses nos rios de Guiné, 1500–1900*. Lisbon: privately published.

Catesby, M. 1771 [1743]. *The Natural History of Carolina, Florida, and the Bahama Islands*. 2 vols. London: B. White.

Catling, D. 1992. *Rice in Deep Water*. London: International Rice Research Institute/Macmillan.

Chaplin, Joyce. 1993. *An Anxious Pursuit: Agricultural Innovation and Modernity in the Lower South, 1730–1815.* Chapel Hill: University of North Carolina.

Charbolin, R. 1977. "Rice in West Africa." In C. L. A. Leakey and J. B. Wills, eds., *Food Crops of the Lowland Tropics.* Oxford: Oxford University Press, pp. 7–25.

Childe, V. G. 1951. *Man Makes Himself.* New York: Mentor.

Clark, V. S. 1949. *History of Manufactures in the U.S.* 2 vols. New York: Peter Smith.

Clowse, Converse. 1971. *Economic Beginnings in Colonial South Carolina, 1670–1730.* Columbia: University of South Carolina.

Coclanis, Peter. 1989. *The Shadow of a Dream.* New York: Oxford University Press.

Connah, Graham. 1987. *African Civilizations.* New York: Cambridge University Press.

Conrad, Robert Edgar. 1994. *Children of God's Fire.* University Park: Pennsylvania State University Press.

Cosgrove, Dennis. 1989. "Geography Is Everywhere: Culture and Symbolism in Human Landscapes." In D. Gregory and R. Walford, eds., *Horizons in Human Geography.* Basingstoke: Macmillan Education, pp. 118–134.

Creel, Margaret W. 1988. *A Peculiar People: Slave Religion and Community Culture among the Gullahs.* New York: New York University Press.

Crone, G. 1937. *The Voyages of Cadamosto.* London: Hakluyt.

Crosby, Alfred W. 1972. *The Columbian Exchange: Biological and Cultural Consequences of 1492.* Westport, Conn.: Greenwood Press.

———— 1986. *Ecological Imperialism: The Biological Expansion of Europe, 900–1900.* New York: Cambridge University Press.

Curtin, Philip. 1969. *The Atlantic Slave Trade.* Madison: University of Wisconsin Press.

———— 1975. *Economic Change in Pre-Colonial Africa.* Madison: University of Wisconsin Press.

———— 1990. *The Rise and Fall of the Plantation Complex.* Cambridge: Cambridge University Press.

Daniel, P. 1985. *Breaking the Land: The Transformation of Cotton, Tobacco, and Rice Cultures since 1880.* Urbana: University of Illinois Press.

Dantzig, Albert van. 1982. "Effects of the Atlantic Slave Trade on Some West African Societies." In J.E. Inikori, *Forced Migration.* London: Hutchinson University Library, pp. 187–201.

David, P. 1980. *Les navétannes: histoire des migrants saisonniers de l'arachide en Sénégambie des origines a nos jours.* Dakar, Senegal: Nouvelles Editions africaine.

Davidson, Basil. 1965. *A History of West Africa.* New York: Doubleday.

Davies, K. G. 1970. *The Royal African Company.* New York: Atheneum.

de Brahm, John Gerar William. 1971. "De Brahm's Report." In Louis de Vorsey, Jr., ed., *Report on the General Survey in the Southern District of North America.* Columbia: University of South Carolina Press, pp. 61–131.

Delany, Martin R., and Robert Campbell. 1969 [1860]. *Search for a Place: Black Separation and Africa.* Edited by Howard Bell. Reprint. Ann Arbor: University of Michigan Press.

Derman, W. 1973. *Serfs, Peasants, and Socialists.* Berkeley: University of California Press.

Dethloff, Henry C. 1988. *A History of the American Rice Industry, 1685–1985.* College Station: Texas A&M Press.

Doar, David. 1970 [1936]. *Rice and Rice Planting in the South Carolina Low Country.* Charleston: Charleston Museum.

Donelha, A. 1977. *An Account of Sierra Leone and the Rivers of Guinea and Cape Verde.* Lisbon: Junta de Investigacões Cientificados.

Donnan, Elizabeth. 1930–1935. *Documents Illustrative of the History of the Slave Trade to America.* 4 vols. Washington, D.C.: Carnegie Institution.

Drayton, John. 1972 [1802]. *A View of South Carolina.* Columbia: University of South Carolina Press.

Duncan, T. B. 1972. *Atlantic Islands: Madeira, the Azores, and the Cape Verdes in Seventeenth Century Commerce and Navigation.* Chicago: University of Chicago Press.

Dusinberre, William. 1996. *Them Dark Days.* Oxford: Oxford University Press.

Earle, Carville. 1992. *Geographical Inquiry and American Historical Problems.* Stanford: Stanford University Press.

Edwards, P. 1967. *Equiano's Travels.* London: Heinemann.

Ferguson, Leland. 1992. *Uncommon Ground: Archaeology and Early African America, 1650–1800.* Washington, D.C.: Smithsonian.

Fernandes, Valentim. 1951. *Description de la Côte Occidentale d'Afrique.* Translation and notes by T. Monod, A. Teixeira da Mota, and R. Mauny. Bissau, Guinea-Bissau: Centro de Estudos de Guiné Portuguêsa.

Flanders, Ralph Betts. 1933. *Plantation Slavery in Georgia.* Chapel Hill: University of North Carolina Press.

Forbes, Jack. 1993. *Africans and Native Americans.* Chicago: University of Chicago Press.

Franke, R., and B. Chasin. 1980. *Seeds of Famine.* Trenton, N.J.: Allanheld.

Funari, Pedro Paulo de Abreu. 1996. "A arqueologia de Palmares." In João José Reis and Flávio dos Santos Gomes, eds., *Liberdade por um fio.* São Paulo: Companhia das Letras, pp. 26–51.

Fyfe, Christopher. 1962. *A History of Sierra Leone.* London: Oxford University Press.

Gallais, Jean. 1967. *Le Delta Intérieur du Niger: étude de géographie régionale.* Dakar, Senegal: Memoires de l'Institut Fondamental d'Afrique Noire.

Gamble, D. 1957. *The Wolof of Senegambia, Together with Notes on the Lebu and the Serer.* Ethnographic Survey of Africa, 14. London: International African Institute.

Gamble, D., and P. E. H. Hair, eds. 1999. *The Discovery of River Gambra by Richard Jobson (1623).* London: Hakluyt.

Gaspar, David B., and Darlene C. Hine, eds. 1996. *More than Chattel: Black Women and Slavery in the Americas.* Bloomington: Indiana University Press.

Gayozo, Raymundo Jozé de Souza. 1818. *Compéndio histórico-político dos princípios da lavoura do Maranhão.* Paris: Fougeron.

Gibb, H. A. R. 1969. *Ibn Battuta: Travels in Asia and Africa, 1325–1354.* London: Routledge & Kegan Paul.

Gilroy, Paul. 1993. *The Black Atlantic: Modernity and Double Consciousness.* Cambridge, Mass.: Harvard University Press.

Glen, James. 1951 [1761]. "A Description of South Carolina: Containing Many Curious and Interesting Particulars Relating to the Civil, Natural, and Commercial History of That Colony." In Chapman J. Milling, ed., *Colonial South*

Carolina: Two Contemporary Descriptions. Columbia: University of South Carolina Press, pp. 2–96.

Glick, Thomas F. 1970. *Irrigation and Society in Medieval Valencia.* Cambridge, Mass.: Harvard University Press.

Golberry, S. M. X. 1803. *Travels in Africa, Performed during the Years 1785, 1786, and 1787, in the Western Countries of This Continent.* 2 vols. Translated by William Mudford. London: R. Bent and J. Mudie.

Grant, D. 1968. *The Fortunate Slave.* New York: Oxford University Press.

Gray, Lewis. 1958. *History of Agriculture in the Southern United States to 1860.* 2 vols. Gloucester, Mass.: Peter Smith.

Grimé, W. E. 1979. *Ethno-botany of the Black Americans.* Algonac, Mich.: Reference Publications.

Grist, D. H. 1968. *Rice.* 4th ed. London: Longmans, Green and Co.

Guida, Giovanni. 1838. *Manuale di risocoltura.* Novara: Tipografia Nazionale di P. Busconi.

Hall, Gwendolyn Midlo. 1992. *Africans in Colonial Louisiana.* Baton Rouge: Louisiana State University Press.

Harlan, Jack. 1975. *Crops and Man.* Madison: Crop Science Society of America.

———— 1989a. "Wild-Grass Seed Harvesting in the Sahara and Sub-Sahara of Africa." In D. R. Harris and G. C. Hillman, eds., *Foraging and Farming: The Evolution of Plant Exploitation.* London: Unwin Hyman, pp. 79–98.

———— 1989b. "The Tropical African Cereals." In D. R. Harris and G. C. Hillman, eds., *Foraging and Farming.* London: Unwin Hyman, pp. 335–343.

Harlan, Jack, J. De Wet, and A. Stemler. 1976. *Origins of African Plant Domestication.* The Hague: Mouton.

Haudricourt, A. 1987. *La technologie science humaine.* Paris: Editions de la Maison des Sciences de l'Homme.

Hemming, John. 1978. *Red Gold.* Cambridge, Mass.: Harvard University Press.

Herskovits, Melville. 1958 [1941]. *The Myth of the Negro Past.* Boston: Beacon.

Herskovits, Melville, and Frances Herskovits. 1971 [1934]. *Rebel Destiny: Among the Bush Negroes of Dutch Guiana.* New York: McGraw-Hill.

Hess, Karen. 1992. *The Carolina Rice Kitchen: The African Connection.* Columbia: University of South Carolina Press.

Heyward, Duncan. 1937. *Seed from Madagascar.* Chapel Hill: University of North Carolina Press.

Hilliard, Sam B. 1978. "Antebellum Tidewater Rice Culture in South Carolina and Georgia." In James Gibson, ed., *European Settlement and Development in North America: Essays on Geographical Change in Honour and Memory of Andrew Hill Clark.* Toronto: University of Toronto Press, pp. 91–115.

Hoehne, F. C. 1937. *Botánica e agricultura no Brasil no século XVI.* São Paulo: Companhia Editora Nacional.

Hopkins, A. G. 1973. *An Economic History of West Africa.* New York: Columbia University Press.

House, Albert Virgil. 1954. *Planter Management and Capitalism in Ante-Bellum Georgia.* New York: Columbia University Press.

Hurault, Jean. 1965. *La vie materielle des noirs réfugiés Boni et des indiens Wayana du Haut-Maroni: Agriculture, économie, et habitat.* Paris: ORSTOM.

Inikori, J. E., ed. 1982. *Forced Migration.* London: African Publishing Company.

Innes, R. Rose. 1977. *A Manual of Ghana Grasses.* Surrey: Ministry of Overseas Development.

Irving, John B. 1969. *A Day on the Cooper River.* Charleston: R. K. Bryant Co.

James, C. L. R. 1989 [1938]. *Black Jacobins.* New York: Vintage Books.

Jefferson, Thomas. 1984. *Thomas Jefferson: Writings.* Edited by M. D. Peterson. New York: Library of America.

Jobson, Richard. 1904 [1623]. *The Golden Trade.* Devonshire: Speight and Walpole.

Jones, Adam. 1983. *From Slaves to Palm Kernels.* Wiesbaden: Franz Steiner.

Jones, W. O. 1959. *Manioc in Africa.* Stanford: Stanford University Press.

Jordan, Terry G. 1981. *Trails to Texas: Southern Roots of Western Cattle Ranching.* Lincoln: University of Nebraska Press.

Joyner, Charles. 1984. *Down by the Riverside.* Urbana: University of Illinois Press.

Kahn, M. C. 1931. *Djuka: The Bush Negroes of Dutch Guiana.* New York: Viking.

Kaplan, Sidney. 1969. "Black Mutiny on the Amistad." In Jules Chametzky and Sidney Kaplan, eds., *Black and White in American Culture.* Amherst: University of Massachusetts Press, pp. 291–297.

Karasch, M. 1996. "Slave Women on the Brazilian Frontier in the Nineteenth Century." In David B. Gaspar and Darleen C. Hine, eds., *More than Chattel.* Bloomington: University of Indiana Press, pp. 79–96.

Kelly, F. 1997. *Early Irish Farming.* Dublin: Dublin Institute for Advanced Studies.

Kemble, Frances. 1984 [1863]. *Journal of a Residence on a Georgia Plantation in 1838–1839.* Athens: University of Georgia Press.

Klein, Herbert S. 1982. "The Portuguese Slave Trade from Angola in the Eighteenth Century." In J. E. Inikori, ed., *Forced Migration: The Impact of the Export Slave Trade on African Societies.* London: African Publishing Company, pp. 21–41.

——— 1983. "Women and Slavery in the Western Sudan." In C. Robertson and M. Klein, eds., *Women and Slavery in Africa.* Madison: University of Wisconsin Press, pp. 67–88.

Kloppenburg, Jack. 1990. *First the Seed.* New York: Cambridge University Press.

Kovacik, Charles, and John Winberry. 1987. *South Carolina: The Making of a Landscape.* Boulder: Westview.

Labat, Père Jean-Baptiste. 1728. *Nouvelle relation de l'Afrique occidentale contenant une description exacte du Sénégal et des Pais situés entre le Cap Blanc et la Rivière de Serrlione, quesqu'à plus de 300 lieues en avant dans les Terres.* 5 vols. Paris.

Landers, Jane. 1999. *Black Society in Spanish Florida.* Urbana: University of Illinois.

Lane, M. 1984. *Architecture of the Old South: South Carolina.* Savannah: Beehive Press.

Lawson, J. 1967 [1709]. *A Voyage to Carolina.* Edited by Hugh Talmadge Lefler. Chapel Hill: University of North Carolina Press.

Lewicki, Tadeusz. 1974. *West African Food in the Middle Ages.* Cambridge: Cambridge University Press.

Linares, Olga. 1992. *Power, Prayer, and Production.* Cambridge: Cambridge University Press.

Littlefield, Daniel C. 1981. *Rice and Slaves.* Baton Rouge: Louisiana State University Press.

Logan, Onnie Lee. 1989. *Motherwit: An Alabama Midwife's Story* (as told to Katherine Clark). New York: Dutton.

Lovejoy, Paul. 1983. *Transformations in Slavery.* Cambridge: Cambridge University Press.

Lovell, Caroline Couper. 1932. *The Golden Isles of Georgia*. Boston: Little, Brown.

MacNeish, Richard S. 1992. *The Origins of Agriculture and Settled Life*. Norman: University of Oklahoma Press.

Mallard, R. Q. 1892. *Plantation Life before Emancipation*. Richmond: Whitte and Shepperson.

Marcus, Jacob R., and Stanley Chyet. 1974. *Historical Essay on the Colony of Surinam 1788*. Cincinnati: American Jewish Archives.

Marques, César Augusto. 1970 [1870]. *Dicionário histórico e geográfico da província do Maranhão*. Rio de Janeiro: Cia. Editôra Fon-Fone Seleta.

Martin, Bernard, and Mark Spurrell. 1962. *The Journal of a Slave Trader (John Newton), 1750–1754*. London: Epworth Press.

Martin, Phyllis. 1972. *The External Trade of the Loango Coast, 1576–1870*. Oxford: Clarendon Press.

McIntosh, Roderick James. 1998. *The Peoples of the Middle Niger*. Malden, Mass.: Blackwell.

McIntosh, S. K., and R. J. McIntosh. 1980. *Prehistoric Investigations in the Region of Jenne, Mali*. Part 2: *The Regional Survey and Conclusions*. Cambridge: Cambridge University Press.

——— 1993. "Cities without Citadels: Understanding Urban Origins along the Middle Niger." In T. Shaw, P. Sinclair, B. Andah, and A. Okpoko, eds., *The Archaeology of Africa: Food, Metals, and Towns*. New York: Routledge, pp. 622–641.

Meillasoux, C. 1983. "Female Slavery." In C. Robertson and M. Klein, eds., *Women and Slavery in Africa*. Madison: University of Wisconsin Press, pp. 49–66.

——— 1991. *The Anthropology of Slavery: The Womb of Iron and Gold*. Chicago: University of Chicago Press.

Merrens, R., ed. 1977. *The Colonial South Carolina Scene*. Columbia: University of South Carolina Press.

Mintz, Sidney, and Richard Price. 1992 [1976]. *The Birth of African-American Culture: An Anthropological Perspective*. Boston: Beacon Press.

Miracle, Marvin. 1966. *Maize in Tropical Africa*. Madison: University of Wisconsin Press.

Mollien, G. 1820. *Travels in Africa*. London: Sir Richard Phillips & Co.

Monod, Th., R. Mauny, and G. Duval. 1959. *De la première découverte de la Guinée: Récit par Diogo Gomes (fin XV siècle)*. Bissau: Centro de Estudos da Guiné Portuguêsa.

Moore, Francis. 1738. *Travels into the Inland Parts of Africa*. London: Edward Cave.

Morgan, Philip D. 1998. *Slave Counterpoint: Black Culture in the Eighteenth-Century Chesapeake and Lowcountry*. Chapel Hill: University of North Carolina Press.

Moritz, L. A. 1958. *Grain Mills and Flour in Classical Antiquity*. Oxford: Oxford University Press.

Mota, A. Teixeira da. 1978. *Some Aspects of Portuguese Colonisation and Sea Trade in West Africa in the 15th and 16th Centuries*. Bloomington: African Studies Program, Indiana University.

Mullin, Michael. 1976. *American Negro Slavery: A Documentary History*. Columbia: University of South Carolina Press.

Nairne, Thomas. 1989 [1710]. "A Letter from South Carolina." In Jack P. Greene, ed., *Selling a New World: Two Colonial South Carolina Promotional Pamphlets*. Columbia: University of South Carolina Press, pp. 33–73.

National Research Council (NRC). 1996. *Lost Crops of Africa*. Washington, D.C.: National Academy Press.

Nunes Dias, Manuel. 1970. *Fomento e mercantilismo: a Companhia Geral do Grão Pará e Maranhão (1755–1778)*. 2 vols. Belém, Brazil: Universidade Federal do Pará.

Orwin, C. S. 1949. *A History of English Farming*. London: Thos. Nelson and Sons.

Otto, John S. 1989. *The Southern Frontiers, 1607–1860*. New York: Greenwood Press.

Pace, A. 1983. *Luigi Castiglioni's Viaggio: Travels in the United States of North America, 1785–87*. Syracuse, N.Y.: Syracuse University Press.

Park, Mungo. 1954 [1799]. *Travels into the Interior of Africa*. London: Eland.

Paulme, Denise. 1954. *Les gens du Riz*. Paris: Librairie Plon.

Pélissier, P. 1966. *Les paysans du Sénégal*. St. Yrieix, France: Imprimerie Fabrègue.

Pereira, Duarte Pacheco. 1937. *Esmeraldo de situ orbis*. Translated by G. H. T. Kimble. London: Hakluyt.

Phillips, Ulrich B. 1918. *American Negro Slavery*. New York: D. Appleton and Co.

Phillipson, D. 1993. *African Archaeology*. Cambridge: Cambridge University Press.

Piso, Wilhelm. 1957. *História natural e médica da India ocidental*. Rio de Janeiro: Instituto Nacional do Livro.

Portères, Roland. 1970. "Primary Cradles of Agriculture in the African Continent." In J. D. Fage and R. A. Oliver, eds., *Papers in African Prehistory*. Cambridge: Cambridge University Press, pp. 43–58.

——— 1976. "African Cereals: Eleusine, Fonio, Black Fonio, Teff, Brachiaria, Paspalum, Pennisetum, and African Rice." In J. Harlan, J. De Wet, and A. Stemler, eds., *Origins of African Plant Domestication*. The Hague: Mouton, pp. 409–452.

Price, Richard, ed. 1979. *Maroon Societies: Rebel Slave Communities in the Americas*. Baltimore: Johns Hopkins University Press.

——— 1983a. *First-Time: The Historical Vision of an Afro-American People*. Baltimore: Johns Hopkins University Press.

——— 1983b. *The Guiana Maroons: A Historical and Bibliographical Introduction*. Baltimore: Johns Hopkins University Press.

Price, Richard, and Sally Price. 1992. *Stedman's Surinam*. Baltimore: Johns Hopkins University Press.

Price, Sally. 1993. *Co-wives and Calabashes*. Ann Arbor: University of Michigan Press.

Pringle, Elizabeth [Pennington, Patience, pseud.]. 1961 [1914]. *A Woman Rice Planter*. Cambridge, Mass.: Harvard University Press.

Ribeiro, Orlando. 1962. *Aspectos e problemas da expansão portuguésa*. Estudos de Ciencias Políticas e Sociais. Lisbon: Junta de Investigações do Ultramar.

Richards, Paul. 1985. *Indigenous Agricultural Revolution*. London: Hutchinson.

——— 1986. *Coping with Hunger*. London: Allen and Unwin.

——— 1996. "Culture and Community Values in the Selection and Maintenance of African Rice." In S. Brush and D. Stabinsky, eds., *Valuing Local Knowledge: Indigenous People and Intellectual Property Rights*. Washington, D.C.: Island Press, pp. 209–229.

Robertson, Claire, and Martin Klein. 1983. "Women's Importance in African Slave Systems." In C. Robertson and M. Klein, eds., *Women and Slavery in Africa*. Madison: University of Wisconsin, pp. 3–28.

Roche, Christian. 1985. *Histoire de la Casamance.* Dakar, Senegal: Karthala.

Rochefoucault-Liancourt, François Alexandre Frederic [Duke of]. 1800. *Travels through the United States of North America, the Country of the Iroquois, and Upper Canada in the Years 1795, 1796, and 1797.* 4 vols. London.

Rodney, Walter. 1970. *A History of the Upper Guinea Coast, 1545 to 1800.* New York: Monthly Review Press.

———— 1982. "African Slavery and Other Forms of Social Oppression on the Upper Guinea Coast in the Context of the Atlantic Slave Trade." In J. E. Inikori, ed., *Forced Migration.* London: African Publishing Company, pp. 6–70.

Roe, Daphne. 1973. *A Plague of Corn: The Social History of Pellagra.* Ithaca, N.Y.: Cornell University Press.

Rogers, George C., and David Chestnutt, eds. 1981–. *The Papers of Henry Laurens.* 14 vols. Columbia: University of South Carolina Press.

Salaman, Redcliffe. 1949. *The History and Social Influence of the Potato.* Cambridge: Cambridge University Press.

Sass, Herbert Ravenel, and D. E. Huger Smith. 1936. *A Carolina Rice Plantation of the Fifties.* New York: Morrow.

Sauer, C. O. 1975. *Seeds, Spades, Hearths, and Herds.* Cambridge, Mass.: MIT Press.

Schwalm, Leslie. 1997. *A Hard Fight for We: Women's Transition from Slavery to Freedom in South Carolina.* Urbana: University of Illinois Press.

Schwartz, Stuart B. 1998. *Sugar Plantations in the Formation of Brazilian Society: Bahia, 1550–1835.* New York: Cambridge University Press.

Sellers, Leila. 1934. *Charleston Business on the Eve of the American Revolution.* Chapel Hill: University of North Carolina Press.

Shange, Ntozake. 1998. *If I Can Cook/You Know God Can.* Boston: Beacon Press.

Shaw, T., P. Sinclair, B. Andah, and A. Okpoko, eds. 1993. *The Archaeology of Africa: Food, Metals, and Towns.* New York: Routledge.

Sheehan, Kate. 1994. In Janice Jorgensen, ed., *Encyclopedia of Consumer Brands.* Vol. 1. Washington, D.C.: St. James Press, pp. 608–609.

Sirmans, M. Eugene. 1966. *Colonial South Carolina: A Political History, 1662–1763.* Chapel Hill: University of North Carolina Press.

Skinner, Elliott P. 1992. *African Americans and U.S. Policy toward Africa, 1850–1924.* Washington, D.C.: Howard University Press.

Smith, Julia Floyd. 1973. *Slavery and Plantation Growth in Antebellum Florida, 1821–1860.* Gainesville: University of Florida Press.

———— 1985. *Slavery and Rice Culture in Low Country Georgia, 1750–1860.* Knoxville: University of Tennessee Press.

Snyder, Francis. 1981. *Capitalism and Legal Change.* New York: Academic Press.

Sobel, Mechal. 1987. *The World They Made Together.* Princeton: Princeton University Press.

Spolverini, Giambattista. 1813. *La coltivazione del riso.* Milan: Tipografia dé Classici Italiano.

Staudenraus, P. J. 1961. *The African Colonization Movement, 1816–1865.* New York: Columbia University Press.

Stewart, Mart A. 1996. *What Nature Suffers to Groe.* Athens: University of Georgia Press.

Stoney, Samuel G. 1938. *Plantations of the Carolina Low Country.* Charleston: Carolina Art Association.

Strickland, James Scott. 1983. " 'No More Mud Work': The Struggle for the Con-

trol of Labor and Production in Low Country South Carolina, 1863–1880."
In Walter J. Fraser and Winfred B. Moore, eds., *The Southern Enigma.* Westport, Conn.: Greenwood Press, pp. 43–62.

Suret-Canale, Jean. 1988. *Essays on African History.* Trenton, N.J.: Africa World
Press.

Swan, D. E. 1975. *The Structure and Profitability of the Antebellum Rice Industry.* New
York: Arno Press.

TeBrake, William H. 1985. *Medieval Frontier: Culture and Ecology in Rijnland.* College Station: Texas A&M University Press.

Thornton, J. 1992. *Africa and Africans in the Making of the Atlantic World, 1400–
1680.* New York: Cambridge University Press.

Trouillot, Michel-Rolph. 1995. *Silencing the Past: Power and the Production of History.* Boston: Beacon Press.

Vavilov, N. I. 1951. *The Origin, Variation, Immunity, and Breeding of Cultivated
Plants: Selected Writings.* New York: Ronald Press.

Vernon, Amelia Wallace. 1993. *African Americans at Mars Bluff, South Carolina.* Baton Rouge: Louisiana State University Press.

Ver Steeg, Clarence. 1984. *Origins of a Southern Mosaic.* Athens: University of
Georgia Press.

Viguier, Pierre. 1939. *La riziculture indigène au Soudan français.* Paris: Larose.

Viveiros, J. de. 1895. *História do comércio do Maranhão, 1612–1895.* 3 vols. São Luís,
Brazil: Edição Facsimilar.

Vlach, John. 1990. *The Afro-American Tradition in Decorative Arts.* Athens: University of Georgia.

——— 1992. *Charleston Blacksmith.* Columbia: University of South Carolina Press.

Voeks, Robert. 1997. *Sacred Leaves of Candomblé.* Austin: University of Texas Press.

Walvin, J. 1994. *Black Ivory.* Washington, D.C.: Howard University Press.

Watson, Andrew M. 1983. *Agricultural Innovation in the Early Islamic World: The
Diffusion of Crops and Farming Techniques, 700–1100.* New York: Cambridge
University Press.

Webster, Pelatiah. 1977. "Journal of a Visit to Charleston, 1765." In H. Merrens,
ed., *The Colonial South Carolina Scene.* Columbia: University of South Carolina
Press, pp. 218–226.

Weiskel, Timothy. 1988. "Toward an Archaeology of Colonialism: Elements in the
Ecological Transformation of the Ivory Coast." In D. Worster, ed., *The Ends of
the Earth.* New York: Cambridge University Press, pp. 141–171.

West, Robert C. 1957. *The Pacific Lowlands of Colombia.* Baton Rouge: Louisiana
State University Press.

Winterbottom, Thomas. 1803. *An Account of the Native Africans in the Neighbourhood of Sierra Leone.* London: C. Whittingham.

Wolf, Eric. 1982. *Europe and the People without History.* Berkeley: University of California Press.

Wood, Betty. 1984. *Slavery in Colonial Georgia.* Athens: University of Georgia
Press.

Wood, Peter. 1974. *Black Majority.* New York: Knopf.

——— 1975. "More Like a Negro Country: Demographic Patterns in Colonial
South Carolina, 1700–1740." In S. L. Engerman and E. D. Genovese, eds.,

Race and Slavery in the Western Hemisphere: Quantitative Studies. Princeton: Princeton University Press, pp. 131–171.

Worster, Donald. 1985. *Rivers of Empire.* New York: Oxford University Press.

———— 1988. *The Ends of the Earth.* New York: Columbia University Press.

Wright, Donald R. 1997. *The World and a Very Small Place in Africa.* Armonk, N.Y.: M. E. Sharpe.

Wright, J. Leitch, Jr. 1981. *The Only Land They Knew.* New York: Free Press.

Articles

Alden, Dauril. 1959. "Manoel Luís Vieira: An Entrepreneur in Rio de Janeiro during Brazil's Eighteenth Century Agricultural Renaissance." *Hispanic American Historical Review,* 39: 521–537.

Allston, R. F. W. 1846. "Memoir of the Introduction and Planting of Rice in South Carolina." *De Bow's Review,* 1: 320–357.

———— 1854. "Essay on Sea Coast Crops." *De Bow's Review,* 16: 589–615.

Alpern, Stanley B. 1992. "The European Introduction of Crops into West Africa in Precolonial Times." *History in Africa,* 19: 13–43.

Andriesse, W., and L. O. Fresco. 1991. "A Characterization of Rice-Growing Environments in West Africa." *Agriculture, Ecosystems, and Environment,* 33: 377–395.

Barnwell, J. W., ed. 1912. "Diary of Timothy Ford, 1785–1786." *South Carolina Historical and Genealogical Magazine,* 13: 181–251.

Becker, Larry, and Roger Diallo. 1996. "The Cultural Diffusion of Rice Cropping in Côte d'Ivoire." *Geographical Review,* 86 (4): 505–528.

Berleant-Schiller, R., and L. Pulsipher. 1986. "Subsistence Cultivation in the Caribbean." *New West Indian Guide,* 60 (1–2): 1–40.

Bullio, Pieraldo. 1969. "Problemi e geografia della risicoltura in Piemonte nei secoli XVII e XVIII." *Annali della Fondazione Luigi Einaudi,* 3: 37–112.

Camus, A., and P. Viguier. 1937. "Riz flottants du Soudan." *Revue de botanique appliquée et d'agriculture tropicale,* 17: 201–203.

Carney, Judith. 1996. "Rice Milling, Gender, and Slave Labour in Colonial South Carolina." *Past and Present,* 153: 108–134.

———— 1998. "The Role of African Rice and Slaves in the History of Rice Cultivation in the Americas." *Human Ecology,* 26 (4): 525–545.

Carney, Judith, and Richard Porcher. 1993. "Geographies of the Past: Rice, Slaves, and Technological Transfer in South Carolina." *Southeastern Geographer,* 33 (2): 127–147.

Carney, Judith, and Michael Watts. 1990. "Manufacturing Dissent: Work, Gender, and the Politics of Meaning in a Peasant Society," *Africa,* 60: 207–241.

Cayouette, J., and S. Darbyshire. 1994. "Taxa Described by Steudel from the Labrador Plants Collected by the Moravian Missionary Albrecht and Distributed by Hohenacker." *Taxon,* 43 (2): 169–171.

Chermont, T. 1885. "Memória sobre a introducção de arroz branco no estado do Gram-Pará." *Revista trimensal do Instituto Histórico Geográphico e Ethnográphico do Brasil,* 48: 770–784.

Chevalier, August. 1925. "Époques auxquelles des plantes cultivés et des mauvaises herbes pantropiques se sont répandues dans les pays chauds de l'ensemble du globe." *Revue de botanique appliquée et d'agriculture tropicale* (1925): 443–448.

────── 1932. "Les céréales des regions subsahariennes et des oasis." *Revue de botanique appliquée et d'agriculture tropicale* (1932): 742–759.

────── 1936. "L'importance de la riziculture dans le domaine colonial français et l'orientation à donner aux récherches rizicoles." *Laboratoire d'agronomie coloniale* (Paris), pp. 27–45.

────── 1937a. "Sur le riz africains du groupe Oryza glaberrima." *Revue de botanique appliquée et d'agriculture tropicale*, 17: 413–418.

────── 1937b. "La culture de riz dans la Vallée du Niger." *Revue de botanique appliquée et d'agriculture tropicale*, 190: 44–50.

────── 1938. "Le Sahara, centre d'origine de plantes cultivés." *Mémoires de la Société de Biogéographie*, 6: 307–322.

Chevalier, A., and O. Roehrich. 1914. "Sur l'origine botanique des riz cultivés." *Comptes rendus de l'Academie de Sciences*, 159: 560–562.

Clifton, J. 1973. "Golden Grains of White: Rice Planting on the Lower Cape Fear." *North Carolina Historical Review*, 50: 365–393.

────── 1981. "The Rice Industry in Colonial America." *Agricultural History*, 55: 266–283.

Coclanis, P., and J. Komlos. 1987. "Time in the Paddies: A Comparison of Rice Production in the Southeastern United States and Lower Burma in the Nineteenth Century." *Social Science History*, 11 (3): 343–354.

Collinson, P. 1766. "Of the Introduction of Rice and Tar in Our Colonies." *Gentleman's Magazine*, June, pp. 278–280.

Cowen, M. 1984. "Early Years of the Colonial Development Corporation: British State Enterprise Overseas during Late Colonialism." *African Affairs*, 83 (330): 63–75.

Crist, Raymond E. 1957. "Rice Culture in Spain." *Scientific Monthly*, 84 (1): 66–74.

Currens, G. 1976. "Women, Men, and Rice: Agricultural Innovation in Northwestern Liberia." *Human Organization*, 35 (4): 355–365.

David, M. 1987. "The Impact of Rural Transformation on the Productive Role of Liberian Women: The Case of Rice Production." *Liberia-Forum*, 3/4: 27–37.

Dresch, J. 1949. "La riziculture en Afrique occidentale." *Bulletin de la Société de Géographie*, 312: 295–312.

Easterby, J. H. 1941. "The South Carolina Rice Factor as Revealed in the Papers of Robert F. W. Allston." *Journal of Southern History*, 7 (2): 160–172.

Ferreira, Alexandre Rodrigues. 1884. "Viagem filosófica ao Rio Negro." *Revista do Instituto Histórico e Geográfico Brasileiro*, 48: 132–137.

Gresham, Charles A., and Donal D. Hook. 1982. "Rice Fields of South Carolina: A Resource Inventory and Management Policy Evaluation." *Coastal Zone Management Journal*, 9: 183–203.

Hahn, S. 1982. "Hunting, Fishing, and Foraging: Common Rights and Class Relations in the Post-Bellum South." *Radical History Review*, 26: 37–64.

Hawley, Norman. 1949. "The Old Plantations in and around the Santee Experimental Forest." *Agricultural History*, 23: 86–91.

Hawthorne, Walter. 1999. "The Production of Slaves Where There Was No State: The Guinea-Bissau Region, 1450–1815," *Slavery and Abolition*, 20 (2): 97–124.

Herskovits, Melville. 1930. "The Culture Areas of Africa." *Africa*, 3: 67–73.

Jones, Adam. 1990. "Decompiling Dapper: A Preliminary Search for Evidence." *History in Africa*, 17: 171–209.

Lecce, Michele. 1959. "Un'azienda risiera veronese nel XVII e XVIII secolo." *Economia e storia*, 1: 64–80.

Lericollais, A., and J. Schmitz. 1984. "La calebasse et la houe," *Cah. ORSTOM*, sér. Sci. Hum., 20 (3–4): 427–452.

Linares, Olga. 1981. "From Tidal Swamp to Inland Valley: On the Social Organization of Wet Rice Cultivation among the Diola of Senegal." *Africa*, 5: 557–594.

Loewald, Klaus G., Beverly Starika, and Paul Taylor. 1957. "Johan Bolzius Answers a Questionnaire on Carolina and Georgia." *William and Mary Quarterly*, 3rd ser., 14: 218–261.

Marzouk-Schmitz, Y. 1984. "Instruments aratoires, systèmes de cultures, et différenciation intra-ethnique." *Cahiers ORSTOM*, sér. Sci. Hum., 20 (3–4): 399–425.

Matory, J. Lorand. 1999. "The English Professors of Brazil: On the Diasporic Roots of the Yorùbá Nation." *Comparative Studies in Society and History*, 41 (1): 72–103.

Mauny, R. 1953. "Notes historiques autour des principales plantes cultivés d'Afrique occidentale." *Bulletin de l'IFAN*, 4 (2): 718.

McIntosh, R. J., and S. K. McIntosh. 1981. "The Inland Niger Delta before the Empire of Mali: Evidence from Jenne-jeno." *Journal of African History*, 22: 1–22.

McIntosh, S. K., and R. J. McIntosh. 1984. "The Early City in West Africa: Towards an Understanding." *African Archaeological Review*, 2: 73–98.

Messedaglia, Luigi. 1938. "Per la storia delle coltura nostre piante alimentari: il riso." *Rivista di storia delle scienze mediche e naturali*, 20: 1–15.

Monastersky, R. 1991. "Satellites Expose Myth of Marching Sahara." *Science News*, 140: 38.

Morgan, Philip D. 1972. "Work and Culture: The Task System and the World of Low Country Blacks, 1700 to 1880." *William and Mary Quarterly*, 3rd ser., 39: 563–599.

Neil, George. 1996. "Archaeologists Uncover 'Rice Trunk.' " *Friends of Drayton Hall Interiors*, 15 (2): 4–5.

Oostinde, Gert. 1993. "The Economics of Surinam Slavery." *Economics and Social History in the Netherlands*, 5: 1–24.

ORSTOM. 1984. "Les instruments aratoires en Afrique tropicale." *Cahiers ORSTOM*, ser. Sci. Hum., 20 (3–4).

Paulme, Denise. 1957. "Des rizicultures africaines: les Baga (Guinée française)." *Les cahiers d'outre-mer*, 39: 257–278.

Porcher, Richard. 1987. "Rice Culture in South Carolina: A Brief History, the Role of the Huguenots, and Preservation of Its Legacy." *Transactions of the Huguenot Society of South Carolina*, 92: 11–22.

Portères, Roland. 1950. "Vieilles agricultures de l'Afrique intertropicale: Centres d'origine et de diversification variétale primaires et berceaux d'agricultures antérieurs au XVIe siècle." *L'agronomie tropicale*, 5 (9–10): 489–507.

——— 1955a. "Presence ancienne d'une varieté cultivée d'*Oryza glaberrima* en

Guyane française." *Journal d'agriculture tropicale et de botanique appliquée*, 11 (12): 680.

——— 1955b. "Historique sur les premiers échantillons d'*Oryza glaberrima* St. recueillis en Afrique." *Journal d'agriculture tropicale et de botanique appliquée*, 11 (10–11): 535–537.

——— 1955c. "Un problème ethno-botanique: relations entre le riz flottant du Rio Nunez et l'origine médinigérienne des Baga de la Guinée française." *Journal d'agriculture tropicale et de botanique appliquée*, 11 (10–11): 538–542.

——— 1960. "Riz subspontanés et riz sauvages en El Salvador (Amérique centrale)." *Journal d'agriculture tropicale et de botanique appliquée*, 7 (9/10): 441–446.

——— 1966. "Les noms des riz en Guinée." *Journal d'agriculture tropicale et de botanique appliquée*, 13 (9): 1–346.

Post, L. 1940. "The Rice Country of Southwestern Louisiana." *Geographical Review*, 30 (4): 574–590.

Price, Richard. 1991. "Subsistence on the Plantation Periphery: Crops, Cooking, and Labour among Eighteenth-Century Suriname Maroons." *Slavery and Abolition*, 12 (1): 107–127.

Ramey, Daina. 1998. " 'She Do a Heap of Work': An Analysis of Female Slave Labor on Glynn County Rice and Cotton Plantations," *Georgia Historical Quarterly*, 82 (4): 707–734.

Raulin, H. M. 1984. "Techniques agraires et instruments aratoires au sud du Sahara," *Cah. ORSTOM*, sér. Sci. Hum., 20 (3–4): 339–358.

Ravenel, Edmund. 1859. "The Limestone Springs of St. John's, Berkeley." *Proceedings of the Elliott Society of Science and Art of Charleston, South Carolina*, Feb. 1, pp. 28–32.

Richards, T. Addison. 1859. "The Rice Lands of the South." *Harper's New Monthly Magazine*, 19, November, pp. 721–738.

Richardson, D. 1991. "The British Slave Trade to Colonial South Carolina." *Slavery and Abolition*, 12: 125–172.

Rochevicz, R. J. 1932. "Documents sur le genre Oryza." *Revue de botanique appliquée et d'agriculture tropicale*, 135: 949–961.

Salley, A. S. 1919. "Introduction of Rice into South Carolina," *Bulletin of the Historical Commission of South Carolina* (Columbia), 6.

Schwartz, Stuart B. 1977. "Resistance and Accommodation in Eighteenth-Century Brazil: The Slaves' View of Slavery." *Hispanic American Historical Review*, 57: 69–81.

Sigaut, F. 1984. "Essai d'identification des instruments à bras de travail de sol" *Cah. ORSTOM*, sér. Sci. Hum., 20 (3–4): 359–374.

Stewart, Mart A. 1991. "Rice, Water, and Power: Landscapes of Domination and Resistance in the Lowcountry, 1790–1880." *Environmental History Review*, 15: 47–64.

Stickney, Gardner. 1896. "Indian Use of Wild Rice." *American Anthropologist*, 9 (4): 115–122.

Swindell, K. 1980. "Serawoolies, Tillibunkas, and Strange Farmers: The Development of Migrant Groundnut Farming along the Gambia River, 1848–95." *Journal of African History*, 21: 93–104.

Szumowski, G. 1957. "Fouilles au norde du Macina et dans la région de Ségou," *Bulletin de l'IFAN*, ser. B (1–2): 224–258.

Tempany, H. A. 1932. "The Italian Rice Industry." *Malaysian Agricultural Journal*, 274–292.

Thilmans, G. 1971. "Le Sénégal dans l'Oeuvre d'Offried Dapper." *Bulletin de l'IFAN*, ser. B., 33: 508–563.

Turner, M. 1993. "Overstocking the Range: A Critical Analysis of the Environmental Science of Sahelian Pastoralism." *Economic Geography*, 69 (4): 402–421.

Tymowski, M. 1971. "Les domaines des princes de Songhay (Soudan occidental): comparaison avec la grande propriété foncière au début de l'époque féodal," *Annales*, 15: 1637–58.

Vaillant, A. 1948. "Milieu cultural et classification des varietés de riz des Guyanes français et hollandaise." *Revue internationale de botanique appliquée et d'agriculture tropicale*, 33: 520–529.

Viguier, Pierre. 1937. "La riziculture indigène au Soudan français. Première Partie." *Annales agricoles d'Afrique Occidentale française et etrangère*, 1: 287–326.

Webber, Mabel L., ed. 1931. "Letters from John Stewart to William Dunlop." *South Carolina Historical and Genealogical Magazine*, 32: 1–75.

Whitten, David. 1982. "American Rice Cultivation, 1680–1980: A Tercentenary Critique." *Southern Studies*, 21 (1): 215–226.

Wilms, Douglas C. 1972. "The Development of Rice Culture in 18th Century Georgia." *Southeastern Geographer*, 12: 45–57.

Wood, Peter. 1974. " 'It was a Negro Taught them': A New Look at African Labor in Early South Carolina." *Journal of Asian and African Studies*, 9: 160–179.

Ph.D. Dissertations and M.A. Theses

Azevedo, Kathleen A. d'. 1974. "Kwi Cooking: Influences of the West African Cooking Tradition." M.A. thesis, Department of Anthropology, California State University at San Francisco.

Carney, Judith. 1986. "The Social History of Gambian Rice Production: An Analysis of Food Security Strategies." Ph.D. dissertation, Department of Geography, University of California, Berkeley.

Dey, Jennie. 1980. "Women and Rice in The Gambia: The Impact of Irrigated Rice Development Projects on the Farming System." Ph.D. dissertation, Department of Sociology, University of Reading.

Morgan, Pat. 1974. "A Study of Tide Lands and Impoundments within a Three River Delta System—The South Edisto, Ashepoo, and Cumbahee Rivers of South Carolina." M.A. thesis, University of Georgia.

Offen, Karl Henry. 1999. "The Miskitu Kingdom Landscape and the Emergence of a Miskitu Ethnic Identity, Northeastern Nicaragua and Honduras, 1600–1800." Ph.D. dissertation, Department of Geography, University of Texas at Austin.

Oliveira, G. C. X. 1993. "Padroes de Variação Fenotípica e Ecologia de Oryzae (Poaceae) Selvagens da Amazônia." M.A. thesis, University of São Paulo.

Pruneau, Leigh Ann. 1997. "All the Time Is Work Time: Gender and the Task System on Antebellum Low Country Rice Plantations." Ph.D. dissertation, Department of History, University of Arizona.

Rosengarten, D. 1997. "Social Origins of the African-American Lowcountry Basket." Ph.D. dissertation, Harvard University.

Reports and Other Documents

Barker, Randolph, and Robert W. Herdt, with Beth Rose. 1985. *The Rice Economy of Asia*. Washington, D.C.: Resources for the Future.

Becker, L., and R. Diallo. 1992. *Characterization and Classification of Rice Agro-Ecosystems in Côte d'Ivoire*. Bouaké, Ivory Coast: West African Rice Development Association.

Food and Agriculture Organization (FAO). 1983. *Rice Mission Report to The Gambia*. Rome: FAO.

Haaland, R. 1979. "Man's Role in the Changing Habitat of Mema under the Old Kingdom of Ghana." ILCA Working Document no. 2. International Livestock Centre for Africa, Addis Ababa.

Moorman, F. R., and N. Van Breeman. 1978. *Rice: Soil, Water, and Land*. Los Baños, Philippines: International Rice Research Institute.

Oka, Hiko-Ichi. 1961. "Report of Trip for Investigations of Rice in Latin American Countries." National Institute of Genetics, Mishima, Japan.

Opala, Joseph A. 1987. *The Gullah*. Freetown, Sierra Leone: United States Information Service.

Porcher, Richard. 1985. "A Field Guide to the Bluff Plantation." O'Brien Foundation, New Orleans.

South Carolina Gazette (SCG). 1733. Advertisement for patent to produce pounding mill by Villepontoux and Holmes, dated July 21–28. South Carolina Historical Society, Charleston.

——— 1738. Advertisement for land sale, dated 19 January. South Carolina Historical Society, Charleston.

United States Census Office. 1864. *Agriculture of the U.S. 1860, 8th Census*. Washington, D.C.: Government Printing Office.

WARDA (West African Rice Development Association). 1980. *Types of Rice Cultivation in West Africa*. Occasional Paper no. 2. Monrovia, Liberia: WARDA.

——— 1995. *WARDA Annual Report*. Bouaké, Ivory Coast: WARDA.

Weil, Peter. 1981. "Agrarian Production, Intensification, and Underdevelopment: Mandinka Women of the Gambia in Time Perspective," paper delivered at a Title XII Conference, Women in Development, University of Delaware, Newark, May 7, 1981.

Index

Winnowing, 7, 53, 111–112, 113, 121, 125
Winterbottom, Thomas, 24
Wittfogel, Karl, 65
Wolof, 15, 36, 70, 85
Women: role in rice cultivation, 1, 19, 23,
 25–27, 28, 31, 49–55, 59, 66, 84, 107,
 110–113, 119–121, 127, 137, 159; as rice
 traders, 15; role in rice processing, 27, 28,
 50, 53, 84, 107, 108, 113–114, 117, 133–

134, 137–139, 142–143, 146–147, 154,
 167; role in rice cooking, 27, 111, 114–
 117, 137; as slaves, 71, 72, 107–108, 117,
 119–121, 127, 133–134, 137–140
Wood, Peter, 3–4, 5, 69, 78, 80, 105, 161
Woodward, Henry, 144

Yams, 11, 16, 74, 75, 150, 159